D0909100

THE EMERGENCE
OF SEXUALITY

ARNOLD I. DAVIDSON

THE EMERGENCE
OF SEXUALITY

*Historical
Epistemology
and the
Formation of
Concepts*

Harvard University Press
CAMBRIDGE, MASSACHUSETTS
LONDON, ENGLAND
2001

Library of Congress Cataloging-in-Publication Data

Davidson, Arnold Ira.
The emergence of sexuality : historical epistemology and the
formation of concepts / Arnold I. Davidson.
p. cm.
Includes bibliographical references and index.
ISBN 0-674-00459-0 (alk. paper)
1. Sex (Psychology)—History.
2. Psychoanalysis and philosophy—History.   I. Title.
BF175.5.S48 D39 2001
155.3—dc21   2001024507

To Diane Brentari
And to the memory of Michel Foucault

CONTENTS

CONTENTS

PREFACE

THE ESSAYS that constitute this book were written, more or less independently of one another, over many years. All of them were first given as lectures, and are marked by the occasions of their presentation. I have not tried to erase their oral quality, nor have I excised a small number of repetitions that appear in related essays. Since the essay/lecture has been my natural form of expression, I have resisted the urge to make this book go contrary to nature. Although they can therefore be read independently of one another, these essays are certainly meant to be mutually supporting, and in many cases arguments are developed at length in one essay that are only hinted at in others. Since I believe that there is an intimate connection between my philosophical standpoint and my historical interpretations, the division of this book into two distinct parts (Essays 1–4 and Essays 5–8) is artificial, even if not arbitrary. Indeed, the distinctiveness of some of the central claims of my historical account is a function of the methodological position developed, and without the specific approach of historical epistemology I do not see how the historical focus articulated here would have been possible. With the methodological apparatus described in the second half of this book, a very particular angle of approach to the history of sexuality becomes possible, a point of entry often invisible to both historians of science and cultural historians of sexuality. Making this kind of history of sexuality visible and justifiable depended on grasping the specificity and virtues of what I have called "historical epistemology."

Furthermore, from my point of view, the value of many of the methodological claims I make is directly supported by the content of the historical essays; the historical interpretations show, in one specific case, the range of benefits that can be derived from this epistemological standpoint.

In each part of this book, there is one essay that, at first glance, seems quite removed from the others—"The Horror of Monsters" in the first part and "The Epistemology of Distorted Evidence" in the second part. If the first three essays of this book primarily take up the history of concepts and scientific reasoning, the kind of history of the emotions outlined in "The Horror of Monsters" seems to me to begin to fill in a gap in the overall ambition of this first part—namely, to understand the constitution of our experience of normativity and its deviations. In "The Horror of Monsters" I shift my focus from the history of scientific reasoning about the normal and the pathological to the relationship between scientific explanation and moral and theological evaluation. Our experience of normativity, structured by both scientific concepts and moral judgments, must be located in more than a single dimension.

A second issue raised by the essays in the first part of this book concerns my claims about psychoanalysis and, more specifically, whether they are compatible with Michel Foucault's seemingly very different attitude toward psychoanalysis. I agree with Georges Canguilhem that we do not yet have a convincing and detailed account of Foucault's relation to psychoanalysis, and, indeed, I believe that it is only now, with the publication of *Dits et écrits* and its gathering together of the many short but crucial discussions concerning psychiatry and psychoanalysis, that we are in a position to be able to write such an account. In *La Volonté de savoir,* where Foucault seems to insist on the continuity of psychoanalysis with the techniques of the Christian confession of the flesh, his main focus is on the effects of power produced by psychoanalysis and on the way in which psychoanalysis fits into the long history of the relations of power exhibited by the will to know. He is hardly concerned with the conceptual structure or the structure of discursive practices peculiar to psychoanalysis. Archeological interests have ceded primary place to genealogical ones.[1] But even given this background, within the space of this preface, I want to point to one passage in *La Volonté de savoir* that complicates one's interpretation of Foucault and that should also help to specify further one source of the differences between my claims and those of Foucault, while indicating that our approaches are not, all things considered, incompatible. As Canguilhem himself noticed, Chapter 4 of Part IV of *La Volonté de savoir* contains an important passage in which Foucault distinguishes psychoanalysis from nineteenth-century medical psychiatry as it had been developing. At the beginning of this chapter Foucault discusses the perversion-heredity-degeneracy ensemble that he says constituted the "solid nucleus of the new technologies of sex" in the nineteenth century, and that already represented an important transformation of the methods practiced by Christianity, without being entirely independent of those methods.[2] He then proceeds to describe what he calls the "singular position of psychoanalysis" (la position singulière de la psychanalyse), but his remarks will be unintelligible to any English reader of the text, since the translation refers to "the strange position of psychiatry."[3] Foucault's whole point here is to distinguish psychoanalysis from psychiatry, and to claim that psychoanalysis effected a "rupture" with respect to the "great system of degeneracy."[4] Whatever criticisms one should make of psychoanalysis, with regard to those nineteenth-century technologies that undertook the medicalization of sex, it was the one that was "rigorously opposed to the political and institutional effects of the perversion-heredity-degeneracy system."[5] Consistent with Foucault's genealogical interests, one sees unambiguously in this discussion his focus on the political and institutional dimensions of the problem, on the technologies of power that are part of the regime of biopower. However, even at this level of analysis, psychoanalysis, according to Foucault, marks a "rupture" with respect to existing political technologies. Although Foucault is not interested, as I am, in the specificity of the psychoanalytic conceptual space, it is remarkable that he chooses the perversion-heredity-degeneracy system as the point of rupture between psychoanalysis and psychiatry. For not only at the level of technologies of power, but also at the level of discursive practices per se, this same system of perversion-heredity-degeneracy represents a fundamental discontinuity between psychiatry and psychoanalysis. My argument in Essay 3, prepared at length in the first essay, is that the psychiatric concept of the sexual instinct is a fundamental component of the perversion-heredity-degeneracy system, and that Freud's overturning of this concept, not just politically but conceptually, constituted, from the perspective of something like Foucault's archeological analysis, what one should think of as a revolution in a style of reasoning. Foucault himself does not make any such claim, since this was not the dimension of analysis that interested him in *La Volonté de savoir,* But he says nothing incompatible with this argument, and indeed leaves more than enough room for its articulation and defense.

In the second half of this book, my essay "The Epistemology of Distorted Evidence," centered on Carlo Ginzburg's historiography, raises questions about the use of evidence that no historical epistemology can afford to ignore. There may be an initial tension felt between this essay and those in which I write from the standpoint of the French tradition of historical epistemology, as if I am caught between two irreconcilable conceptions of evidence, historical proof and even truth, one of which, to put it in the crudest possible terms, is more or less absolutist, the other one being thoroughly relativist. I myself feel no insuperable conflict, as some people have, between my admiration for Ginzburg's work and the continuous invocation of Foucault, and I do not think that the absolutist/relativist distinction marks out any stakes of ultimate significance in what others have made into an almost Manichean battle. I believe that the relevant distinction here, between conditions of validity and conditions of possibility, is of crucial help in resolving the initially felt tension.

The questions about evidence, proof, and truth claims in the essay on Ginzburg concern the problem of *conditions of validity,* of how one determines that a given statement is true or false. The questions about truth, concepts, and reasoning in the more Foucault-inspired chapters concern the problem of *conditions of possibility,* of how a statement becomes a possible candidate for either truth or falsehood.[6] One must distinguish between these two levels of conditions in order to see how to reconcile historical epistemology with the kinds of historiographical claims made by Ginzburg. Briefly stated, within the conceptual space articulated by a style of reasoning, which will allow a large range of statements that can be either true or false, the conditions of validity for a particular statement may be quite objective. Indeed, I think that although the psychiatric style of reasoning did create new categories of true and false statements, within these new conditions of possibility, there were agreed-on criteria, and widespread agreement, about how to determine, for example, that the claim that someone suffered from a sexual perversion was true. Conditions of validity for a particular statement can be objective, independent from political and ideological changes, even while one maintains, at another level, that styles of reasoning and associated conceptual spaces may (even if relatively rarely) undergo radical transformation. Ginzburg wants to combat the view that truth is a merely ideological notion, based on specific political interests and reducible to relations of power, as though historical proof were a surface expression of relations of force. I see nothing in the version of historical epistemology that I have advanced that is ultimately contrary to the kinds of arguments developed in "The Epistemology of Distorted Evidence." Neither styles of reasoning nor conceptual spaces are simple expressions of social interests, and, as one should thus expect, my historical accounts contain virtually no social history. That is the reason why I find the label "social construction" utterly inappropriate as a description of my work. Once some such distinction as that between conditions of validity and conditions of possibility is made, the assumed unbridgeable dichotomy will be seen to have been badly located, a function of overly crude as well as misplaced divisions.

Of course it is true that many people seem to believe that the use of Foucault's work *requires* the rejection of what might be thought to be a more traditional practice of history, a view that continues to strike me as bizarre and that is contrary to anything I ever heard Foucault say. Some historians have rejected Foucault, Foucault did reject the work of some historians, but the philosophical motivations of his work coexisted with a vital interest in the writing of history as practiced by historians.

If I were forced to summarize my approach to the history of sexuality (questions of horror and monsters aside) and if I had to say how I made use of historical epistemology in this approach (questions of evidence aside), I suppose I would say something like the following. It is not because we became preoccupied with our true sexuality that a science of sexuality arose in the nineteenth century; it is rather the emergence of a science of sexuality that made it possible, even inevitable, for us to become preoccupied with our true sexuality. Thus our existence became a sexistence, saturated with the promises and threats of sexuality. Historical epistemology attempts to show how this new form of experience that we call "sexuality" is linked to the emergence of new structures of knowledge, and especially to a new style of reasoning and the concepts employed within it.

If this book as a whole sometimes seems to fall between various disciplines, then it may have achieved one of its goals. The idea that academic disciplines need to be kept pure seems to me to have produced an enormous amount of wasted energy—and even more bad work. Even though I always undertake my work from within philosophy, the writings and criticisms of colleagues outside of philosophy have certainly made this a better book.

One final word about sources and translations. The essays in this book that were written earliest make use of standard English translations of texts. As time went on, I became increasingly suspicious of many existing English translations, and more and more obsessive about conceptual precision in translation. Thus the last essays, which were originally presented in French anyway, contain translations for which I alone can be held responsible, and resolutely ignore the fact that, in some cases, canonical English translations already exist

The debts I have accrued during the writing of this book are considerable. Some of the essays contain specific acknowledgments, but there is no better moment to acknowledge some ongoing debts to places and people. I am grateful to the Center for the Humanities, Stanford University, the Institute for the Humanities, University of Michigan, and the Wissenschaftskolleg, Berlin, for fellowships that helped to support this work. And I am grateful to the University of Chicago for its continuous support of my research. The research staff of the History Division of the National Library of Medicine provided early, crucial help.

Among historians of science, Mario Biagioli, Lorraine Daston, and Peter Galison have each played an important role in helping me to overstep disciplinary boundaries from philosophy to the history of science. Conversations with each of them have contributed in many ways to the writing of this book. In addition, Peter Galison was, in a certain sense, my first real colleague when I began teaching at Stanford, and our conversations have continued uninterruptedly since that time.

At the University of Chicago, my colleagues in the Department of Philosophy and the Committee on the Conceptual Foundations of Science have created that rare atmosphere in which one can actually work. I am especially grateful to Dan Brudney and Jan Goldstein for many years of discussion on the topics of this book. I have benefited from Dan Brudney's intellectual advice for over twenty years now. My fellow editors, and the extraordinary staff, of *Critical Inquiry* have provided a combination of intellectual provocation and fun that I can no longer imagine doing without. Tom Mitchell and Joel Snyder, and often both of them together, have argued with me about virtually everything. Without my daily conversations with Tom Mitchell, everyday life would have been much less bearable.

David Halperin and David Wellbery each played significant roles in the initial development of some of these ideas. Were it not for Ian Hacking's early support, and the help I received from him and from his writings, I doubt I would have been able to pursue this work. Discussions with Hilary Putnam over many years have been an unfailing source of inspiration. Over the past five years, endless phone conversations with Jim Conant on every imaginable topic have provided continuity, sanity, and unending intellectual pleasure. Stanley Cavell has played a singular role in the development of my work; although his influence is often explicit in these pages, virtually nothing could adequately indicate its depth or extent. Among my French colleagues, I want to single out François Delaporte and Sandra Laugier for years of helpful discussion. Most recently, even when my work was far removed from his, I have profited enormously from Pierre Hadot, and I am glad to have been able to revive his early essays on Wittgenstein in these pages. Students, both undergraduate and graduate, at Stanford University, Princeton University, the University of California at Davis, and the University of Chicago, as well as audiences at dozens of universities, have had an influence on this work that I can hardly calculate.

Large parts of the work on this book were done in places outside of Chicago—Paris, Florence, Berlin, Barcelona, Lisbon, Rio de Janeiro. Many years ago I began using the great bookstores of the world as substitute research libraries. Thus I am grateful to Marzocco and La Libreria Francese in Florence, La Procure and Compagnie in Paris, Romänische Buchhandelung in Berlin, Libraria Laie in Barcelona. Livraria de Portugal in Lisbon, and Contra Capa in Rio de Janeiro for providing frequently needed research opportunities. Fortunately, the most extraordinary bookstore in the world is no more than two hundred meters from my apartment in Chicago, and I am profoundly grateful to the Seminary Cooperative Bookstore and its manager, Jack Cella, for answering an uncountable number of questions.

The happiest stretches of working on this book were spent in Travalle, Italy, and were it not for the hospitality and generosity of Arnolfo and Renata Biagioli that happiness would have been unimaginable.

My parents maintained their support, even in the face of idiosyncrasies and inconveniences that were not always easy to bear.

Since my desire to write my own books is almost always overwhelmed by my infinite interest in reading other people's books, I partly owe the existence of this book to those friends who have repeatedly urged its existence on me. And Lindsay Waters' years of intellectual and moral support, as well as his persistence, cannot go unmentioned.

This book is dedicated to two people—to Diane Brentari, for every conceivable reason, and to whom I can only repeat the words of Vergílio Ferreira: "O vocabulário do amor é restrito e repetitivo, porque a sua melhor expressão é o silêncio. Mas é deste silêncio que nasce todo o vocabulário do mundo"; and to Michel Foucault, whose writings, conversations, and encouragement many years ago first made me think that I just might have something to say.

THE EMERGENCE
OF SEXUALITY

1

Closing Up the Corpses

I

In *The Birth of the Clinic*, Michel Foucault charts the emergence and the effects of the conjunction of pathological anatomy and clinical medicine, and he emphasizes the significance of pathological anatomy as a foundation for the description and classification of diseases.[1] At the beginning of the nineteenth century, assertions like that of Bouillaud in his *Philosophie médicale* were to determine the fate of medicine:

> If there is an axiom in medicine it is certainly the proposition that there is no disease without a seat. If one accepted the contrary opinion, one would also have to admit that there existed functions without organs, which is a palpable absurdity. The determination of the seat of disease or their localization is one of the finest conquests of modern medicine.[2]

The history of this fine conquest is replete with surprises and ironies, the complete story of which still remains to be fully recounted. But we can summarize the hopeful, revolutionary enthusiasm of the pathological anatomists with the words of Bichat:

> For twenty years, from morning to night, you have taken notes at patients' bedsides on affections of the heart, the lungs and the gastric vis-

cera, and all is confusion for you in the symptoms which, refusing to yield up their meaning, offer you a succession of incoherent phenomena. Open up a few corpses: you will dissipate at once the darkness that observation alone could not dissipate.[3]

And so Foucault concludes that "the great break in the history of Western medicine dates precisely from the moment clinical experience became the anatomo-clinical gaze."[4]

One of the great breaks in the history of Western psychiatry comes precisely during the time when the anatomo-clinical gaze is in steady decline. The story of psychiatry's emergence, in the nineteenth century, as an autonomous medical discipline, and specifically its autonomy from neurology and cerebral pathology, is, in part, the history of this decline. Pathological anatomy could not serve psychiatry either as an explanatory theory for so-called mental diseases or disorders or as the foundation for the classification and description of these diseases. But the gradual and virtually anonymous disappearance of pathological anatomy in psychiatry is not merely the history of decline. For with this decline came the proliferation of whole new kinds of diseases and disease categories, a revitalization and reworking of nosologies the consequences of which stamp us even today. Foremost among these new disease categories was the class of functional diseases, of which sexual perversion and hysteria were the two most prominent examples. Although the hope that these functional diseases would yield to pathological anatomy was held out long after there was any evidence for this hope, in clinical practice, and later in theory as well, these diseases were fully describable simply as functional deviations of some kind; in the case of sexual perversion, for instance, one was faced with a functional deviation or abnormality of the sexual instinct. Admitting pure functional deviations as diseases was to create entire new species of diseased individuals, and to radically alter our conceptions of ourselves.

In this essay I focus on the diseases of sexual perversion and try to show how the history of this disease category is intertwined with the fall of pathological anatomy. The results of this history determine some of our concepts of mental disease today, as shown, for example, by the third edition of the diagnostic and statistical manual of the American Psychiatric Association. More important, the effects of this history have helped to determine how we now categorize ourselves, have contributed to our current epistemology of the self. We are all potentially perverts. How has this come to be?

II

It is convenient to divide the history of sexual perversion into three stages, each stage depending upon a different understanding of what these diseases were thought to be diseases of. It is perhaps best to think of each stage as characterized by a different mode or form of explanation, the third stage constituting a decisive break with the first two, since it inaugurates an entirely new style of reasoning about perversion. In the first, most short-lived stage, sexual perversion was thought to be a disease of the reproductive or genital organs, a disease whose basis was some anatomical abnormality of these organs. The second stage, although in clinical practice recognizing perversions to be abnormalities of the sexual instinct, insisted that the psychophysiology of the sexual instinct (and so of its diseases as well) would eventually, with advances in knowledge, come to be understood in terms of the neurophysiology and neuroanatomy of the brain. These first two stages of explanation shared a commitment to the anatomo-pathological style of reasoning. The third stage took perversions to be pure functional deviations of the sexual instinct, not reducible to cerebral pathology. Perversions were to be viewed and treated at the level of psychology, not at the grander level of pathological anatomy. The psychiatric style of reasoning emerged clearly and definitively at this third stage.

Of course, this three-stage structural partition does not precisely coincide with historical chronology; the three forms of explanation were often mixed together, sometimes even in the same article. But they are capable of being distinguished and it will help our understanding to so distinguish them. More specifically, the second and third stages are not separated by some exactly datable dividing line. Indeed, these two stages overlap to such an extent that many of the psychiatrists who are most responsible for our current conception of the perversions were also strongly wedded to the dominance of brain pathology. So although for analytical and historiographical reasons we must carefully separate these last two stages, as a matter of historical account no such neat division will be found.

In the years between 1870 and 1905 psychiatry was caught between two conceptual grids; in one of which it was aligned with neurology, in the other with psychology. Most psychiatric disease categories, including the perversions, were swept along in this battle over what kind of science psychiatry was to be. The fact that the majority of the great European psychiatrists at the end of the nineteenth century were trained as neurologists meant that they paid at least theoretical homage to their mother discipline. But it was not merely biographical considerations that prompted a constant appeal to the neural sciences. During this span of time, no one really knew what it would mean to conceive of diseases like perversion in purely functional terms. It would be like admitting functions without organs, which, as Bouillaud reminds us, was a palpable absurdity. So the hold of pathological anatomy remained to mask the fact that this palpable absurdity was already reality. In fact, the professions of these brain anatomists in almost no way affected the description and classification of the perversions. From very near the beginning of psychiatry's emergence as an academic discipline, functional diseases were a recognized part of clinical experience. Theories about the neuropathology of the brain had no clinical effects; they were part of an almost useless conceptual space. So although we can, and should, distinguish between perversions as functional deviations ultimately reducible to brain disease and perversions as pure functional diseases, if we look at the *descriptions* of those who advocate these second and third modes of explanation, they are practically identical. The real break, the new style of reasoning, is to be located at that point when the sexual instinct and its functional diseases were introduced together. Functional diseases were diseases of something—not an organ, but an instinct.[5]

III

In one of the earliest articles on what we have come to call perversion, probably the earliest article in French, Dr. Michea takes up the case of Sergeant Bertrand, accused of having violated female cadavers.[6] Although like all of the discussions prior to 1870, Michea's is concerned primarily with the question of Bertrand's legal and moral responsibility for his actions, his article is distinguished by the fact that he does consider, in passing, the classification of what he names *les déviations maladives de l'appétit vénérien*. He classifies these deviations into four kinds, in order of their frequency: first, Greek love, the love of an individual for someone of his own sex; second, bestiality; third, the attraction for an inanimate object; and fourth, the attraction for human cadavers.[7] Michea's paper is significant in that he argues that Bertrand suffers not from vampirism or destructive monomania but from some deviation of the venereal appetite, some kind of erotic monomania. Arguments of this type were crucial in providing grounds for isolating diseases of sexuality as distinct morbid entities, and thus not reducing them to mere effects of other, prior disease processes. But for our purposes, the most interesting aspect of Michea's short paper is his discussion and explanation of "Greek love," to which he devotes, by far, the greatest space. (Indeed, Michea claims that there is only one previous case in judicial records of the attraction for human cadavers, the disease from which Bertrand is supposed to suffer.) After arguing that Greek love should be considered an unhealthy deviation of the venereal appetite, Michea wonders what might explain this strange disorder. His explanation relies on the work of Weber, a professor of anatomy and physiology, who has recently described, in great detail, the location and anatomy of the "masculine uterus." Michea points out that Weber's description of the masculine uterus has already been successfully used by Akermann to explain a hermaphrodite.[8] On the basis of this successful application of Weber's anatomical discovery, Michea concludes:

> If these anatomical facts are verified, if, above all, one proceeded to discover that the masculine uterus can have sometimes a greater and sometimes a lesser development, one would perhaps be justified in establishing a relation of causality between these facts and the feminine tendencies that characterize the majority of individuals who engage in Greek love.[9]

Nothing could be more natural than to expect these feminine tendencies to have some anatomical basis; and nothing could constitute a more appropriate anatomical basis than a masculine uterus. The uterus, that almost always diseased female organ, was responsible for masculine deviations as well!

Although perhaps extraordinary in some of its details, Michea's form of explanation is not as uncommon as one might have expected. Writing in English in 1888, J. G. Kiernan puts great emphasis on the biological facts of bisexuality and hermaphroditism in the lowest orders of life.[10] Combining these facts with the fact that the human embryo is not originally sexually differentiated, Kiernan proposes to explain sexual perversions according to a "principle of atavism":[11]

> The original bisexuality of the ancestors of the race shown in the rudimentary female organs of the male could not fail to occasion functional if

not organic reversions when mental or physical manifestations were inter-
fered with by disease or congenital defect.[12]

Or as he puts it later:

> Males may be born with female external genitals and vice versa. The low-
> est animals are bisexual and the various types of hermaphroditism are
> more or less complete reversions to the ancestral type.[13]

Writing a year later in *Medical and Surgical Reporter,* G. Frank Lydston
elaborates on the observations and hypothesis of Kiernan:

> It is puzzling to the healthy man and woman, to understand how the
> practices of the sexual pervert can afford gratification. If considered in the
> light of reversion of type, however, the subject is much less perplexing.
> That maldevelopment, or arrested development, of the sexual organs
> should be associated with sexual perversion is not at all surprising; and
> the more nearly the individual approximates the type of fetal develop-
> ment which exists prior to the commencement of sexual differentiation,
> the more marked is the aberrance of sexuality.[14]

Whether it be the increased development of the masculine uterus or the
failed development of sexual differentiation, the forty-two years between
Michea and Lydston persist in anatomo-pathological explanations of the
perversions. The explanatory ideal here is that of physical hermaphroditism. Since it was natural to suppose that all behavioral disorders had an
organic basis, and since the behavioral manifestations in question were diseases of sexuality, it seemed inevitable that the sexual organs themselves
must be the seat of the perversions. And it was no accident that the vast
majority of the clinically reported cases of perversion were cases of "contrary sexual instinct" or homosexuality. Male organs led to male behavior
and female organs to female behavior. Investigate the anatomy of the organs and behavioral science would be on a secure foundation. How this explanatory ideal of physical hermaphroditism was to explain the other perversions was never clear. But these other perversions were sufficiently rare
in comparison with contrary sexual instinct that they could be theoretically
neglected, at least at first, without much worry. This straightforward style
of pathological anatomy wished to trace the behavioral abnormalities of
perverts back to some gross physical deformity (or deficiency) of the reproductive organs, and in this way a clear and epistemologically satisfying

causal link would be established between organs and functions. The anatomy of the body would continue to be explanatorily supreme.

Medical doctors took great solace in this brute physicalism, insisting on the power of their science to explain even the most bizarre acts. Their attitude is clearly expressed by Lydston, whose article was originally delivered as a clinical lecture to the College of Physicians and Surgeons, Chicago, Illinois. Here is a synoptic passage:

> The subject has been until a recent date studied solely from the standpoint of the moralist, and from the indisposition of the scientific physician to study the subject, the unfortunate set of individuals who are characterized by perverted sexuality have been viewed in the light of their moral responsibility rather than *as the victims of a physical and incidentally of a mental defect.* It is certainly much less humiliating to us as atoms of the social fabric to be able to attribute the degradation of these poor unfortunates to a physical cause, than to a wilful viciousness over which they have, or ought to have, volitional control. Even to the moralist there should be much satisfaction in the thought that a large class of sexual perverts are physically abnormal rather than morally leprous . . . the sexual pervert is generally a physical aberration—a lusus naturae.[15]

Most of the cases of contrary sexual instinct reported in the nineteenth-century medical literature explicitly record the anatomy of the reproductive organs of these unfortunate patients. And to the consternation of the pathological anatomists, the conclusion is virtually always the same—genital organs, normal; no physical malformations of the reproductive organs. Physical hermaphroditism could no more explain homosexuality than it could any of the other perversions. This grossest level of anatomy proved to be, in this arena, a useless explanatory space. Julien Chevalier had gotten the surprising conclusion correct when he wrote of "sexual inversion" in 1885: "It is characterized by the absence of anatomo-pathological lesions of the sexual organs."[16] But if pathological anatomy was to survive this startling claim, it had to retreat. And it quickly found its site of retreat in the brain.

IV

In the second edition of his acclaimed *Mental Pathology and Therapeutics,* Wilhelm Griesinger, holder of the first chair of psychiatry in Germany, and founder of the *Archiv für Psychiatrie und Nervenkrankheiten,* began with the following proclamation:

> The first step towards a knowledge of the symptoms [of insanity] is their locality—to which organ do the indications of the disease belong? What organ must necessarily and invariably be diseased where there is madness? The answer to these questions is preliminary to all advancement in the study of mental disease.
>
> Physiological and pathological facts show us that this organ can only be the brain; we therefore primarily, and in every case of mental disease, recognize a morbid action of that organ.[17]

Fewer than ten pages later, commenting on the state of knowledge in brain anatomy, Griesinger continues:

> Cerebral pathology is, even in the present day, to a great extent in the same state which the pathology of the thoracic organs was in before the days of Laennec. Instead of proceeding in every case from the changes of structure of the organ, and being able to deduce in an exact manner the production of the symptoms from the changes in the tissue, it has very often to deal with symptoms of which it can scarcely give an approximation to the seat, and of whose mode of origin it is completely ignorant. It must keep to the external phenomena, and establish the groups of diseases according to something common and characteristic in the symptoms altogether independently of their anatomical basis.[18]

Griesinger admits that although in many diseases of insanity anatomical change in the brain "cannot be ocularly demonstrated by pathological anatomy, still, on physiological grounds it is universally admitted."[19] And he frankly acknowledges, at the beginning of his chapter on the forms of mental disease, that "a classification of mental diseases *according to their nature*—that is, according to the anatomical changes of the brain which lie at their foundation—is, at the present time, impossible."[20]

Writing about diseases of sexuality almost twenty years later, Paul Moreau, a prominent French chronicler of aberrations, claims:

> Genital excitation, physical or psychical, is the result of a special physiological or pathological excitement, resulting from the localization or aug-

mentation of a real morbid process to a center of genital functions. But this center, where is it?—In the cortex, the cerebellum, the medulla?

On this point we confess our ignorance and with Esquirol we repeat: we know nothing about it.[21]

Yet again, over twenty-five years later, Eugene Kraepelin, in the seventh edition of his textbook for psychiatrists, insists:

The principle requisite in the knowledge of mental diseases is an accurate definition of the separate disease processes. In the solution of this problem one must have, on the one hand, knowledge of the physical changes in the cerebral cortex, and on the other of the mental symptoms associated with them. Until this is known we cannot hope to understand the relationship between mental symptoms of disease and the morbid physical processes underlying them, or indeed the causes of the entire disease process. . . . Judging from experience in internal medicine, the safest foundation for a classification of this kind is that offered by pathological anatomy. Unfortunately, however, mental diseases thus far present but very few lesions that have positive distinctive characteristics, and furthermore there is the extreme difficulty of correlating physical and mental morbid processes.[22]

I have reproduced these pronouncements, separated by forty-five years, because they present us with a significant problem: How are we to understand this obsession with brain anatomy coupled as it is with the constant admission of its theoretical and clinical uselessness? A naive hypothesis is that at the end of the nineteenth century, after the work of Paul Broca and others, brain anatomy was just beginning to prove fruitful. Thus, this hypothesis continues, although brain pathology was perhaps not yet helpful in the classification and explanation of mental diseases, these physicians knew that with the slow progress of scientific knowledge it would soon become, both theoretically and clinically, of supreme importance. There was good evidence, so the claim concludes, on which to base an optimistic prediction about the explanatory power of the brain sciences. I have called this hypothesis "naive" because it takes at face value and as the whole story the statements of these neuropsychiatrists. I have no doubt that Griesinger and his descendants would have replied as this hypothesis suggests.[23] But their own avowed replies are not an accurate index of the historical circumstances. At this time in the history of psychiatry only certain kinds of statements about disease processes could count as either true or false; not every such statement was a possible candidate for the status of truth or falsehood.[24] Specifically, explanations of disease states had to be referred to organs; any explanation not of this type was not so much false as not even in the domain of the true and false. An explanation that did not at least attempt to anatomically localize the disease was more a part of theology than of science.[25] Since it was believed that there were distinct diseases of sexuality, and since these diseases could not be explained by defects of the reproductive organs, the only plausible organ that remained to provide an explanation was the brain. The dominance of brain pathology was as much a consequence of a complicated web of epistemic and conceptual conditions as it was of any empirical evidence. Indeed, for these early psychiatrists it does not seem as if anything could have counted as evidence against the proposition that sexual perversions are ultimately traceable to brain disease. Postmortem examinations that demonstrated no pathological lesions, and should have constituted such evidence, were always explained away; the necessary changes in brain structure were undoubtedly "so fine that with ordinary instruments they are not demonstrable postmortem."[26] Whatever evidence was to be amassed had to be placed within the given framework of pathological anatomy. To affirm explicitly that sexual perversions or other mental diseases were functionally autonomous from the brain would have been to pass from basic truth to palpable absurdity, something beyond falsity.[27]

The epistemological stranglehold of pathological anatomy on psychiatry is perhaps best illustrated by Moriz Benedikt's *Anatomical Studies upon Brains of Criminals.*[28] In this book Benedikt reproduces, in extraordinarily painstaking detail, the results of his investigations of the anatomical structure of the brains of twenty-two criminals. Believing that we think, feel, desire, and act according to the anatomical construction and physiological development of our brain, Benedikt hopes that his dissections of criminals' brains will furnish the "foundation stones of a Natural History of Crime."[29] He considers the brains of various kinds of criminals from different races—some habitual thieves, murderers, a banknote counterfeiter, someone who killed the husband of his priest's concubine at the priest's instigation, and numerous others. Whatever interest there may be in the details of his presentations, his conclusion is remarkable:

THE BRAINS OF CRIMINALS EXHIBIT A DEVIATION FROM THE NORMAL TYPE,
AND CRIMINALS ARE TO BE VIEWED AS AN ANTHROPOLOGICAL VARIETY OF
THEIR SPECIES, AT LEAST AMONG THE CULTURED RACES.[30]

The idea that criminals are an anthropological variety of their species, because of their atypical brains, is an idea that we today find no more than
amusing. But Benedikt found little amusement in his results. Concerned
with criminal deviation, and starting from the framework of pathological
anatomy, he found the "evidence" necessary for the logical conclusion. We
should be concerned less with his evidence than with his style of explanation and his epistemic framework. Benedikt himself was sometimes aware
of this framework:

> It is self-evident that the observations here collected are the result of the
> a priori conviction that the constitutional ("eigentliche") criminal is a
> burdened ("belastetes") individual; that he has the same relation to crime
> as his next blood kin, the epileptic, and his cousin, the idiot, have to their
> encephalopathic condition.[31]

It is this a priori conviction that sets the stage for neuropsychiatry. The sexual pervert was no less burdened an individual than the criminal, epileptic,
or idiot. I do not know how many anatomical investigations were performed upon the brains of perverts. But we should be more surprised if
there were not such dissections than if there were. Given the explicit theoretical conception of perversion common at this time, Benedikt's kind of
anatomical investigation would have been the ideal diagnostic and explanatory tool.

Yet I have claimed that pathological anatomy did not substantially influence the clinical description and classification of the perversions. Indeed,
the only person to even attempt a classification of the perversions on an anatomical basis was Paul Magnan, a distinguished medical psychologist and
a sometime collaborator with J. M. Charcot. In a presentation to the
Société médico-psychologique in 1885, Magnan divided the perversions
into four classes, hoping that his anatomical classification would help to reduce the confusion that surrounded these aberrations.[32] Perversions were to
be understood, according to him, as (1) spinal, (2) posterior spinal cerebral
(nymphomania and satyriasis), (3) anterior spinal cerebral (contrary sexual
instinct), and (4) anterior cerebral (erotomania). As ultimately unsatisfac-

tory as it was, Magnan's classification was at least headed in the right direction, assuming, of course, that pathological anatomy was as useful as was always claimed. But even in Magnan's hands this classification was more nominal than real. His explanation for why the different perversions were classified as they were was less than sketchy, and his classifications had, at most, a minimal influence on his presentation of cases. Magnan was better known among his colleagues for his extended description of contrary sexual instinct *(inversion du sens génital)* and for his linking of this perversion with degeneracy; in this respect his views were quite common and his work followed a long line of predecessors, beginning with Carl Westphal.[33] In fact, Falret, commenting on Magnan's 1885 presentation, mentions nothing about his supposed anatomical classification, but rather insists (as did Magnan) on the importance of the hereditary character of the perversions. Although Magnan's classification was adopted by a few other French physicians, it was without much effect.[34] His classification never really caught on, and no one offered any more sophisticated anatomical classifications in its place. Magnan's attempt was offered more out of theoretical necessity than as a result of any genuine evidence or insight. His was a last effort to keep pathological anatomy alive.

V

The best way to understand the nineteenth-century obsession with perversion is to examine the notion of the sexual instinct, for, as I have said, the actual conception of perversion underlying clinical thought was that of a functional disease of this instinct. That is to say, the class of diseases that affected the sexual instinct was precisely the sexual perversions. Of course, the pathological anatomists did not want the notion of a sexual instinct to escape their grasp. Griesinger himself had said that "there is nothing inconsistent in seeking to discover in certain parts of the brain the seat of the sensual instincts."[35] And Krafft-Ebing, in *Psychopathia Sexualis,* asserts that the sexual instinct is a function of the cerebral cortex, although he admits that no definite region of the cortex has yet been proven to be the exclusive seat of this instinct.[36] He speculates that since there is a close relation between the olfactory sense and the sexual instinct, these two centers must be close together in the cerebral cortex. Indeed, he accepts Mackenzie's observations that masturbators are subject to nosebleeds, and that "there are affections of the nose which stubbornly resist all treatment until the concomitant (and causal) genital disease is removed."[37] But besides these rather vague remarks, Krafft-Ebing says nothing that would help one to determine the anatomical foundation of the sexual instinct, or to lead one to believe that it was actually possible to find distinct cerebral lesions associated with the diseases of this instinct.

The appropriate way to understand the sexual instinct is in functional terms, not in anatomical ones. Without such a functional understanding, there would have been no conceptual foundation for classifying certain phenomena as perversions or diseases of the instinct. And Richard von Krafft-Ebing himself, as I shall show, understood the sexual instinct in this functional way; his pathological anatomy here is just so much window dressing. One of the most explicit recognitions of the importance of this functional characterization of the sexual instinct, a characterization shared by all the significant clinical work on perversion, appears in M. P. Legrain's *Des anomalies de l'instinct sexuel et en particulier des inversions du sens génital,* published in 1896:

> The sexual instinct is a physiological phenomenon in every normal being endowed with life. It is a need of a general order and in consequence it is useless to look for its localization, as one has done, in any particular part whatever of the organism. Its seat is everywhere and nowhere. . . . This instinct is therefore independent of the structure itself of the external genital organs, which are only instruments in the service of a function, as the stomach is an instrument in the service of the general function of nutrition.[38]

By acknowledging the subservience of the genital organs to the function of the sexual instinct, Legrain makes overt what by 1896 nobody should have doubted. And by claiming that the seat of the sexual instinct was everywhere and nowhere, he told us to look for its diseases everywhere and nowhere. This "everywhere and nowhere" sometimes had a more common name in psychiatric discussions—it went under the name of *personality.* A functional understanding of the instinct allowed one to isolate a set of disorders or diseases that were disturbances of the special functions of the instinct. Paul Moreau (de Tours), in a book that influenced the first edition of Krafft-Ebing's *Psychopathia Sexualis,* argued that the clinical facts forced one to accept, as absolutely demonstrated, the psychic existence of a sixth sense, which he called the genital sense.[39] Although the notion of a genital sense may appear ludicrous, Moreau's characterization was adopted by subsequent French clinicians, and his phrase *sens génital* was preserved, by Charcot among others, as a translation of our "sexual instinct." So Carl Westphal's *conträre Sexualempfindung* became *inversion du sens génital.* The genital sense is just the sexual instinct, masquerading in different words. Its characterization as a sixth sense was a useful analogy. Just as one could become blind or have acute vision or be able to discriminate only a part of the color spectrum, and just as one might go deaf or have abnormally sensitive hearing or be able to hear only certain pitches, so too this sixth sense might be diminished, augmented, or perverted. What Moreau hoped to demonstrate was that this genital sense had special functions, distinct from the functions served by other organs, and that just as with the other senses, this sixth sense could be psychically disturbed without the proper working of other mental functions, either affective or intellectual, being harmed.[40] A demonstration such as Moreau's was essential in isolating diseases of sexuality as distinct disease entities.

The *Oxford English Dictionary* reports that the first modern medical use in English of the concept of perversion occurred in 1842 in Robley Dunglison's *Medical Lexicon:* "'Perversion,' one of the four modifications of function in disease; the three others being augmentation, diminution, and abolition."[41] The notions of perversion and function are inextricably intertwined. Once one offers a functional characterization of the sexual instinct, perversions become a natural class of diseases; and without this characterization there is really no conceptual room for this kind of disease. Whatever words of pathological anatomy he and others offered, it is clear that Krafft-Ebing understood the sexual instinct in a functional way. In his *Textbook on Insanity* Krafft-Ebing is unequivocal in his claim that life presents two instincts, those of self-preservation and sexuality; he insists that abnormal life presents no new instincts, although the instincts of self-preservation and sexuality "may be lessened, increased or manifested with perversion."[42] The sexual instinct was often compared with the instinct of self-preservation, which manifested itself in appetite. In a section entitled "Disturbances of the Instincts," Krafft-Ebing first discusses the anomalies of the appetites, which he divides into three different kinds. There are increases of the appetite (hyperorexia), lessening of the appetite (anorexia), and perversions of the appetite, such as a "true impulse to eat spiders, toads, worms, human blood, etc."[43] Such a classification is exactly what one should expect from a functional understanding of the instinct. Anomalies of the sexual instinct are similarly classified as lessened or entirely wanting (anaesthesia), abnormally increased (hyperaesthesia), and perverse expression (paraesthesia); in addition there is a fourth class of anomalies of the sexual instinct, which consists in its manifestation outside of the period of anatomical and physiological processes in the reproductive organs (paradoxia).[44] In both his *Textbook on Insanity* and *Psychopathia Sexualis*, Krafft-Ebing further divides the perversions into sadism, masochism, fetishism, and contrary sexual instinct.[45]

In order to be able to determine precisely what phenomena are functional disturbances or diseases of the sexual instinct, one must also, of course, specify what the normal or natural function of this instinct consists in. Without knowing what the normal function of the instinct is, everything and nothing could count as a functional disturbance. There would be no principled criterion to include or exclude any behavior from the disease category of perversion. So one must first believe that there is a natural function of the sexual instinct and then believe that this function is quite determinate. One might have thought that questions as momentous as these would have received extensive discussion during the nineteenth-century heyday of perversion. But, remarkably enough, no such discussion appears. There is virtually *unargued unanimity* both on the fact that this instinct does have a natural function and on what that function is. Krafft-Ebing's view is representative here:

> During the time of the maturation of physiological processes in the reproductive glands, desires arise in the consciousness of the individual, which have for their purpose the perpetuation of the species (sexual instinct). . . . With opportunity for the natural satisfaction of the sexual instinct, every expression of it that does not correspond with the purpose of nature—i.e., propagation—must be regarded as perverse.[46]

Nineteenth-century psychiatry silently adopted this conception of the function of the sexual instinct, and it was often taken as so natural as not to need explicit statement. It is not at all obvious why sadism, masochism, fetishism, and homosexuality should be treated as species of the same disease, for they appear to have no essential features in common.[47] Yet if one takes the natural function of the sexual instinct to be propagation, it becomes possible to see why they were all classified together as perversions. They all manifest the same kind of perverse expression, the same basic kind of functional deviation. Thus this understanding of the instinct permits a *unified* treatment of perversion, allows one to place an apparently heterogeneous group of phenomena under the same natural disease kind.[48] Had anyone denied either that the sexual instinct has a natural function or that this function is procreation, diseases of perversion, as we understand them, would not have entered psychiatric nosology.

I have already indicated that most nineteenth-century clinical reports of perversion were cases of so-called contrary sexual instinct, and I have offered a hypothesis to explain why this may have been so. In the rest of my discussion of the medical literature on perversion I shall concentrate on these cases, other forms of perversion requiring a separate treatment (which I have provided elsewhere). We can conveniently place the origin of contrary sexual instinct, as a medicopsychological diagnostic category, in 1870, with the publication of Carl Westphal's "Die conträre Sexualempfindung" in *Archiv für Psychiatrie und Nervenkrankheiten*. Westphal's attachment to pathological anatomy did not prevent him from giving the first modern definition of homosexuality. He believed that contrary sexual instinct was a congenital perversion of the sexual instinct, and that in this perversion "a woman is physically a woman and psychologically a man and, on the other hand, a man is physically a man and psychologically a woman."[49] I have called this the first modern definition because it presents a purely psychological characterization of homosexuality, and, detached from Westphal's meager explanatory speculations, it provides us with the clinical conception of this perversion operative in almost all of the subsequent medical literature. Later issues of the *Archiv* contained similar reports of contrary sexual instinct, and some of Krafft-Ebing's most important early work appeared in this journal.

With the publication of Charcot and Magnan's paper in *Archives de Neurologie* in 1882, an epidemic of contrary sexual instinct, equal to that of Germany, was soon to plague France.[50] An Italian case appeared in 1878;[51] and the first case in English, in 1881.[52] The latter case was reported by a German physician and some English-speaking psychiatrists did not consider it "a contribution to the study of this subject by English science."[53] In 1883, J. C. Shaw and G. N. Ferris, writing in the *Journal of Nervous and Mental Diseases*, summarize all of the German, French, Italian, and English cases, and conclude that there have been eighteen documented cases of contrary sexual instinct, to which they add one more, bringing the grand total to nineteen.[54] Westphal's psychological characterization of homosexuality is, in effect, the psychiatric transformation of a previous, although nonmedical, understanding of this disorder. Karl Heinrich Ulrichs, a Hanoverian lawyer, had achieved some notoriety with his autobiographical description of contrary sexual instinct, published in the middle 1860s. Ulrichs gave the name "urnings" to those who suffered from these desires, and supposed that a woman's soul dwelled in a man's body *(anima muliebris in virili corpore inclusa).*[55] And of course, throughout the 1870s and 1880s, there were the obligatory anatomical claims that these desires were the result of "the brain of a woman in the body of a man and the brain of a man in the body of a woman."[56] These three ideas of same-sex sexual behavior represent three central places where the phenomenon was thought to reside—the soul, the brain, and the psyche or personality. And, although not always in this historical sequence, theology, pathological anatomy, and psychiatry each took its own opportunity to lay claim to a complete explanation of perverse desires.

The significance of a psychological description of homosexuality is amply illustrated by *Psychopathia Sexualis:*

> After the attainment of complete sexual development, among the most constant elements of self-consciousness in the individual are the knowledge of representing a definite sexual personality and the consciousness of desire, during the period of physiological activity of the reproductive organs (production of semen and ova), to perform sexual acts corresponding with that sexual personality—acts which, consciously or unconsciously, have a procreative purpose. . . .
>
> With the inception of anatomical and functional development of the generative organs, and the differentiation of form belong to each sex, which goes hand in hand with it (in the boy as well as in the girl), rudiments of a mental feeling corresponding with the sex are developed.[57]

With this picture of the definite sexual personality in hand, Krafft-Ebing says of contrary sexual instinct:

> It is purely a psychical anomaly, for the sexual instinct does in no wise correspond with the primary and secondary sexual characteristics. In spite of the fully differentiated sexual type, in spite of the normally developed

and active sexual glands, man is drawn sexually to the man, because he has, consciously or otherwise, the instinct of the female toward him, or vice versa.[58]

The normal sexual instinct expresses itself in a definite personality or character; functional disorders of the instinct will express themselves as psychical anomalies. Since the sexual instinct was thought to partake of both somatic and psychic features, any functional abnormality of the instinct could be expected to manifest itself psychically. In this way, these functional disorders and psychology were very closely connected. As Albert Moll says, "To understand the homosexual urge we should consider the genital instinct not as a phenomenon apart from the other functions but rather as a psychic function."[59]

During this period of near-frenetic psychiatric classification, many attempts were made to provide detailed classifications of different degrees and kinds of homosexuality. Psychiatrists were not content with single categories, but rather subdivided the perversions into innumerable kinds so that, before long, the psychiatric world was populated by a plethora of strange beings.[60] Krafft-Ebing believed that, "clinically and anthropologically," there were four degrees of development of homosexuality:

1. With the predominant homosexual feeling there are traces of heterosexual sensibility (psychosexual hermaphroditism).
2. Exclusive inclination to the same sex (homosexuality).
3. The whole psychic existence is altered to correspond with the abnormal sexual feeling (effemination and viraginity).
4. The form of the body approaches that which is in harmony with the abnormal sexual feeling. However, there are never actual transitions to hermaphrodites.[61]

It is important to note here that the degrees or kinds of homosexuality are differentiated according to psychic features, namely, the degree of homosexual sensibility or feeling that is present. Only the rarest and most severe form of homosexuality is accompanied by any somatic changes, and even these changes are subordinate to the abnormal sexual feeling.

This psychological/functional understanding of contrary sexual instinct is not limited to the German medical literature of the time. In 1896 Legrain could warn us not to make a mistake about the true sex (le sexe vrai) of a "uranist." Even though registered at birth as a man, if in his contacts with men, he has the feelings that men normally have toward women, then he is a woman.[62] Psychological characteristics, expressions of the sexual instinct, are decisive for the categorization of the sexes:

> And this psychical differentiation is a fact of principal importance, for in my view in it alone rests the categorization of the sexes; as long as it is not a complete fact, the individual is really sexually neutral, whatever his genital structure.[63]

This priority of the psychological provided some of the conditions necessary for statements such as Kraepelin's:

> It [contrary sexual instinct] is more prevalent in certain employments, such as among decorators, waiters, ladies' tailors; also among theatrical people. Moll claims that women comedians are regularly homosexual.[64]

It is clear from what Kraepelin says later that he does not believe that these employments are causally responsible for this perversion of the sexual instinct. Rather, he must believe that once the psychic anomalies of the perversion are manifest, one tends to choose employment that is more appropriate to these psychical abnormalities.[65] With remarks like these, the death of pathological anatomy is secured.

One of the most notable facts about this early psychiatric literature on perversion is that no explanatory framework is proposed to account for purely functional diseases. None of the writers I am familiar with ever suggests that these so-called functional diseases are not true diseases, are not part of the legitimate domain of medical science. Yet, at the same time, there was no already clearly formulated concept of disease under which they could readily fall. Clinical practice came first; explanatory theory lagged far behind. No doubt the circumstances are complicated by the fact that all of the early writers expressed an allegiance to pathological anatomy. But even after pathological anatomy became an obvious explanatory failure, psychiatry did not regroup and address itself to the question of whether these perversions were really diseases. One unequivocal path to take would have been to claim that precisely because no anatomical changes underlay the perversions, they could not be considered diseases, and physicians must leave their regulation to others more qualified. But clinical practice had already constituted the perversions as diseases, and by the time the hold of pathological anatomy was loosened, they were already a recognized part of psychiatric nosology. This precedence of clinical practice to theory is officially endorsed by the American Psychiatric Association, whose *Diagnostic and Statistical Manual* is meant to be theoretically neutral.[66] But such theoretical neutrality is as unprincipled as it is expansive; indeed, its expansiveness is partially a function of its lack of principle. On a straightforward interpretation, it sanctions the view that whatever psychiatrists do in fact treat as diseases are diseases. So what could not become a disease? The American Psychiatric Association recognizes telephone scatologia, among others, as a psychosexual disorder. Moreover, phenomena do not exhibit their disease status to everyone's untutored vision. To count something as a disease is to make a theoretical classification. The hope of reading diseases straight off of nature, independent of theory, is as philosophically naive as it is historically suspect.

One of the first comprehensive attempts to provide an explanatory framework for functional diseases is Morton Prince's 1898 paper, "Habit Neuroses as True Functional Diseases."[67] Prince considers the whole class of diseases for which there are no anatomical changes different in kind from those that occur in health (sexual perversion being one subclass of functional disease). Not surprisingly, his explanations are of a thoroughly psychological nature, relying mainly on the laws of association. Simply put, his theory was that phenomena may become so strongly associated that their occurrence together is automatic, independent of volition. He thought that we may

> by a process of education be taught to respond to our environment or to internal stimuli in such a way as to generate painful sensations or undesirable motor effects. . . . The painful (disagreeable, undesirable) motor and sensory and other phenomena thus developed constitute so-called disease.[68]

He refers to these diseases as habit neuroses, association neuroses, neuromimesis, or true functional diseases.[69] Prince's framework bears a striking resemblance to Sigmund Freud's attempt to "pass over into the field of psychology" to explain that other great functional disease, hysteria. Freud's explanations also rely on the effects of associations in the genesis of mental disorders, and were published in French five years earlier than Prince's paper.[70] Both papers help to culminate the gradual process by which psychiatry became independent of neurology and annexed itself instead to psychology. I have given these two examples (there are others as well) so as not to be accused of claiming that there were no theories of functional diseases. The important point is that theories of this kind were developed after the fact, after the recognition, in standard psychiatric manuals, of whole new disease categories. These new diseases appeared almost full-blown in clinical practice, and silently, anonymously, became part of psychiatric nomenclature. The effect of this quiet, undisturbed recognition was vastly to enlarge psychiatric therapy and intervention. Psychiatry was not to be concerned solely with the extreme forms, the limits, of the human condition, such as madness. Instead, the entire domain of the unnatural and abnormal was to become its province. And one need not have waited until Freud's *Three Essays on the Theory of Sexuality*[71] to realize that this clinical arena was as common as it was "unnatural"; no one was to escape the psychiatric gaze.

VI

In a groundbreaking essay on the traditional philosophical problem of other minds, Stanley Cavell concludes by saying:

> We don't know whether the mind is best represented by the phenomenon of pain, or by that of envy, or by working on a jigsaw puzzle, or by a ringing in the ears. A natural fact underlying the philosophical problem of privacy is that the individual will take *certain* among his experiences to represent his own mind—certain particular sins or shames or surprises of joy—and then take his mind (his self) to be unknown so far as *those* experiences are unknown.[72]

Nineteenth-century psychiatry took sexuality to be the way in which the mind is best represented. To know a person's sexuality is to know that person. Sexuality is the expression of the individual shape of the personality. And to know sexuality, to know the person, one must know its anomalies. Krafft-Ebing was quite clear about this point:

> These anomalies are very important elementary disturbances, since *upon the nature of sexual sensibility the mental individuality in greater part depends.*[73]

Sexuality individualizes, turns one into a specific kind of human being—a sadist, masochist, homosexual, fetishist. This link between sexuality and individuality explains some of the passion with which psychiatry investigated the perversions. The more details one has about these anomalies, the better one is able to penetrate the covert individuality of the self. The second edition of Dr. Laupts's book on homosexuality announces the first thirteen volumes in a "Bibliothèque des Perversions Sexuelles."[74] Here one can read about the perversions of one's choice, gathering as much information as possible about the most profound truths of the individual.

VII

The question I now wish to ask is: Were there any perverts before the later part of the nineteenth century? Strange as it may sound, the answer to this question is, *no.* Perversion and perverts were an invention of psychiatric reasoning and of the psychiatric theories I have surveyed. (I again restrict myself to the case of homosexuality, but a similar history could be recounted for the other perversions.) I do not wish to be misunderstood—intercourse between members of the same sex did not begin, I dare say, in the nineteenth century; but homosexuality, as a disease of the sexual instinct, did. One will not be able to understand the importance of these new diseases of sexuality if one conflates contrary sexual instinct with sodomy. Sodomy was a legal category, defined in terms of certain specifiable behavior; the sodomite was a judicial subject of the law. Homosexuality was a psychic disease of the instinct, of one's sensibility, not to be reduced to merely behavioral terms. Westphal's "conträre Sexualempfindung" is literally a contrary sexual sentiment or sensation, in which the notion of behavior plays, at most, a subsidiary role; the homosexual is a medical patient of psychiatry. Psychiatrists were forever concerned with carefully distinguishing sodomy from homosexuality; Laupts's book reports the views of D. Stefanowski, which are representative of attempts to differentiate the two. Stefanowski gives a point-by-point comparison of pederasty and "uranism," of which the following are some of the more interesting contrasts. In pederasty "the manner of feeling and acting in matters of love remains masculine, the inclination for women exists everywhere," and "the outward appearance always remains masculine; the tasks and habits remain manly"; on the other hand, in uranism "the manner of feeling and acting is completely feminine: it is accompanied by an envy and hatred toward women," and "the outward look sometimes becomes entirely effeminate; the tastes, habits, and pursuits become those of a woman." Moreover, "pederasty can sometimes be restrained and repressed by a vigorous effort of the will," while "uranist passion is completely outside of the domain of the will." Finally, "pederasty as a vice or profession should be repressed and forbidden by the law, male prostitution should be strictly prohibited"; but "uranism, as an innate moral deformity, can never be punished or prosecuted by the law; still its manifestations must necessarily be repressed, in the name of public morality, but one should judge its manifestations as an expression of a diseased state, as a sort of partial mental illness."[75] These passages make clear how distinct homosexuality and sodomy were considered to be. Homosexuality was a disease, a "perversion" strictly speaking, whereas sodomy was a vice, a problem for morality and law, about which medicine had no special knowledge. The crucial distinction in this area of investigation was made by Krafft-Ebing:

> *Perversion* of the sexual instinct . . . is not to be confounded with *perversity* in the sexual act; since the latter may be induced by conditions other than psychopathological. The concrete perverse act, monstrous as it may be, is clinically not decisive. In order to differentiate between disease (perversion) and vice (perversity), one must investigate the whole personality of the individual and the original motive leading to the perverse act. Therein will be found the key to the diagnosis.[76]

Every psychiatrist writing during this period acknowledged the difference between perversion and perversity, even if they also quickly admitted that it often proved difficult to distinguish the two. Only minutely detailed examination could help to determine that a given patient was a genuine pervert, and not merely evil or wicked. Before the later part of the nineteenth century, questions of sexual perversity were not cloaked in silence or secrecy, but were dealt with primarily in treatises of moral philosophy, moral theology, and jurisprudence, and not in medicine. A good example is the work of Immanuel Kant. Besides his three great critiques on epistemology, moral philosophy, and aesthetic judgment, Kant wrote on just about every imaginable topic that was philosophically interesting. His *Anthropology from a Pragmatic Point of View* (1798) contains a discussion of mental illness in which he distinguishes between hypochondria, mania, melancholia, delirium, and other forms of mental derangement.[77] Not a word about sexual perversion appears anywhere in this book, however, even though there are chapters on the cognitive powers, the appetitive powers, temperament, character, and a section on the character of the sexes. But matters of sex did not escape Kant's pen, for if we turn to a book published a year earlier, *The Doctrine of Virtue,* which is Part II of *The Metaphysic of Morals,* we find Kant devoting an entire section to "carnal self-defilement" in his chapter "Man's Duties to Himself as an Animal Being."[78] Moreover, he explicitly considers whether the sexual power may be used without regard for nature's purpose in the intercourse of the sexes (namely, procreation), and he uses the concept of "unnatural lust" here.[79] So it is not as if Kant was silent on the topic of sexual deviations, as if he was subject to some pre-Victorian reticence. It is rather that the epistemic and conceptual conditions necessary to formulate the notion of *diseases of sexuality* did not yet obtain, and sexual unnaturalness could no more be seen unequivocally through the lens of medicine than could any other fundamentally moral problem. The reassignment in regulating the perversions, from law/morality to medicine, was not simply a new institutional division of labor; it was to signal a fundamental transformation, and the inauguration of whole new ways of conceptualizing ourselves.

Perversion was not a disease that lurked about in nature, waiting for a psychiatrist with especially acute powers of observation to discover it hiding almost everywhere. It was a disease created by a new (functional) understanding of disease, a conceptual shift, a shift in reasoning, that made it possible to interpret various types of activity in medicopsychiatric terms. There was no natural morbid entity to be discovered until clinical psychiatric practice invented one.[80] Perversion was not a disease candidate until it became possible to attribute diseases to the sexual instinct, and there were no possible diseases of the sexual instinct before the nineteenth century; when the notion of diseases of this instinct loses its last remaining grasp upon us, we will rid the world of all of its perverts.[81]

Of course, I do not for a moment deny that nineteenth-century psychiatry took itself to be discovering a real disease, and not inventing one. Many of the books I have discussed include entire chapters attempting to demonstrate the presence of these diseases throughout history. Moreau, for instance, after one such historical excursion, insists that we need no longer ascribe these frightful debaucheries to the anger of God or to the rebellion of Satan against God. We can now regard them from a scientific point of view, in conformity with "modern ideas."[82] This particular reinterpretation of history was part of the "retrospective medicine" that was so prominent during the nineteenth century, and which consisted in the reinterpretation of misunderstood past phenomena according to medical categories.[83] Charcot, to take a more famous instance, was another one of the practitioners of this revisionist medicine, and his *Les Démonaiques dans l'art*, written with Paul Richer, argues that artistic representations of demonic possession are in fact representations of hysteria.[84] So we need not be at all surprised to find it repeatedly claimed that these sexual perversions can be seen everywhere in history. These claims, however, should not detain us; all we find before the nineteenth century are descriptions of sodomy, as an actual reading of these pre–nineteenth-century descriptions will confirm. Perversion is a thoroughly modern phenomenon.

VIII

I want to discuss very briefly one last problem before drawing some conclusions. One of the concepts most often linked to sexual perversion is that of the degenerate. This concept derives from B. A. Morel and is understood by him to be an unhealthy deviation from the normal type of humanity; one of the essential characteristics of degeneracy is its hereditary transmissibility.[85] The theory of degeneracy was used as a pseudoexplanatory framework for practically every serious psychopathological state dealt with by nineteenth-century psychiatry. Degeneracy functioned as one of the central ties between what Foucault has called the anatomo-politics of the human body and the bio-politics of the population.[86] Everybody from Westphal to Charcot considered sexual perversion to be one instance of this ever present degeneracy. Krafft-Ebing took the functional anomalies of the sexual instinct to be "functional signs of degeneration";[87] Kraepelin, in his grand classificatory scheme of psychopathology, placed contrary sexual instinct under the general category of "constitutional psychopathological states (insanity of degeneracy)."[88] One advantage of regarding perversion as an inherited degenerate state was that, under this hypothesis, it was difficult to doubt that it was a true disease. Since the etiology of perversion was thought to be constitutional, independent of volition and cultivation, the distinction between perversity and perversion was in principle easily drawn. Yet with this clear advantage of allowing, even requiring, psychiatry to treat perversion as a disease came an unfortunate disadvantage "from a social and therapeutic point of view."[89] It was natural to assume that it was impossible to modify or remove a congenital, inherited condition, and so the theory of degeneracy led to "therapeutic nihilism and social hopelessness."[90] As Kraepelin put it, "There can be no thought of treatment of an anomaly like this, which has developed with the development of the personality and has its origin deep within it."[91] How was psychiatric intervention to be justified in a case where, as a matter of theory, there could be little therapeutic efficacy? Since there was no hope in attempting to treat these patients, psychiatry might seem severely limited in how it could exercise its knowledge and power over the perversions. A. von Schrenck-Notzing was perhaps the first to argue in detail that extraneous influences and education were actually the most significant etiological factors in the genesis of the perversions.[92] He treated thirty-two homosexual patients with hypnotic suggestion and found that 70 percent were greatly improved and 34 percent were cured.[93] As he puts it in the preface to his book,

> The favorable results obtained in "congenital" urnings by psychical treatment in the hypnotic state placed before me the alternative either to assume that suggestion is capable of influencing congenital abnormalities of the mind or to prove that in the idea of homo-sexuality at present prevalent the hereditary factor is overestimated, to the disadvantage of educational influences.[94]

He chose, without hesitation, the latter alternative, emphasizing that individuals who actually suffered from contrary sexual instinct found the theory of heredity convenient, for they "find in it a very welcome excuse for their peculiarity."[95] Von Schrenck-Notzing said that the aim of his book was to demonstrate that "useful members of society can be made of such perverted individuals," and he hoped that his work would "open to workers in the domain of suggestive therapeutics a new and productive field of activity and humane striving!"[96] Morton Prince also recognized that the educational theory of the perversions offered "hope and possibilities," possibilities of successful therapeutic intervention that brought with them that social hopefulness that has always been so much a part of American psychiatry.[97] But Prince insisted as well that the theory that perversion was acquired or cultivated, owing to the effect of education, unconscious mimicry, external suggestion, example, and so forth, had its own unfortunate disadvantages. On this theory, weren't perversions really vices rather than diseases, perversity instead of true perversion?[98] And if this was so, then there was still a difficulty in justifying psychiatric intervention. How could psychiatry legitimately interfere in purely moral problems; ought it not to be limited to real mental diseases, to the domain of medical science?[99] The matrix of psychiatric power/knowledge would be maximized if one could claim both that sexual perversion was not congenital and that it was a disease. If it was not congenital, then therapeutic intervention could be efficacious; if it was a disease, then therapeutic intervention would be required. This is exactly where Prince relied on his theory of habit neuroses and true functional diseases. He believed that in order to maintain that perversion, although acquired, was nevertheless a disease, one had to demonstrate that intensely cultivated habits could eventually become automatic, independent of volitional control. The pervert was then subject to "real imperative sensations and ideas."[100]

> Analogy with what takes place in other fields of the nervous system would make it intelligible that sexual feelings and actions may by constant repetition (cultivation) become associated together and developed into the sort of quasi-independent neural activities, which may then become practically independent of the will—or, in other words, a psychosis.[101]

Prince could then argue that, given this theory, it is up to "counter-education to replace the morbid processes by healthy ones."[102] Under countereducation one could include almost anything one pleased, and so psychiatry was on its way to an unlimited disciplinary regulation of the sexual life. This theory of perversion as an acquired disease induced one to leave completely the domain of pathological anatomy and embed oneself firmly in psychology. Morton Prince, after all, founded both the *Journal of Abnormal Psychology* (1906) and the American Psychopathological Association (1910). The sexual personality was created so much the better to control the body.

IX

It was Immanuel Kant who argued that we can never know the self as it is in itself, but only as it appears to us.[103] Kant thought that he could give a deduction that would exhibit the determinate and unchanging categories through which everything, including our own self, must appear to us. Even if we reject Kant's own deduction, we ought not to reject his basic idea.

The categories and conceptualizations of the self determine not only how others view us, but also how each person conceives of him- or herself. And conceptions of ourselves greatly influence how we actually behave. Part of Foucault's "genealogy of subject in Western civilization" must consist in an investigation of the origin of new categories of the self.[104] These categories may come from the strangest and most diverse places. Ian Hacking has shown that the grand statistical surveys of the early nineteenth century provided many new classifications of the self.[105] It will not be as surprising to be told that psychiatry is another fertile source for new conceptualizations of the self. The concept of perversion, once exclusively a part of specialized nineteenth-century discussions, became, in the twentieth century, a dominant way of organizing our thought about our own sexuality. People diagnosed as perverts came to think of themselves as diseased, as morbid, an experience that was not possible before the heyday of the pervert that I have described. Westphal believed that contrary sexual instinct was always accompanied by consciousness of the morbidity of the condition.[106] Being classified as a pervert could alter everything from one's self-conception to one's behavior to one's social circumstances. And even those of us who are not full-fledged perverts have had to reconceive of ourselves; every little deviation of the sexual instinct may be a sign of our impending perversion. We are all possible perverts. It is perversion as a possible way of being, a possible category of the self, that is the legacy of nineteenth-century psychiatry. The notion of perversion has so penetrated our framework of categories that it is now as natural and unquestioned to think of oneself as a pervert as it was once odd and questionable.

Ian Hacking has argued that

> the organization of our concepts, and the philosophical difficulties that arise from them, sometimes have to do with their historical origins. When there is a radical transformation of ideas, whether by evolution or by an abrupt mutation, I think that whatever made the transformation possible leaves its mark upon subsequent reasoning.[107]

The problem of perversion is a case in point. All of our subsequent reasoning about perversion is afflicted by the historical origins of the concept. Moreover, we cannot think away the concept of perversion, even if we no longer claim to believe that there is any natural function of the sexual instinct. We are prisoners of the historical space of nineteenth-century psychiatry, "shaped by pre-history, and only archeology can display its shape."[108] The archeology of perversion is a crucial stage in understanding the history of the twentieth-century self. Perhaps there will come a time when we can think to ourselves, "How do I love thee; let me count the ways," and no longer fear our possible perversion.

2

Sex and the Emergence of Sexuality

SOME YEARS AGO a collection of historical and philo-
sophical essays on sex was advertised under the slogan: Philosophers are interested in sex again. Since that time the history of sexuality has become an
almost unexceptionable topic, occasioning as many books and articles as
anyone would ever care to read. Yet there are still fundamental conceptual
problems that get passed over imperceptibly when this topic is discussed,
passed over, at least in part, because they seem so basic or obvious that it
would be time badly spent to worry too much about them. However, without backtracking toward this set of problems, one will quite literally not
know what one is writing the history of when one writes a history of sexuality.

An excellent example of some of the most sophisticated current writing
in this field can be found in *Western Sexuality*, a collection of essays that resulted from a seminar conducted by Philippe Ariès at the Ecole des hautes
études en sciences sociales in 1979–80.[1] As one would expect, *Western Sexuality* is characterized by a diversity of methodological and historiographical
approaches—social history, intellectual history, cultural history (which one
historian I know refers to as the history of bad ideas), historical sociology,
the analysis of literary texts, and that distinctive kind of history practiced
by Michel Foucault and also in evidence in the short essay by Paul Veyne.

One perspective virtually absent from this collection is the history of science, and since I believe that the history of science has a decisive and irreducible contribution to make to the history of sexuality, it is no accident that I am going to focus on that connection. But the history of sexuality is also an area in which one's historiography or implicit epistemology will stamp, virtually irrevocably, one's first-order historical writing. It is an arena in which philosophical and historical concerns inevitably run into one another.

In his 1979 Tanner lectures, Foucault writes that he is concerned with the problem of "the relations between experiences (like madness, illness, transgression of laws, sexuality, self-identity), knowledge (like psychiatry, medicine, criminology, sexology, psychology), and power (such as the power which is wielded in psychiatric and penal institutions, and in all other institutions which deal with individual control)."[2] The question that he places at the center of his work is, "In what way are those fundamental experiences of madness, suffering, death, crime, desire, individuality connected, even if we are not aware of it, with knowledge and power?"[3] In the preface to the second volume of his *History of Sexuality*, attempting to explain the chronological displacement from the eighteenth and nineteenth centuries (the focus of the first volume) to the period of antiquity (in the second and third volumes), Foucault emphasizes that the period around the nineteenth century "when this singular form of experience, sexuality, took shape is particularly complex."[4] In particular, the formation of domains of knowledge and the role of various normative systems had a determining effect on the constitution of this experience. For a number of reasons, Foucault decided to address himself "to periods when the effect of scientific knowledge and the complexity of normative systems were less, . . . in order eventually to make out forms of relation to the self different from those characterizing the experience of sexuality. . . . Rather than placing myself at the threshold of the formation of the *experience of sexuality*, I tried to analyze the formation of a certain mode of relation to the self in the *experience of the flesh*."[5]

Foucault's distinction between the experience of sexuality and the experience of the flesh is meant to mark the fact that our experience of sexuality has a specific and distinctive historical genesis. Although we take it to be a natural phenomenon, a phenomenon of nature not falling within the domain of historical emergence, our experience of sexuality is a product of systems of knowledge and modalities of power that bear no claim to ineluctability. And an analysis of late antiquity and early Christianity would reveal, according to Foucault, an experience of the flesh quite distinct from, and not to be confused with, our experience of sexuality. The conflation of these experiences is the result of a coarse epistemology whose consequence is a disfiguring, disabling anachronism. Much the same idea is expressed in Veyne's article, "Homosexuality in Ancient Rome," when he argues that the ancient Roman world did not view the experience of homosexuality as "a separate problem," that the question was never homosexuality per se, but being free and not being a passive agent. What we find is "a world in which one's behaviour was judged not by one's preference for girls or boys, but by whether one played an active or a passive role."[6] If we want to isolate the problem of homosexuality, we must jump to the nineteenth century to find it.

I want to concentrate on the relation between forms of experience and systems of knowledge, on the way in which what we have come to call "sexuality" is the product of a system of psychiatric knowledge that has its own very particular style of reasoning and argumentation. No complete account of the genesis of sexuality can ignore modalities of nineteenth-century power, what Foucault calls biopower, that have detailed and precise relations to our experience of sexuality, a topic about which I shall have almost nothing to say. But the emergence of sexuality and the emergence of a new psychiatric style of reasoning bear such an intimate connection to each other that our experience must remain opaque until this connection is fully articulated.

In order to provide some understanding, even if only at an intuitive level, of how I understand the notion of a style of reasoning or argumentation, let me give an example of two radically different styles of reasoning about disease—what I call the anatomical and psychiatric styles of reasoning. Like Foucault, I am concerned with how systems of knowledge shape us as subjects, how these systems literally make us subjects. In modern times, categories of sexuality have partially determined how we think of ourselves, the shape of ourselves as subjects. If we take the example of sexual identity and its disorders, we can see two systems of knowledge, exhibiting two styles of reasoning, as they come to be instantiated in the nineteenth century. The particular case of the anatomical style of reasoning that I will consider is one that Foucault has made famous with his publication of the memoirs of the nineteenth-century French hermaphrodite, Herculine Barbin. Foucault claims in his introduction to the memoirs that in the Middle Ages both canon and civil law designated those people "hermaphrodites" in whom the two sexes were juxtaposed in variable proportions. In some of these cases the father or godfather determined the sex of the child at the time of baptism. However, later, when it was time for these hermaphrodites to marry, they could decide for themselves whether they wished to retain the sex that had been assigned them or whether to choose instead the opposite sex. The only constraint was that they could not change their minds again: they had to keep the sex that they had chosen until the end of their lives.[7] Although Foucault's account applies to only one kind of medieval hermaphrodite (and because of its brevity simplifies complex relations between the legal, religious, and medical treatment of hermaphroditism in the Middle Ages and Renaissance),[8] his claim simply echoes that of, for example, Ambroise Paré's 1573 *Des monstres et prodiges*.[9]

As Foucault emphasizes, in the eighteenth and into the nineteenth century, all apparent hermaphrodites came to be treated as pseudo-hermaphrodites, and it became the task of the medical expert to decipher "the true sex that was hidden beneath ambiguous appearances" (*HB,* p. viii), to find the one true sex of the so-called hermaphrodite. It is in this context that the case of Herculine Barbin must be placed. Adelaide Herculine Barbin, also known as Alexina or Abel Barbin, was raised as a woman but was eventually recognized as really being a man. Given this determination of his true sexual identity, Barbin's civil status was changed, and, unable to adapt to his new identity, he committed suicide. The details of the case are fascinating, but my concern is with how medical science determined Herculine's real sexual identity. Here are some remarks from the doctor who first examined Barbin, and who published a report in 1860 in the *Annales d'hygiène publique et de médicine légale*. After describing Barbin's genital area, Dr. Chesnet asks,

What shall we conclude from the above facts? Is Alexina a woman? She has a vulva, labia majora, and a feminine urethra. . . . She has a vagina. True, it is very short, very narrow; but after all, what is it if not a vagina? These are completely feminine attributes. Yes, but Alexina has never menstruated; the whole outer part of her body is that of a man, and my explorations did not enable me to find a womb. . . . Finally, to sum up the matter, ovoid bodies and spermatic cords are found by touch in a divided scrotum. *These are the real proofs of sex.* We can now conclude and say: Alexina is a man, hermaphroditic, no doubt, but with an obvious predominance of masculine sexual characteristics. (*HB,* pp. 127–128; my emphasis)

Notice that the real proofs of sex are to be found in the anatomical structure of Barbin's sexual organs.

Writing nine years later in the *Journal de l'anatomie et de la physiologie de l'homme,* Dr. E. Goujon definitively confirms Chesnet's conclusions by using that great technique of pathological anatomy, the autopsy. After discussing Barbin's external genital organs, Goujon offers a detailed account of his internal genital organs:

Upon opening the body, one saw that only the epididymis of the left testicle had passed through the ring; it was smaller than the right one; the vasa deferentia drew near each other behind and slightly below the bladder, and had normal connections with the seminal vesicles. Two ejaculatory canals, one on each side of the vagina, protruded from beneath the mucous membrane of the vagina and traveled from the vesicles to the vulvar orifice. The seminal vesicles, the right one being a little larger than the left, were distended by sperm that had a normal consistency and color. (*HB,* pp. 135–136)

All of medical science, with its style of pathological anatomy, agreed with Auguste Tardieu when he claimed in his revealingly titled book, *Question médico-légale de l'identité dans ses rapports avec les vices de conformation des organes sexuels,* that "to be sure, the appearances that are typical of the feminine sex were carried very far in his case, but both science and the law were nevertheless obliged to recognize the error and to recognize the true sex of this young man" (*HB,* p. 123).[10]

Let me now bypass a number of decades. It is 1913, and the great psychologist of sex, Havelock Ellis, has written a paper called "Sexo-Aesthetic Inversion" that appears in *Alienist and Neurologist.* It begins as follows:

By "sexual inversion," we mean exclusively such a change in a person's sexual impulses, the result of inborn constitution, that the impulse is turned towards individuals of the same sex, while all the other impulses and tastes may remain those of the sex to which the person by anatomical configuration belongs. There is, however, a wider kind of inversion, which not only covers much more than the direction of the sexual impulses, but may not, and indeed frequently does not, include the sexual impulse at all. This inversion is that by which a person's tastes and impulses are so altered that, if a man, he emphasizes and even exaggerates the feminine characteristics in his own person, delights in manifesting feminine aptitudes and very especially, finds peculiar satisfaction in dressing himself as a woman and adopting a woman's ways. Yet the subject of this perversion experiences the normal sexual attraction, though in some cases the general inversion of tastes may extend, it may be gradually, to the sexual impulses.[11]

After describing some cases, Ellis writes further,

The precise nature of aesthetic inversion can only be ascertained by presenting illustrative examples. There are at least two types of such cases; one, the most common kind, in which the inversion is mainly confined to the sphere of clothing, and another, less common but more complete, in which cross-dressing is regarded with comparative indifference but the subject so identifies himself with those of his physical and psychic traits which recall the opposite sex that he feels really to belong to that sex, although he has no delusion regarding his anatomical conformation.[12]

In categorizing disorders, Ellis' clear separation of two distinct kinds of things, anatomical configuration and psychic traits, provides a surface manifestation of a profound and wide-ranging epistemological mutation. It is what makes possible sexo-aesthetic inversion, as a disease, in the first place.

Ellis' discussion descends from the psychiatric style of reasoning that begins, roughly speaking, in the second half of the nineteenth century, a period during which rules for the production of true discourses about sexuality change radically. Sexual identity is no longer exclusively linked to the anatomical structure of the internal and external genital organs. It is now a matter of impulses, tastes, aptitudes, satisfactions, and psychic traits. There is a whole new set of concepts that makes it possible to detach questions of sexual identity from facts about anatomy, a possibility that only came about with the emergence of a new style of reasoning. And with this new style of reasoning came entirely new kinds of sexual diseases and disorders.

As little as 150 years ago, psychiatric theories of sexual identity disorders were not false, but rather were not even possible candidates of truth-or-falsehood.[13] Only with the birth of a psychiatric style of reasoning were there categories of evidence, verification, explanation, and so on, that allowed such theories to be true-or-false. And lest you think that Ellis' discussion is outdated, I should point out that the third edition of the *Diagnostic and Statistical Manual of Mental Disorders* of the American Psychiatric Association discusses disorders of sexual identity in terms that are almost conceptually identical to those of Ellis. It calls these disorders, "characterized by the individual's feelings of discomfort and inappropriateness about his or her anatomic sex and by persistent behaviors generally associated with the other sex," *gender identity disorders*.[14] We live with the legacy of this relatively recent psychiatric style of reasoning, so foreign to earlier medical theories of sex. So-called sex change operations were not only technologically impossible in earlier centuries; they were conceptually impossible as well. Before the second half of the nineteenth century persons of a determinate anatomical sex could not be thought to be really, that is, psychologically, of the opposite sex. Anatomical sex exhausted one's sexual identity; psychological considerations could not have provided the basis for "sex reassignment surgery" since these considerations were not so much as relevant to the question of one's sexual identity. Our current medical concept of sex reassignment would have been unintelligible or incoherent since it could not cohere with the style of reasoning about sexual identity.

The anatomical style of reasoning took sex as its object of investigation and concerned itself with diseases of structural abnormality, with pathological changes that resulted from some macroscopic or microscopic anatomical change. It is for this reason that hermaphroditism most visibly exemplifies this mode of reasoning. But for sexuality to become an object of clinical knowledge, a new style of psychiatric reasoning was necessary. Ellis' discussion already *takes for granted* the new style of reasoning and so treats sexuality and its attendant disorders, such as sexo-aesthetic inversion, as if they were naturally given. Even as sophisticated a historian as Ariès can conflate these different objects of clinical investigation, with the inevitable historical confusion that results. Writing about homosexuality he declares, "The anomaly condemned was one of sexual ambiguity, the effeminate man, the woman with male organs, the hermaphrodite."[15] But any attempt to write a unified history that passed from hermaphroditism to homosexuality would solder together figures that an adequate historical epistemology must keep separate. The hermaphrodite and the homosexual are as different as the genitalia and the psyche. The notion of a style of reasoning helps us to see how this is so.

Indeed, I do not think it would be going too far to defend the claim, paradoxical though it may seem, that sexuality itself is a product of the psychiatric style of reasoning. Sexuality only became a possible object of psychological investigation, theorizing, and speculation because of a distinctive form of reasoning that had a historically specific origin; or to put it another way, statements about sexuality came to possess a positivity, a being true-or-false, only when the conceptual space associated with the psychiatric style of reasoning was first articulated. A somewhat pedestrian, though still surprising, confirmation of this claim is in fact provided by looking at the origin of the word "sexuality." The very word "sexuality," as well as our concept of sexuality, first appears, according to the *Oxford English Dictionary*, in the late nineteenth century. The *O.E.D.* gives as its first example of "sexuality," defined as "possession of sexual powers, or capability of sexual feelings," a statement from 1879 made in J. M. Duncan's *Diseases of Women:* "In removing the ovaries, you do not necessarily destroy sexuality in a woman." Nothing could be a better illustration of my claim that sexuality is an object distinct from the anatomical style of reasoning about diseases. A woman's sexuality is not reducible to facts about, or to the existence of, her reproductive system, and given this understanding it was necessary to have a way of conceptualizing sexuality that permitted one to say something about it without invoking, in any essential way, those anatomical facts. It is the psychiatric style of reasoning that made such talk possible in medicine, that made it possible to make statements such as Duncan's. Without this style of reasoning we would be forever talking about sex, not about sexuality.

Despite Foucault's remarks to the contrary at the end of Volume 1 of *The History of Sexuality,* I think it is of decisive epistemological importance to distinguish carefully between sex and sexuality, where the former is understood, as the *O.E.D.* defines it, as "either of the two divisions of organic beings distinguished as male and female respectively"; an example of this usage is the statement in Crooke's *Body of Man* from 1615, "If wee respect the . . . conformation of both the sexes, the male is sooner perfected . . . in the wombe." The *O.E.D.* gives as another definition of "sex" what is in effect a further specification of the first definition, "the sum of those differences in the structure and function of the reproductive organs on the ground of which beings are distinguished as male and female, and of the other physiological differences consequent on these"; an example of this usage is a remark of H. G. Wells from a 1912 book on marriage: "The young need . . . to be told . . . all we know of three fundamental things; the first of which is God, . . . and the third sex." These uses are closely connected with the use of the verb "to sex," which the *O.E.D.* defines as "to determine the sex of, by anatomical examination."

Although they are closely related, I am concerned primarily with the concepts of sexuality and sex rather than with the words "sexuality" and "sex." A good example of how the same word may be used to express two distinct concepts is given by the only instance I know of where the notion of sexuality is linked to biology instead of psychology. This occurs in Buck's *Handbook of Medical Science* from 1888: "According to a strict biological definition sexuality is the characteristic of the male and female reproductive elements (genoblasts), and sex of the individuals in which the reproductive elements arise. A man has sex, a spermatozoon sexuality." This statement is so bizarre as to produce puzzlement eventuating in silence. Can a spermatozoon be heterosexual, homosexual, or bisexual? Can it suffer from deviant sexuality, or abnormally increased or decreased sexuality? Can it have masochistic, sadistic, or fetishistic sexual desires? The answer to these questions is neither yes nor no, since the questions get their sense from the psychiatric style of reasoning, which has no application whatsoever to a spermatozoon. We quite literally do not understand the claim that "a man has sex, a spermatozoon sexuality," for there is no such thing as sexuality outside of the psychiatric style of reasoning. The irreducible weirdness or incomprehensibility of Buck's claim is a good example of how specific concepts are produced by distinctive styles of reasoning, of how we think about sexuality, and of how we distinguish between sex and sexuality. In looking for the origin of our concept of sexuality, we do well to heed Oscar Wilde's advice that "it is only shallow people who do not judge by appearances." We should examine the word "sexuality" in the sites in which it is used, that is, we must look at the sentences in which "sexuality" appears, and see what is done with these sentences by the various people who use them. Typically, at least when we are dealing with an epistemological break, we will find that the concept under investigation enters into systematic relation with other very specific concepts, and that it is used in distinctive kinds of sentences to perform regular, because often repeated, functions. What we must avoid is the attempt to go behind the appearances, to offer some subtle hermeneutic reconstruction that ignores or overrides the surface of sentences.

If anyone believes that I have so far been talking only about words and not about things, that I have not exited from concepts to the world, it will be helpful at this point to recall some examples of Wittgensteinian criteria. In the most compelling discussion I know of Ludwig Wittgenstein's notions of criteria and grammar, Stanley Cavell, in *The Claim of Reason,* brings into focus a number of examples, one of which concerns the grammar of "pain":

> And pain can be deadened (not altered, as an opinion), or obtunded (not dampened, as a mood); you can locate certain pains, or have to, by prodding, i.e., by activating them, causing them afresh, focussing them; we speak of someone as in pain, but not as in pleasure (and as in mourning and in ecstasy, but not as in joy or in rage); you can cause pain but not pleasure, which is given and is taken (like pride and courage, but unlike happiness, which can only be found; though you can make someone proud and happy, and so also ashamed and unhappy); and so on.[16]

Is it only part of our concept of pain that we say it can be deadened or obtunded, but not altered or dampened, that we say someone is in pain but not in pleasure, that we cause pain but give pleasure? Or is it in the nature of pain itself that we can say these things of it? Cavell's grammar of pain is meant to show that any such facile distinction collapses under the weight of this example. And in this same chapter, entitled "What a Thing Is (Called)," contrasting what he calls the Austinian kind of object and the Wittgensteinian kind of object, he shows more specifically that "if you do not know the grammatical criteria of Wittgensteinian objects, then you lack, as it were, not only a piece of information or knowledge, but the possibility of acquiring any information about such objects *überhaupt;* you cannot be told the name of that object because there is as yet no *object* of that kind for you to attach a forthcoming name to."[17] In these terms, I can formulate my claim by saying that sexuality is a Wittgensteinian object and that no one could know the grammatical criteria of this object before the emergence of the psychiatric style of reasoning, which is to say that before this time there was as yet no object for us to attach the name "sexuality" to.

I recognize that I am defending a very strong, counterintuitive, even seemingly unnatural, thesis here, so let me try to increase its plausibility. I want to approach this issue by discussing some aspects of Leo Steinberg's brilliant book, *The Sexuality of Christ in Renaissance Art and in Modern Oblivion*.[18] Although I am going to focus almost exclusively on a conceptual inadequacy in Steinberg's account, I do not for a moment wish to diminish the major achievement of his book, which transcends the boundaries of any single discipline, articulating issues that take the reader far from the province of art history. His book has an almost unlimited interest, and the kind of provocations it allows is a certain indication of its very rare virtues. The title of Steinberg's book should give us pause since, according to the claim I have just put forward, it seems as though there could not be any such thing as the *sexuality* of a person, Christ included, in the Renaissance. A careful reading of his book shows unambiguously that it is not about the sexuality of Christ, but about the sex of Christ, the representation of Christ's genitalia in Renaissance art. Indeed, Steinberg's argument requires that the paintings he discusses be about the sex of Christ, the fact of his sex.

To briefly summarize his argument, Steinberg believes that these representations of Christ are motivated by the centrality of an incarnational theology, that the representation of the penis of the infant or adult Christ gives visible reality to the mystery of the incarnation. For Christ to redeem humanity by his death, he had to be a man in every respect, and these Renaissance paintings represent him as such: "The rendering of the incarnate Christ ever more unmistakably flesh and blood is a religious enterprise because it testifies to God's greatest achievement. And this must be the motive that induces a Renaissance artist to include, in his presentation of the Christ Child, even such moments as would normally be excluded by considerations of modesty—such as the exhibition or manipulation of the boy's genitalia" (*SC*, p. 10). As Steinberg succinctly puts it later in his book, "the evidence of Christ's sexual member serves as the pledge of God's humanation" (*SC*, p. 13). And as he himself recognizes, the dogma of the incarnation requires that Christ be "both deathbound and sexed" (*SC*, p. 13), and these artists allow us to see that he is sexed, by anatomical examination; the argument requires nothing at all about Christ's sexuality. The anatomical fact of Christ's sex, the representation of his penis, is paralleled by Renaissance discussions and sermons about Christ's circumcision and, as André Chastel has pointed out, by the reliquary of the holy foreskin, called the Relic of the Circumcision, in the Holy of Holies at the Lateran, which was stolen in 1527 during the sack of Rome. Again, there is much about sex but nothing about sexuality in these traditions. At one point in his review of Steinberg's book, Chastel accuses him of "an unjustified transfer of a current conception to a description of the situation in the fifteenth and sixteenth centuries."[19] But the most blatant and far-reaching such transfer, overlooked by Chastel, occurs in the very title of his work. Of course, one might think that Steinberg is simply being careless in his choice of words, that nothing significant turns on this choice, since whatever words he uses, he clearly means "sex." But his choice of "sexuality," whether careless or studied, covers something of genuine significance that is all too naturally missed. It is this automatic and immediate application of concepts, as though concepts have no temporality, that allows, and often requires, us to draw misleading analogies and inferences that derive from a historically inappropriate and conceptually untenable perspective. So let me turn to some representations of sex and sexuality in order to underline their radical differences.

The iconographical representation of sex proceeds by depiction of the body, more specifically by depiction of the genitalia. The iconographical representation of sexuality is given by depiction of the personality, and it most usually takes the form of depiction of the face and its expressions. Figures 2.1 through 2.5, all of which appear in Steinberg's book, represent the sex of Christ by explicitly drawing attention to the fact of his genitalia. Figure 2.1 depicts Saint Anne manipulating Christ's genitalia as Mary and Joseph look on. The work as a whole bears no trace of scandal or blasphemy, and I believe Steinberg is correct in interpreting Anne's palpation of Christ's penis as "palpable proof" of "God's descent into manhood" (*SC*, p. 8). Notice that Christ's profile is barely visible, his face turned toward Mary and not a prominent or significant part of the woodcut. The lengths or depths to which some will go to deny what is visibly evident is rather remarkable. One art historian reviewing Steinberg's book has said the following about his interpretation of the Baldung woodcut:

> The gesture [of Saint Anne] is at the very least ambiguous, in that the
> fingers could well be behind the penis, and not touching it at all. Indeed,
> given that her other fingers are around his knee, this is the most likely

FIGURE 2.1 Hans Baldung Grien, *Holy Family*, 1511.

reading. . . . If they [Baldung's contemporaries] had initially supposed
that St Anne was fondling Christ's penis, they would surely have looked
again to see if another, less wildly inappropriate reading was possible.
They would have noticed not only the position of the other fingers, but
would also have observed that her right hand is under the child's back
and that she is bending forward to take him from her daughter. This is a
familiar subject; and once we recognise it, we can see that the ambigu-
ously placed left hand cannot possibly be touching the genitals. Baldung's
composition is a little awkward, but it does not represent a subject unique
in European art.[20]

This description, even while acknowledging that Baldung's composition is
a "little awkward," shows a reviewer who exemplifies modern oblivion.
First of all, Steinberg's reading is not in the least "wildly inappropriate"
when framed by his readings of dozens of other paintings and by the visual
evidence of the other 245 reproductions in his book. Furthermore, the alternative reading that the fingers "could well be behind the penis" which is
supposed to be made "most likely" by the fact that "her other fingers are
around his knee" is hardly likely at all. If Saint Anne's fingers were actually
around Christ's knee, it would be more natural for her thumb to be extended, which it is not, and for her wrist to be angled more toward her
body. Moreover, and most important, the placement of her left hand is
more than a little awkward if Saint Anne is lifting Christ from Mary's arms.
If, on this interpretation, the supporting right hand is actually doing the
lifting, then the position of the other hand is entirely unmotivated. The alternative interpretation is that the left hand is supposed to be participating
in the lifting. But if one simply places one's hands in the exact position of
Saint Anne's and then attempts to lift an infant from the angle from which
she is purported to be lifting Christ, one all too quickly sees that the most
straightforward function of this placement of the left hand would be to
strain or dislocate the child's left knee or hip. Steinberg's historical erudi-
tion in interpreting paintings is not made at the expense of the perspicacity
of his eye.

Figure 2.2, a painting by Veronese, depicts, going clockwise, Mary, Saint
Joseph, Saint John, and Saint Barbara, with the infant Jesus in the middle.
The central image of the painting is Jesus' self-touch, a motif which recurs
in many other Renaissance paintings. Although in passing Steinberg de-

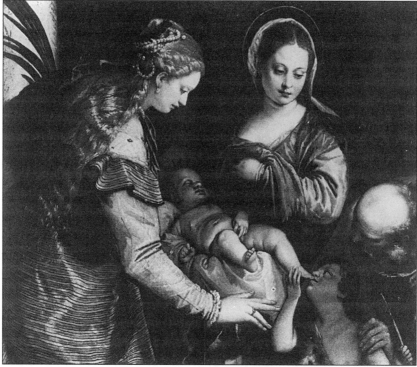

FIGURE 2.2 Paolo Veronese, *Holy Family with Saint Barbara and the Infant Saint John,* c. 1560.

scribes the infant Jesus in this painting as a "contented baby," the expression on his face is actually rather minimal, bordering on blank, his "contentment" being more a lack of restlessness than anything else. The other central image of the painting is Saint John kissing the infant's toe. There is a long tradition of Christian exegesis and interpretation in which the head and feet represent respectively the divine and the human. So Saint John's kissing Jesus' foot draws attention to his humanity as does the self-touch, and this is enhanced by the gazes of all the protagonists (nobody looks at Jesus' face) and by the fact that his upper body is shadowed in a way that his lower body is not. Moreover, as Steinberg points out in another context, "feet" is a standard biblical euphemism for genitalia—Saint Jerome refers to "'the harlot who opens her feet to everyone who passes by'" (*SC,* p. 144).[21] Figure 2.3 is one of three paintings by Maerten van Heemskerck depicting Christ, the mystical Man of Sorrows. All three paintings, not to mention others discussed by Steinberg, clearly exhibit a phallic erection.

FIGURE 2.3 Maerten van Heemskerck, *Man of Sorrows,* ca. 1525–1530.

Even though we take erection to represent sexuality, the presence of rising desire, no such equation can be found here, where the symbolic value of erection is quite different. Steinberg speculates, not at all wildly, that in these paintings erection should be equated with resurrection: "If the truth of the Incarnation was proved in the mortification of the penis, would not

FIGURE 2.4 Mattia Preti (?), *Dead Christ with Angels.*

the truth of the Anastasis, the resuscitation, be proved by its erection? Would not this be the body's best show of power?" (*SC*, p. 91). Whatever one ultimately thinks about these depictions, one looks in vain for any expression of sexuality. Figures 2.4 and 2.5 depict a hand-on-groin gesture of the dead Christ. Although this motif raises many interpretive problems, discussed at length by Steinberg (see *SC*, excursis 38), suffice it to say that dead men can have no sexuality, even if the dead man is Christ exhibiting, by the gesture of his left hand, his sex, his humanity. My motive for reproducing these illustrations is that, like all of Steinberg's iconographical evidence, they can be fully interpreted without invoking the notion of sexuality; indeed, to invoke this notion is to misrepresent what is being depicted.

Contrast these representations with some illustrations from nineteenth-century psychiatric texts.[22] Consider, first, Figure 2.6, which is from an 1879 article by the Hungarian pediatrician S. Lindner, cited and discussed in the second of Freud's *Three Essays on the Theory of Sexuality*.[23] The central feature of the drawing is the depicted relationship between thumb sucking and genital stimulation, which relationship is intended to exhibit one of the essential components of infantile sexuality. The upper left arm/

FIGURE 2.5 David Kindt, *Lamentation*, 1631.

shoulder and right hand of the girl are contiguous in a way that suggests one single, interconnected, even continuous motion linking thumb sucking and genital manipulation. The drawing demonstrates, as Freud was to emphasize, that sexuality is not to be confused with the genitals, that the facts of sexuality encompass far more than the fact of one's sex. Think of Lindner's reasons for accompanying his article with this drawing—there is no need for visible proof of the little girl's sex; it is not as though one is faced with a hermaphrodite; the fact that one views a female child is unproblematic and unambiguous. But how could Lindner demonstrate the facts of infantile sexuality to his doubting pediatric colleagues? It is that problem to which this drawing is meant to respond. It links, so to speak, by ocular proof the psychological pleasure and satisfaction in thumb sucking with the satisfaction one takes in genital stimulation. There is no plausible explanation of the drawing that doesn't invoke the psychology of sexuality as opposed to the anatomy of sex. Furthermore, the expression on the girl's face, although perhaps showing contentment (it is difficult to determine unequivocally) is primarily one of distraction and self-absorption. Her eyes never fully meet ours; the lack of direction in her gaze expresses her preoccupation with her own activity. This kind of infantile self-absorption more subtly demonstrates another aspect of infantile sexuality—the psychiatric style of reasoning calls it "autoerotism." Figures 2.7 through 2.9 illustrate the psychiatric emphasis on the face and its expressions as the way of representing derangements of the personality. From "Happy, Hilarious Mania" to "impulsive insanity," physiognomy was the key to personality. As James Shaw, author of a series of late-nineteenth-century articles entitled "Facial Expression as One of the Means of Diagnosis and Prognosis in Mental Disease," put it:

FIGURE 2.6 From S. Lindner, "Das Saugen an den Fingern, Lippen, etc. bei den Kindern (Ludeln). Eine Studie," *Jb. Kinderheilk,* 1879.

The face having been examined in repose, it is necessary, in order to study the facial reaction, to engage the patient in conversation, or if he is suffering from much intellectual weakness, to ask him a question or make some statement or movement calculated to arouse his attention, and then to watch the changes of facial expression carefully, or to note their absence. . . . Attention to these simple directions, together with a general knowledge of the facial signs given below, will enable any practitioner to refer most cases to one of the ten great symptomatic groups into which I have divided mental cases for the purposes of this monograph. Many cases will be further capable of diagnosis as to the subdivisions etiological,

FIGURE 2.7 James Crichton Browne, "Happy, Hilarious Mania," ca. 1869.

FIGURE 2.8 Manic depression. The manic state is on the left, the depressive state on the right. From Theodor Ziehen, *Psychiatrie für Arzte und Studierende bearbeitet,* 1894.

pathological, or symptomatic, to which they belong, and in most others the medical man will be put on the way to a diagnosis to be confirmed by the patient's speech, conversation, conduct, and anamnesia (personal and family history).[24]

For my immediate purposes, Figure 2.10 is most interesting. It is the only photograph of sexual perversion among the fifty-five photographs reproduced in Shaw's *Physiognomy of Mental Diseases and Degeneracy.* Here is Shaw's commentary on this photograph: "The young deaf mute represented . . . is the subject of a mild form of sexual perversion, leading him to object to wear male attire except under compulsion. His face suggests effeminacy, and his sloping shoulders strengthen the impression. It is often the case that male sexual perverts resemble females, and *vice versa.*"[25] There is obviously no question that the resemblance here is one of sexuality, not of sex. The pervert's tastes, impulses, desires, dispositions, and so forth, exhibit feminine sexuality, all emblematized by the effeminacy of his face. A statement such as Duncan's that removing the ovaries does not necessarily destroy a woman's sexuality, thus divorcing sexuality from sex, was part of the conceptual space that made it possible for males to exhibit feminine

FIGURE 2.9 Three studies of impulsive insanity. From Henri Dagonet, *Nouveau traité élémentaire et pratique des maladies mentales,* 1876.

FIGURE 2.10 Sexual perversion with deaf-mutism. From James Shaw, *The Physiognomy of Mental Diseases and Degeneracy,* 1903.

sexuality and vice versa, made it possible for there to be kinds of sexuality that did not correspond to an individual's sex.

Let me return briefly to Steinberg in order to anticipate, without fully answering, a possible objection to my account. There is a sustained Christian tradition of discussions of Christ's virginity and chastity, a tradition present in many Renaissance sermons, and it might appear that this tradition is explicitly directed to Christ's sexuality, not merely to his sex. After all, how is one to understand chastity except by reference to sexuality? But as Steinberg emphasizes, chastity consists of physiological potency under check; it is a triumph of the will over the flesh and is exemplary because of the volitional abstinence in the face of the physiological possibility of sexual activity (see *SC*, p. 17 and excursis 15). Commenting on a painting of Andrea del Sarto, Steinberg notices that he "contrasts the Christ Child's stiffer member with that of St. John—a differentiation which suggests the likeliest reason for the motif: it demonstrates in the Infant that physiological potency without which the chastity of the man would count for nought" (*SC*, p. 79). Chastity and virginity are moral categories denoting a relation between the will and the flesh; they are not categories of sexuality. Although we tend to read back our own categories of sexuality into older moral categories, partly because it is often so difficult for us to distinguish them precisely, it is crucial to my argument that we separate the two. Blurring the two kinds of categories leads to epistemological and conceptual lack of differentiation, and results in the historiographical infection that the great French historian of science Georges Canguilhem has called the "virus of the precursor."[26] We perpetually look for precursors to our categories of sexuality in essentially different domains, producing anachronisms at best and unintelligibility at worst. The distinction between categories of morality and sexuality raises extraordinarily difficult issues, but I think it could be shown, for example, that even Aquinas' discussion of the parts or species of lust in Part 2.2, Question 154 of the *Summa Theologica* ought not to be assimilated to a discussion of sexuality. One must not suppose that in nineteenth-century psychiatry moral deviation was simply transformed into disease. And in the case of chastity one must carefully distinguish it from what Richard von Krafft-Ebing called "anaesthesia of the sexual instinct" in *Psychopathia Sexualis:* "Here all organic impulses arising from the sexual organs, as well as all impulses, and visual, auditory, and olfactory sense impressions fail to sexually excite the individual."[27] This is a disorder of sexuality, not a triumph of the will but a form of psycho-pathology. Christ most assuredly did not suffer from it. Of course, in concentrating on the Renaissance and the nineteenth century, I have passed over many intervening years. But Steinberg's book is of such importance and can be used to cast such a clear light on the epistemological contrast I wish to draw that a detailed discussion of it is worth our conceptual focus. (The eighteenth century raises its own intriguing problems and would require an entirely separate discussion.)

Here is one final piece of visual evidence for the newly emerging psychiatric style of representing diseases. It was not uncommon for medical texts up through the nineteenth century to include drawings depicting hermaphrodites (Figure 2.11). These poor creatures were shown exhibiting their defective anatomy, the pathological structure of their organs revealing, for all to see, the condition of their diseased sexual identity. Their ambiguous status was an ambiguous anatomical status. But not too many decades later, when a new style of reasoning appeared, we find the radically different iconography of sexual diseases to which I have pointed. A further exemplification of this new iconography is the frontispiece to D. M. Rozier's tract on female masturbation (Figure 2.12), a nineteenth-century book published, significantly enough, at the threshold of the emergence of the psychiatric style of reasoning.[28] Opening this book, the reader is confronted by a drawing of a young woman. Her head is stiffly tilted toward her left, and her eyes are rolled back, unfocused, the pupils barely visible. She is a habitual masturbator. The depicted portion of her body looks normal, but we can see her psyche, her personality, disintegrating before our eyes. She stands as an emblem of psychiatric disorders, so distinct from her anatomically represented predecessors.

Since there are more seemingly problematic cases for my account than I can possibly discuss here, I want to take one example, returning again to a Renaissance document, in order to show how I would defend my claims against some apparent counterinstances of historical importance. A useful place to begin is with a conversation between Foucault and some members of the department of psychoanalysis at the University of Paris/Vincennes that took place after the publication of the first volume of Foucault's *History of Sexuality*. Toward the end of this conversation, Alan Grosrichard questions Foucault as follows:

FIGURE 2.11 A hermaphrodite. From James Paris du Plessis, "A Short History of Human Prodigies and Monstrous Births . . . ," unpublished manuscript, early seventeenth century.

Grosrichard: Does what you say in your book about perversions apply equally to sado-masochism? People who have themselves whipped for sexual pleasure have been talked about for a very long time . . .

Foucault: Listen, that's something that's hard to demonstrate. Do you have any documentation?

Grosrichard: Yes, there exists a treatise *On the Use of the Whip in the Affairs of Venus,* written by a doctor and dating, I think, from 1665, which gives a very complete catalogue of cases. It's cited precisely at the time of the convulsions of St Médard, in order to show that the alleged miracle actually concealed a sexual story.[29]

FIGURE 2.12 A masturbator. From D. M. Rozier, *Des habitudes secrètes ou des maladies produites par l'onanisme chez les femmes,* 1830.

Foucault goes on to make the claim that, nevertheless, the pleasure in having oneself whipped was not catalogued in the seventeenth century as a disease of the sexual instinct, and the issue then drops—too soon, in my opinion, to see what is really at stake. Foucault's account of perversion was to have been worked out in what he originally announced as the fifth volume of his *History of Sexuality*, to be titled, appropriately enough, *Perverts*. But he soon reconceived the topics for his projected history of sexuality and so never provided much historical detail to support his claims about perversion. An account of the emergence of sexuality must be supplemented by the story of the emergence of perversion as a disease category, something I have attempted elsewhere.[30] Or to be more precise, our experience of sexuality was born at the same time that perversion emerged as the kind of deviation by which sexuality was ceaselessly threatened. I have argued not only that our medical concept of perversion did not exist prior to the mid-nineteenth century but also that there were no perverts before the existence of this concept. This shift from the emergence of a concept ("perversion") to the emergence of a kind of person (the pervert), to return to an issue I have already mentioned, is underwritten by the doctrine that Ian Hacking has called "dynamic nominalism." Hacking argues that in many domains of the human sciences, "categories of people come into existence at the same time as kinds of people come into being to fit those categories, and there is a two-way interaction between these processes." Dynamic nominalism shows how "history plays an essential role in the constitution of the objects, where the objects are the people and ways in which they behave," since the human sciences "bring into being new categories which, in part, bring into being new kinds of people."[31] Hacking gives multiple personality as an example of making up people and provides other examples from the history of statistics.[32] Perverts and the history of perversion are a still further example of making up people. Our experience of sexuality is all that there is to sexuality itself, and this experience was decisively and quite recently formed by a set of concepts or categories, among them "perversion," and an associated style of reasoning.

Since the problem raised by Grosrichard is a good test case for my claims, I want to turn directly to the treatise he mentions. In 1629 (or, according to some sources, 1639) John Henry Meibomius, "a physician of Lubeck," wrote a short treatise entitled "On the Use of Flogging in Medical and Venereal Affairs, the Function of the Reins and Loins." It begins with a catalog of cases of whipping that bear no relation to any question of sexuality. Meibomius asserts that whipping has been used as a cure for melancholy, madness, to help lean persons "to plump their bodies," to cure relaxed limbs, to forward the eruption of smallpox, and to cure obstructions in the belly. After listing these cases, which he takes to be uncontroversial, he turns to the question of "persons who are stimulated to venery by strokes of the rod, and worked into a flame of lust by blows."[33] He establishes the veracity of this kind of case through the testimony of other physicians as well as through his own medical experience. Here is one instance he cites:

> I subjoin a new and late instance, which happened in this city of Lubeck, where I now reside. A citizen of Lubeck, a cheesemonger by trade, was cited before the magistrates, among other crimes, for adultery, and the fact being proved, he was banished. A courtesan, with whom this fellow had often an affair, confessed before the Deputies of the State, that he could never have a forcible erection, and perform the duty of a man, till she had whipped him on the back with rods; and that when the business was over, that he could not be brought to a repetition unless excited by a second flogging. (*FVA*, pp. 20–21)

Having thus established the truth of these instances, he next considers "what reason can be given for an action so odd and uncommon." He first entertains the astrological explanation, namely, that "the man's propensity to Venus was caused in his geniture, and destined to flogging by opposite and threating rays of the stars," only to reject it immediately since "the heavens and the stars are universal causes, and so cannot occasion such particular effects in one or two individuals" (*FVA*, p. 21). He next examines the explanation by custom, the idea that these odd and uncommon acts are due to vicious habits practiced in childhood, "a strange instance of what a power the force of education has in grafting inveterate ill habits on our morals." But this explanation is also rejected because not all youths who are engaged in this practice continue it habitually; and moreover, "neither is it probable that all those boys we mentioned began their youth with exposing their chastity to sale with this reciprocal communication of vice, and used rods at the first to provoke lechery" (*FVA*, p. 22). The most adequate explanation of these strange cases, according to Meibomius, can be found by examining the physiology and anatomy of the reins and loins. After discussing in some detail the anatomical relations between the reins, loins, the seminal arteries and veins, and the testicles, as well as determining the way in which "each in a different manner, are appropriated as well for the elaborating of the seed as for performing the work of generation" (*FVA*, p. 23), Meibomius concludes:

> that stripes upon the back and loins, as parts appropriated for the generating of the seed, and carrying it to the genitals, warm and inflame those

parts, and contribute very much to the irritation of lechery. From all which, it is no wonder that such shameless wretches, victims of a detested appetite such as we have mentioned [masturbation], or others exhausted by too frequent repetition, their loins and their vessels being drained, have sought a remedy by flogging. For it is very probable that the refrigerated parts grow warm by such stripes, and excite a heat in the seminal matter, and that the pain of the flogged parts, which is the reason that the blood and spirits are attracted in greater quantity, communicate heat also to the organs of generation, and thereby the perverse and frenzical appetite is satisfied. Then nature, though unwilling, is drawn beyond the stretch of her common power, and becomes a party to the commission of such an abominable crime. (*FVA*, p. 30)[34]

In the next paragraph, Meibomius' underlying aim in writing this treatise becomes clearer. As a physician, he has evidently cured a number of men, otherwise unable to perform the act of generation, with this treatment of stripes and strokes upon the back. This remedy seems to have become the object of much discussion and questioning among both fellow physicians and laypersons. Meibomius admits that perhaps some of those who come to him for treatment are simply exhausted by excess venery and request his treatment merely so that they can continue the "same filthy enjoyment." But he demands of those who question this practice, "You must, in all conscience, also ask: whether a person who has practised lawful love, and yet perceives his loins and sides languid, may not, without the imputation of any crime, make use of the same method, in order to discharge a debt which I won't say is due, but to please the creditor?" (*FVA*, p. 30). Meibomius wants to vindicate his practice by arguing that the use of whips in the affairs of Venus can be a justified therapeutic modality, one that physician and patient can practice without the imputation of any crime to either one.

These quotations already allow us to anticipate my argument that Meibomius' treatise is not a counterexample to the claim that perversion does not emerge as a medical phenomenon until the nineteenth century. Before I set out this argument, however, let me remind you how masochism was understood by nineteenth-century psychiatry. For this understanding, we do best to turn again to Krafft-Ebing's *Psychopathia Sexualis*, since Krafft-Ebing was, after all, the inventor of the concept of masochism. Here is what Krafft-Ebing says at the beginning of his section on masochism:

By masochism I understand a peculiar perversion of the psychical sexual life in which the individual affected, in sexual feeling and thought, is controlled by the idea of being completely and unconditionally subject to the will of a person of the opposite sex; of being treated by this person as by a master, humiliated and abused. This idea is colored by lustful feeling; the masochist lives in fantasies, in which he creates situations of this kind and often attempts to realize them. By this perversion his sexual instinct is often made more or less insensible to the normal charms of the opposite sex—incapable of a normal sexual life—psychically impotent. But this psychical impotence does not in any way depend upon a horror of the opposite sex, but upon the fact that the perverse instinct finds an adequate satisfaction differing from the normal, in woman, to be sure, but not in coitus. (*PS,* pp. 86–87)

Krafft-Ebing is unequivocal in his assertions that masochism is a special kind of psychopathological disorder that affects the functioning of the sexual instinct in a very particular way. The normal direction of the sexual instinct is blocked in masochism, and this instinct and the psychical sexual life are redirected to an abnormal path which Krafft-Ebing characterizes by a number of distinctive features. Masochism is one mode of functional deviation of the sexual instinct that picks out a *kind of individual.* Krafft-Ebing's world of sexual psychopathology is peopled not merely by individuals who want to be flagellated but by masochistic individuals, a very specific kind of diseased creatures. If we were to list the ways of expressing or instantiating sexuality in Krafft-Ebing's universe, masochism would be on that list. Being a masochist is, in *Psychopathia Sexualis,* a possible way of conceiving of oneself, a possible way of being a person.[35]

Returning to Meibomius' treatise, we find, first of all, that there is not even the slightest implication that people who are whipped, even for venereal purposes, suffer from a disease or disorder which manifests itself in a desire for such whippings. In 1629 there was no possible disease which consisted in the pleasure in having oneself whipped; the very idea of such a disease could not be conceptualized. It is only one of many similar ironies in the history of medicine that far from being a disease, the whipping of patients, even the desire of some patients for these whippings, was thought to be therapeutically efficacious and justified. Moreover, there is absolutely no indication in Meibomius' pamphlet that men who are whipped in venereal affairs constitute a distinct kind of individual, different from other people because of special features of their personality. Anybody may be a candidate for this therapy, depending solely upon whether his languid loins can be, so to speak, activated in no other, simpler way. The question for Meibomius and his interlocutors is whether the lust whipping arouses is always morally prohibited, whether it can ever be so aroused "without the imputation of any crime." The question is not whether there is some kind of person for whom only such whipping provides an adequate psychological satisfaction.

This reading of the treatise is further supported by two additional essays appended to it when it was reprinted in 1669. In neither of these essays is there any anticipation of the set of concepts necessary to describe the phenomenon of masochism. Indeed, all three essays, when not attempting to produce a physiological explanation of the effects caused by whipping, fit squarely into the tradition of moral philosophy and theology that deals with the nature and kinds of lust. Although I cannot discuss this tradition in any detail here, I want to make a few, general background remarks. In Book 12 of the *City of God* Augustine uses the theological concept of perversion to describe evil acts of the will. The will is perversely affected when it fails to adhere to God, when it defects from the immutable to mutable good. Perversion is not intrinsically connected with lust, but describes any act of the will that is contrary to God and so is contrary to nature.[36] In Part 2.2, Question 154 of the *Summa Theologica,* Aquinas argues that there are unnatural vices that are a determinate species of lust, since they are contrary not merely to right reason, which is common to all lustful vices, but, in addition, "contrary to the natural order of the venereal act as becoming to the human race."[37] However, even in Aquinas' fascinating attempt to distinguish kinds of lust, it is clear that distinct species of lust do not map onto distinct kinds of individuals; we are all subject to all the kinds of lust, and the principle by which we distinguish lusts from one another does not permit us to distinguish different types of people from one another. In this tradition of moral theology, one classifies kinds of sins, not primarily kinds of individuals and certainly not kinds of disorders.

In fact, Krafft-Ebing was quite concerned with the issue of flagellation as it came to be discussed in moral philosophy and theology. He devotes a section of *Psychopathia Sexualis* to distinguishing carefully between passive flagellation and masochism, insisting that the former is a perversity, and therefore an appropriate topic of ethical and legal discussion, while only the latter is a genuine perversion, a medical phenomenon:

> It is not difficult to show that masochism is something essentially different from flagellation, and more comprehensive. For the masochist the principal thing is subjection to the woman; the punishment is only the expression of this relation—the most intense effect of it he can bring upon himself. For him the act has only a symbolic value, and is a means to the end of mental satisfaction of his peculiar desires. On the other hand, the individual that is weakened and not subject to masochism and who has himself flagellated, desires only a mechanical irritation of his spinal centre. (*PS*, p. 93)

Krafft-Ebing goes on to specify further the characteristics that distinguish the masochist from the "weakened debauchee" who desires passive flagellation, the most significant of these characteristics being psychological. He concludes by claiming that masochism bears to simple flagellation a relation analogous to that between inverted sexual instinct and pederasty; both of these relations are examples of the more general contrast between perversion and perversity, and hence of disease and moral deviation. The phenomenon of masochism, like the general phenomenon of perversion, is a thoroughly modern phenomenon. As Krafft-Ebing remarks, without any further comment, the perversion of masochism was, up until the time of Leopold von Sacher-Masoch, "quite unknown to the scientific world as such" (*PS*, p. 87).

Let me return one last time to Meibomius' treatise to make a final conceptual point. In this treatise, the adjective "perverse" occurs twice, once in the phrase "perverse and frenzical appetite" and a second time in the phrase "vices of perverse lust" (*FVA*, pp. 30, 22). The context of both occurrences makes it clear that "perverse" is used as a general term of disapprobation, although precisely what the disapproval consists in is not further specified. Indeed, if one looks at lexical patterns in the treatises of moral philosophy and theology that discuss perversion, and even in the pre–nineteenth-century medical works that seem to deal with this topic, the adjectival, adverbial, and verb forms, "perverse," "perversely," and "to pervert," appear to occur far more predominantly than either the noun form "perversion" or, especially, the noun form "pervert." However, I do not want merely to claim that the numerical occurrences of the noun form are far fewer than adjective, adverb, and verb, although in the works I have examined this appears to be the case. But even apart from looking at and counting lexical patterns, I think it can be argued that the noun had a conceptually derivative place in moral theology but a conceptually central place in nineteenth-century medicine. One could confirm this claim by studying, for instance, the use of this term in Augustine's *City of God.* And just about the time that Meibomius' treatise was published, a common use in English of the noun "pervert" was as an antonym to "convert"—a pervert being one that is turned from good to evil, and a convert being the contrary. This usage clearly implies that the primary phenomenon is to be located in the perverse choices and actions of the individual, someone being a pervert or convert depending on the person's ethical choices.

In Krafft-Ebing's *Psychopathia Sexualis,* however, we have a book devoted to the description, indeed the constitution, of four types of characters: the homosexual or invert, the sadist, the masochist, and the fetishist. That is to say, we have a book that sets forth the intrinsic distinguishing characteristics of a new kind of person—the pervert. Krafft-Ebing insisted that to diagnose the pervert correctly one "must investigate the whole personality of the individual" (*PS,* p. 53). He continually emphasizes that diagnosis cannot proceed simply by examining the sexual acts performed. One must rather investigate impulses, feelings, urges, desires, fantasies, tendencies, and so on, and the result of this investigation will be to mark off new kinds of persons, distinct and separate from the normal heterosexual individual. It is the pervert who is primary, perverse choices and actions being subordinated to a conceptually subsidiary role. If in psychiatry the conceptual focus moves from perverse choice to the pervert, and if linguistic forms reflect such conceptual changes, then it should come as no surprise that we find more distinctive and frequent use there of "pervert" and even "perversion."

Connected with this new focus is the fact that nineteenth-century psychiatry often took sexuality to be the way in which the mind is best represented. To know a person's sexuality is to know that person. Sexuality is the externalization of the hidden, inner essence of personality. And to know sexuality, to know the person, we must know its anomalies. Krafft-Ebing was quite clear about this point. In his *Text-book of Insanity,* a massive book that covers the entire field of mental abnormality, he writes, "These anomalies are very important elementary disturbances, since *upon the nature of sexual sensibility the mental individuality in greater part depends.*"[38] Sexuality individualizes, turns one into a specific kind of human being—a sadist, masochist, homosexual, fetishist. This link between sexuality and individuality explains some of the passion with which psychiatry constituted the pervert. The more details we have about the anomalies of perversion, the better we are able to penetrate the covert individuality of the self. Only a psychiatrist, after meticulous examination, could recognize a real pervert. Or to be more accurate, it was also thought that there was one other kind of person who could recognize a true pervert, even without meticulous examination: as if by a kind of hypersensitive perception, a pervert could recognize one of his own kind. Of course, much more historical detail would be needed to produce an unequivocally convincing argument that proves the conceptual shift from perverse choice to the pervert. But anyone who reads a few dozen of the relevant texts in moral theology and psychiatry will, I think, be fully struck by what Foucault once called their "different epistemological texture."[39]

Much of my discussion has been concerned with a rupture in styles of reasoning within medicine, a break from pathological anatomy in all its forms to the emergence of psychiatric reasoning. This rupture delineates a problematic internal to the history of medicine. However, my discussion of Meibomius' treatise and the issues it raises, as well as of Steinberg's remarks on the chastity of Christ, opens up a companion problem, one not internal to the history of medicine but rather centered on medicine's appropriation of an initially related, but unmedicalized domain. It is not that medicine simply took over the study of what had once been a part of morality; moral deviation did not merely transform itself into disease. Instead, the moral phenomenon of the perversity of the will furnished a point of reference that both opened the way for and provided an obstacle to the medical constitution of perversion. This problematic, which has barely begun to be worked out in detail, concerns a crossing of the "threshold of scientificity."[40] Foucault, in *The Archaeology of Knowledge,* has very precisely described the questions that must be answered in attempting to understand how such a threshold can be crossed. Describing not his own position but that of Canguilhem and Gaston Bachelard, the kind of history of science he calls an "epistemological history of the sciences," Foucault writes:

> Its purpose is to discover, for example, how a concept—still overlaid with metaphors or imaginary contents—was purified, and accorded the status and function of a scientific concept. To discover how a region of experi-

ence that has already been mapped, already partially articulated, but is still overlaid with immediate practical uses or values related to those uses, was constituted as a scientific domain. To discover how, in general, a science was established over and against a pre-scientific level, which both paved the way and resisted it in advance, how it succeeded in overcoming the obstacles and limitations that still stood in its way.[41]

I know of no better succinct description of what is at stake at this level of analysis. An adequate history of the psychiatric emergence of sexuality will have to look not only to shifts in styles of reasoning within medicine but also to the multilayered relations between our ethical descriptions of sexual practices and their scientific counterparts.

3

How to Do the History of Psychoanalysis: A Reading of Freud's Three Essays on the Theory of Sexuality

I HAVE TWO primary aims in this essay, aims that are inextricably intertwined. First, I want to raise some historiographical and epistemological issues about how to write the history of psychoanalysis. Although they arise quite generally in the history of science, these issues have a special status and urgency when the domain is the history of psychoanalysis. Second, in light of the epistemological and methodological orientation that I am going to advocate, I want to begin a reading of Freud's *Three Essays on the Theory of Sexuality,* one whose specificity is a function of my attachment to this orientation, to a particular way of doing the history of psychoanalysis. Despite the enormous number of pages that have been written on Freud's *Three Essays,* it is very easy to underestimate the density of this book, a density at once historical, rhetorical, and conceptual. This underestimation stems in part from historiographical presumptions that quite quickly misdirect us away from the fundamental issues.

In raising questions about the historiography of the history of science, I obviously cannot begin at the beginning. So let me begin much further along, with the writings of Michel Foucault. I think of the work of Foucault, in conjunction with that of Gaston Bachelard and Georges Canguilhem, as exemplifying a very distinctive perspective about how to write the history of science. In the English-speaking world, perhaps only the work of Ian Hacking both shares this perspective and ranks with its French counterparts in terms of originality and quality. No brief summary can avoid eliding the differences between Bachelard, Canguilhem, Hacking, and Foucault; indeed, the summary I am going to produce does not even fully capture Foucault's perspective, which he called "archaeology."[1] But this sketch will have to do for the purposes I have in mind here, whose ultimate aim is to reorient our approach to the history of psychoanalysis.

In a 1977 interview, Foucault gave what we might take to be a one-sentence summary of his archeological method: "'Truth' is to be understood as a system of ordered procedures for the production, regulation, distribution, circulation and operation of statements."[2] Given this characterization of his standpoint, we should think of Foucault as having undertaken in his archeological works to write a history of statements that claim the status of truth, a history of these systems of ordered procedures. The attempt to write such a history involves isolating certain kinds of discursive practices—practices for the production of statements—which will be "characterized by the delimitation of a field of objects, the definition of a legitimate perspective for the agent of knowledge, and the fixing of norms for the elaboration of concepts and theories. Thus, each discursive practice implies a play of prescriptions that designate its exclusions and choices."[3] Foucault's project, announced in the foreword to the English edition of *The Order of Things,* was to write the history of what Hacking has called the *immature sciences*—those sciences that, in Foucault's words, are "considered too tinged with empirical thought, too exposed to the vagaries of chance or imagery, to age-old traditions and external events, for it to be supposed that their history could be anything other than irregular"[4]—from the standpoint of an archeology of discursive practices.[5] Foucault made the claim, perhaps commonplace now, but bold and even radical when he first wrote, that this kind of knowledge possesses a well-defined regularity, that a history of this knowledge can exhibit systems of rules, and their transformations, which make different kinds of statements possible. These rules are, however, never formulated by the participants in the discursive practice; they are not available to their consciousness but constitute what Foucault once called the "positive unconscious of knowledge."[6]

If these rules are both relatively autonomous and anonymous, if they make it possible for individuals to make the claims they do when they do, then the history of such rules and such knowledge will not look like the sort of history with which we are most familiar. It will not, for example, necessarily group sets of regularities around individual works and authors; nor will it rest content with the ordinary boundaries of what we think of as a science or a discipline. It will rather force regroupings of statements and practices into "a new and occasionally unexpected unity."[7] Because Foucault wanted to describe discursive practices from the standpoint of archeology, the theme of discontinuity was prominent in some of his major works. The unearthing of discontinuities between systems of knowledge is not an assumption of his method but a consequence of it. If one sets out to describe the historical trajectories of the sciences in terms of anonymous rules for the formation and production of statements, then what looked continuous from some other perspective now may very well appear radically discontinuous. Problems of periodization and of the unity of a domain may be almost entirely transformed: one will find, for example, that new kinds of statements which seem to be mere incremental additions to scientific knowledge are in fact made possible only because underlying rules for the production of discourse have significantly altered. However, the method of archeology also makes possible the discovery of new continuities, overlooked because of a surface appearance of discontinuity. Archeology makes no presumption about the predominance of discontinuity over continuity in the history of knowledge; but it does make it extremely likely that what had been taken to be natural groupings of thought will turn out, at this new level of analysis, to be quite unnatural indeed.

In other writings, I have tried to adopt and adapt Foucault's archeological perspective, using it to write a history of nineteenth-century psychiatric theories of sexuality.[8] I have argued that starting around 1870 a new psychiatric style of reasoning about diseases emerges, one that makes possible, among other things, statements about sexual perversion—about homosexuality, fetishism, sadism, and masochism—that then quickly become commonplaces in discussions of sexuality. The appearance and proliferation of these statements were a direct consequence of this new style of reasoning, which we can think of, in Foucault's terms, as the birth of a new discursive practice. An epistemologically central constituent of a style of reasoning, as I interpret it, is a set of concepts linked together by specifiable rules that determine what statements can and cannot be made with the concepts.[9] So to write a history of nineteenth-century psychiatry by way of this notion requires writing a history of the emergence of a new system of concepts and showing how these concepts are internally related by a set of rules to form what we might think of as a determinate conceptual space. We want to see what concepts, connected in what particular ways, allowed statements about sexual perversions that had never been made before, allowed the creation of a new object of medical discourse—sexuality. Thus I have urged that we need a conceptual history of sexuality, without which we cannot know what was being talked about when the domain of psychiatric discourse became fixated on sexuality.

This same kind of method was employed by Heinrich Wölfflin in his *Principles of Art History: The Problem of the Development of Style in Later Art*. Wölfflin characterized the differences between classic and baroque art in terms of two distinct systems of determining concepts. He tried to show the way in which the features of classic art were linked together to form a specific classic visual space, while opposing features were linked together to form a distinctive baroque visual space.[10] It is no surprise that Paul Veyne, in his inaugural lecture at the Collège de France, has conjoined the names of Wölfflin and Foucault; nor is it a surprise, when we remember the derivative role that great men in the history of science play in Foucault's work, that Arnold Hauser has referred to Wölfflin's art history as "art history without names."[11]

Whatever the plausibility of an art history without names, and whatever the general applicability of this methodological perspective in the history of science, a thoroughgoing skepticism about its usefulness for writing the history of psychoanalysis might well persist. Since psychoanalysis is so completely intertwined with the name of Sigmund Freud, it is natural to object that writing its history without his name would not be to write its history at all. It is, no doubt, a peculiar feature of psychoanalysis, a feature that requires a more detailed account than I can provide here, that no matter what one takes as the last word of psychoanalysis, its first and second words are always the words of Freud. And this is not merely because Freud was the originator of psychoanalysis but primarily because the central concepts, claims, and problems of psychoanalysis have not received deeper specification beyond their congealment in his texts. So there is an obvious sense in which any history of psychoanalysis must continuously invoke the name of Freud. This fact, however, does not, and should not, settle the question of what form this invocation should take. Wölfflin was not reluctant to discuss the great works of classic and baroque art; he wanted to demonstrate that this greatness was not incompatible with their artists being subject to specifiable constraints. "Not everything is possible at all times," Wölfflin famously remarked, and his art history, without names, was meant to conceptualize the limits of the artistically possible in a given historical period and to show how a change in constraints could lead to a reorganization of the limits of the possible.[12] To do this successfully, Wölfflin had to operate at a level distinct from individual biography and psychology. In writing the history of psychoanalysis, I want to preserve this level, one whose articulation requires a history of a structurally related system of concepts, a conceptual space, that lies below, or behind, the work of any particular author, even great works of great authors.

Two competing myths about Freud have gradually developed. The first myth, that of official psychoanalysis, depicts Freud as a lonely genius, isolated and ostracized by his colleagues, fashioning psychoanalysis singlehandedly and in perpetual struggle with the world at large. The history of psychoanalysis under the sway of this myth has become the story of Freud as triumphant revolutionary. The second, opposing myth pictures Freud as getting all of his ideas from someone else—usually Wilhelm Fliess, although the names of Jean Martin Charcot, Havelock Ellis, and Albert Moll, among many others, are also mentioned frequently—and taking credit for what were in fact no more than minor modifications in previously developed theories. This is the myth of the career discontents, and the history of psychoanalysis dominated by it has become the story of Freud as demagogue, usurper, and megalomaniac. To the first myth, one can reply *ex nihilo nihil fit,* which is as appropriate a slogan in the history of science as in theology. The second myth derives its strength from an impoverished reading of Freud and an equally impoverished notion of how to read Freud. When applied to the *Three Essays on the Theory of Sexuality,* this myth proceeds by showing that, for example, Richard von Krafft-Ebing employed the idea of libido and Ellis the idea of autoerotism, that Fliess made central use of the notion of bisexuality, that Moll discovered infantile sexuality years before Freud, that Iwan Bloch talked about erotogenic zones, and so on, ad infinitum. Since Freud was fully aware of these writings, the story continues, how could he be anything other than a usurper, with a kingdom made of stolen materials?

Both of these myths, mirror images of each other, depend on the same kind of historiographical presumptions, unacknowledged, prejudicial, and, in my opinion, misguided. Whether Freud did or did not discover infantile sexuality, whatever his own changing assessment of his indebtedness to Fliess, whether he was the first, second, or third to use the word *Trieb* when speaking of sexuality, all of these claims, both pro and con, are radically inadequate if we want to understand his place in the history of psychiatry. Both myths rely on an inappropriate invocation of his name; both misplace the role that such invocation should have in writing the history of psychoanalysis. Freud's biography, his personal drama, and whom he read in what year are all topics that, of course, are interesting and important. But they will not allow us accurately to ground the question whether he was an originator of thought or merely a conserver, and sometimes extender, of other people's ideas.

How we characterize Freud's place in the history of psychiatry ought to depend not on who said what first, but on whether the structure of concepts associated with Freud's writings continues, extends, diverges from, or undermines the conceptual space of nineteenth-century psychiatry. What we need, as I have indicated, is a history of the concepts used in psychoanalysis, an account of their historical origins and transformations, their rules of combination, and their employment in a mode of reasoning.[13] This task presumes, first, that we can isolate the distinctive concepts of nineteenth-century psychiatry, articulate their rules of combination, and thereby discern their limits of the possible. We must then undertake the very same enterprise for Freud's work, which, with sufficient detail, should enable us to see more clearly whether Freud's conceptual space continues or breaks with that of his predecessors. Although Freud may use much the same terminology as many of the people we know he read, the structure of concepts he employs, what I have been calling his conceptual space, may nevertheless deviate to greater or lesser extent from theirs.

These methodological remarks, however brief and abstract, should stand or fall depending on whether or not they enable us to produce a philosophically enlightening, historically plausible account of the issues at hand. If they do not directly guide us toward a more adequate reading of Freud, then their interest will remain but brief and abstract. So I now want to turn to some of the historical questions that this archeological method dictates. This is the place to acknowledge the somewhat misleading implications of the title of this essay. I will not even attempt anything like a complete reading of the *Three Essays*. I want to focus exclusively on the problems encountered in reading the first essay, "Sexual Aberrations." Given the structure of Freud's book, I will obviously have to look at passages in the other essays as well, but I will discuss these only when, and insofar as, they are relevant to excavating Freud's conceptualization of the sexual perversions. The scope of my task is limited here by my desire to approximate to a comprehensive reading only of this first essay. In order to do even that, I will have to start before Freud, with the prevailing concept of sexual perversion in the literature of nineteenth-century psychiatry. So let me try to demarcate the conceptual space of which perversion was an element that dominated European psychiatry at the time Freud was writing the *Three Essays*.[14]

During the second half of the nineteenth century there was a virtual explosion of medical discussions about the sexual perversions, what Foucault has called an incitement to discourse, an immense verbosity.[15] These discussions saturated European and, eventually, American psychiatric concerns, resulting in an epidemic of perversion that seemed to rival the recent cholera outbreaks. Despite many differences between these loquacious psychiatrists, differences both theoretical and clinical, all shared the concept of perversion that underpinned these discussions—the perversions were a *shared object* of psychiatric discourse about which there were commonly recognized and fully standardized forms of reasoning. The best way to begin to understand the nineteenth-century conceptual space encircling perversion is to examine the notion of the sexual instinct, for the conception of perversion underlying clinical thought was that of a functional disease of this instinct. That is to say, the class of diseases that affected the sexual instinct was precisely the sexual perversions. A functional understanding of the instinct allowed one to isolate a set of disorders or diseases that were disturbances of its special functions. Moreau (de Tours), in a book that influenced the first edition of Krafft-Ebing's *Psychopathia Sexualis,* argued that the clinical facts forced one to accept as absolutely demonstrated the psychic existence of a sixth sense, which he called the genital sense.[16] Although the notion of a genital sense may appear ludicrous, Moreau's characterization was adopted by subsequent French clinicians, and his phrase "sens genital" was preserved, by Charcot among others, as a translation of our "sexual instinct." The genital sense is just the sexual instinct, masquerading in different words. Its characterization as a sixth sense was a useful analogy. Just as one could become blind, or have acute vision, or be able to discriminate only a part of the color spectrum, and just as one might go deaf, or have abnormally sensitive hearing, or be able to hear only certain pitches, so too this sixth sense might be diminished, augmented, or perverted. What Moreau hoped to demonstrate was that this genital sense had special functions distinct from those served by other organs and that, just as with the other senses, this sixth sense could be psychically disturbed without the proper working of other mental functions, either affective or intellectual, being harmed.[17] A demonstration such as Moreau's was essential in isolating diseases of sexuality as distinct morbid entities.

The *Oxford English Dictionary* reports that the first modern medical use in English of the concept of perversion occurred in 1842 in Dunglison's *Medical Lexicon:* "*Perversion,* one of the four modifications of function in disease: the three others being augmentation, diminution, and abolition."[18] The notions of perversion and function are inextricably connected. Once one offers a functional characterization of the sexual instinct, perversions become a natural class of diseases; without this characterization there is really no conceptual room for this kind of disease. It is clear, for instance, that Krafft-Ebing understood the sexual instinct in a functional way. In his *Text-book of Insanity* Krafft-Ebing is unequivocal in his claim that life presents two instincts, those of self-preservation and sexuality; he insists that abnormal life presents no new instincts, although the instincts of self-preservation and sexuality "may be lessened, increased, or manifested with perversion."[19] The sexual instinct was often compared with the instinct of self-preservation, which manifested itself in appetite. In his section on "Disturbances of the Instincts," Krafft-Ebing first discusses the anomalies of the appetites, which he divides into three different kinds. There are increases of the appetite ("hyperorexia"), lessening of the appetite ("anorexia"), and perversions of the appetite, such as a "true impulse to eat spiders, toads, worms, human blood, etc." (*TI*, p. 80; see also pp. 77–81). Such a classification is exactly what one should expect on a functional understanding of the instinct. Anomalies of the sexual instinct are similarly classified as lessened or entirely wanting ("anesthesia"), abnormally increased ("hyperesthesia"), and perversely expressed ("paresthesia"); in addition there is a fourth class

of anomalies of the sexual instinct which consists in its manifestation outside of the period of anatomical and physiological processes in the reproductive organs ("paradoxia") (see *TI*, p. 81).[20] In both his *Text-book of Insanity* and *Psychopathia Sexualis,* Krafft-Ebing further divides the perversions
into sadism, masochism, fetishism, and contrary sexual instinct (see *TI*,
pp. 83–86 and *PS*, pp. 34–36).

To be able to determine precisely what phenomena are functional disturbances or diseases of the sexual instinct, one must also, of course, specify in
what the normal or natural function of this instinct consists. Without
knowing the normal function of the instinct, everything and nothing could
count as a functional disturbance. There would be no principled criterion
to include or exclude any behavior from the disease category of perversion.
So one must first believe that there is a natural function of the sexual instinct and then believe that this function is quite determinate. We might
think that questions as momentous as these would have received extensive
discussion during the heyday of perversion in the nineteenth century. But,
remarkably enough, no such discussion appears. There is virtually *unargued unanimity* both on the fact that this instinct does have a natural function and on what that function is. Krafft-Ebing's view is representative
here:

> During the time of the maturation of physiological processes in the re-
> productive glands, desires arise in the consciousness of the individual,
> which have for their purpose the perpetuation of the species (sexual in-
> stinct). . . .
>
> With opportunity for the natural satisfaction of the sexual instinct, every
> expression of it that does not correspond with the purpose of nature—
> i.e., propagation—must be regarded as perverse.   (*PS,* pp. 16, 52–53)[21]

Should anyone doubt the representativeness of Krafft-Ebing's conception, let me cite a long passage from Moll's *Perversions of the Sex Instinct*
(1891), since Moll is considered by Frank Sulloway, among others, to be a
direct anticipator of Freud.[22] Although Moll disputed many of Krafft-
Ebing's specific claims, the degree of unspoken agreement on the appropriate conception of perversion is remarkable. Moll believed that many of the
theories of homosexuality with which he was familiar (homosexuality being
the most clinically well documented of the sexual perversions) did not suf-

ficiently take into account the analogy between the sexual instinct and other functions:

> To understand the homosexual urge we should consider the genital instinct not as a phenomenon apart from the other functions but rather as a psychic function. The morbid modifications of the genital instinct would appear to be less incomprehensible if we were to admit that almost all the other functions whether physical or psychic may be susceptible to similar modifications. The sexual anomalies strike us as singular because most individuals who possess the attributes of the masculine sex have a sexual urge for women. But one must not be led astray by the frequence and regularity of this phenomenon. From a teleological point of view, that is from the point of view of the reproduction of the species, we consider *natural* the urge that the normal man feels for woman. Still in certain pathological conditions the organs do not meet the end assigned to them. The teeth are meant to grind food yet there are men who have no teeth or who have very few of them. The function of the liver is to secrete bile which is diverted into the intestine, and in certain disorders of the liver or of the bile ducts the bile is not secreted and does not reach the intestine. The function of hunger is to remind the organism that it needs food. However, there are pathological states in which the sensation of hunger is absent, although the stomach continues to function normally. It is the same with the absence of the sexual urge for women in a man possessing normal genital organs. We can hardly establish a connection between man's genital organs and his urge for women except from a teleological point of view. Otherwise, one does not see why men should be urged to have connections with women since ejaculation of the sperm may be brought about in quite other ways. It would be rather surprising to see the genital instinct not presenting the same morbid anomalies as the other functions.[23]

Like that of other late nineteenth-century psychiatrists, Moll's teleological *façon de parler* was mixed with, and presumably grounded in, evolutionary considerations. But my concern is not with why Moll said what he did but rather with exactly what he said. In this respect, his conception and Krafft-Ebing's are quite literally interchangeable.

Nineteenth-century psychiatry silently adopted this conception of the function of the sexual instinct. It was often taken as so natural as not to need explicit statement since it was the only conception that made sense of psychiatric practice.[24] It is not at all obvious why sadism, masochism, fetishism, and homosexuality should be treated as species of the same disease, for they appear to have no essential features in common. However, if one takes the natural function of the sexual instinct to be propagation, and if one takes the corresponding natural, psychological satisfaction of this instinct to consist in the satisfaction derived from heterosexual, genital intercourse, then it becomes possible to see why they were all classified together as perversions. Sadism, masochism, fetishism, and homosexuality all exhibit the same kind of perverse expression of the sexual instinct, the same basic kind of functional deviation, which manifests itself in the fact that psychological satisfaction is obtained primarily through activities disconnected from the natural function of the instinct. As Moll succinctly states it, emphasizing the psychological constituent of this natural function, "we ought to consider the absence of heterosexual desires morbid even when the possibility of practicing normal coition exists."[25] This understanding of the instinct permits a unified treatment of perversion, allowing one to place an apparently heterogeneous group of phenomena under the same natural disease-kind. Had anyone denied either that the sexual instinct has a natural function or that this function is procreation, diseases of perversion, as they were actually understood, would not have entered psychiatric nosology.

With this conceptual and historical background, we can place the opening two paragraphs of Freud's first essay in proper perspective:

> The fact of the existence of sexual needs in human beings and animals is expressed in biology by the assumption of a "sexual instinct," on the analogy of the instinct of nutrition, that is of hunger. Everyday language possesses no counterpart to the word "hunger," but science makes use of the word "libido" for that purpose.
>
> Popular opinion has quite definite ideas about the nature and characteristics of this sexual instinct. It is generally understood to be absent in childhood, to set in at the time of puberty in connection with the process of coming to maturity and to be revealed in the manifestations of an irresistible attraction exercised by one sex upon the other; while its aim is supposed to be sexual union, or at all events actions leading in that direction. We have every reason to believe, however, that these views give a

very false picture of the true situation. If we look into them more closely we shall find that they contain a number of errors, inaccuracies and hasty conclusions.[26]

In describing popular opinion about the sexual instinct, Freud's use of the analogy of hunger indicates, as it did throughout the nineteenth century, the functional conception of this instinct. Moreover, just as we should expect, the natural function of the sexual instinct is expressed by an irresistible attraction of the sexes toward each other, an attraction whose ultimate aim is sexual union. Freud's use of the phrase "popular opinion" can easily mislead a reader to think that this conception of the sexual instinct defines popular as opposed to learned opinion. But however popular this opinion was, it was exactly the view of those psychiatrists, listed in the first footnote of this first essay, from whom Freud says his information has been derived.[27] If the argument of Freud's first essay is that these views "give a very false picture of the true situation," then we can expect Freud's conclusions to place him in opposition to both popular and, more important, medical opinion. The problem is how precisely to characterize this opposition.

In the last paragraph of this preliminary section of the first essay, Freud introduces what he calls "two technical terms." The *sexual object* is "the person from whom sexual attraction proceeds," while the *sexual aim* is "the act towards which the instinct tends" (*T*, pp. 135–136). Freud's motivation for introducing these terms is not merely, as he explicitly states it, that scientific observation uncovers many deviations in respect of both sexual object and sexual aim. More significantly, these are precisely the two conceptually basic kinds of deviations we should expect of those writers who subscribed to the popular conception of the sexual instinct. Deviations with respect to sexual object are deviations from the natural attraction exercised by one sex upon the other; deviations with respect to sexual aim are deviations from the natural goal of sexual union. The remainder of the first essay is structured around this distinction between sexual object and sexual aim, and the central role of this distinction is itself firmly dependent on the view of the sexual instinct that Freud will argue is false. I emphasize this point because one must recognize that Freud's opposition to the shared opinion concerning the sexual instinct is an opposition from within, that his argument unfolds while taking this shared opinion as given. Freud's opposition, let me say in anticipation, participates in the mentality that it criticizes. This decisive starting point, Freud's immanent criticism, will show itself in his final formulations and conclusions, specifically in their ambiguities and hesitations.

I want to proceed by reminding you of the general outlines of the next two sections of the first essay, in many ways the core of this essay. The next section discusses deviations in respect of the sexual object. Under this category Freud includes the choice of children and animals as sexual objects, but his most detailed discussion is of inversion, the deviation to which nineteenth-century psychiatrists had themselves devoted the most attention. After describing different degrees of inversion, Freud argues that inversion should not be regarded as an innate indication of nervous degeneracy—an assessment which was widespread, even if not universal, in the nineteenth century. The overturning of the theory of degeneracy as the explanation of nervous disorders was of central importance in the history of nineteenth- and early–twentieth-century psychiatry, and Freud played a role here, as did many others.[28] Indeed, Freud insisted that the choice between claiming inversion to be innate and claiming it to be acquired is a false one, since neither hypothesis by itself gives an adequate explanation of the nature of inversion. Freud immediately turns, in a section both complicated and problematic, to the role of bisexuality in explaining inversion, and I shall not even attempt to discuss this section now. Despite the recent attention that has been given to the notion of bisexuality in the development of Freud's early psychoanalytic thought, his remarks in this section become more and more puzzling the more carefully they are studied.

Freud next describes the characteristics of the sexual object and sexual aims of inverts and ends this whole section on deviations in respect of the sexual object with an extraordinary conclusion, a conclusion more innovative, even revolutionary, than I suspect he was able to recognize.

> It has been brought to our notice that we have been in the habit of regarding the connection between the sexual instinct and the sexual object as more intimate than it in fact is. Experience of the cases that are considered abnormal has shown us that in them the sexual instinct and the sexual object are merely soldered together—a fact which we have been in danger of overlooking in consequence of the uniformity of the normal picture, where the object appears to form part and parcel of the instinct. We are thus warned to loosen the bond that exists in our thought be-

tween instinct and object. It seems probable that the sexual instinct is in the first instance independent of its object; nor is its origin likely to be due to its object's attractions. (*T,* pp. 147–148)

In the nineteenth-century psychiatric theories that preceded Freud, both a specific object and a specific aim formed part and parcel of the instinct. The nature of the sexual instinct manifested itself, as I have said, in an attraction to members of the opposite sex and in a desire for genital intercourse with them. Thus inversion was one unnatural functional deviation of the sexual instinct, a deviation in which the natural object of this instinct did not exert its proper attraction. By claiming, in effect, that there is no natural object of the sexual instinct, that the sexual object and sexual instinct are merely soldered together, Freud dealt a conceptually devastating blow to the entire structure of nineteenth-century theories of sexual psychopathology. In order to show that inversion was a real functional deviation and not merely a statistical abnormality without genuine pathological significance, one had to conceive of the "normal" object of the instinct as part of the very content of the instinct itself. If the object is not internal to the instinct, then there can be no intrinsic clinico-pathological meaning to the fact that the instinct can become attached to an inverted object. The distinction between normal and inverted object will not then coincide with the division between the natural and the unnatural, itself a division between the normal and the pathological. Since the nature of the instinct, according to Freud, has no special bond with any particular kind of object, we seem forced to conclude that the supposed deviation of inversion is no more than a mere difference. Indeed, Freud's very language is indicative of the force of this conclusion. He says, "Experience of the cases that are *considered* abnormal," thus qualifying "abnormal" in a rhetorically revealing manner.[29] These cases of inversion are *considered* abnormal because of a certain conception of the sexual instinct in which one kind of object is a natural part of the instinct itself. Unhinged from this conception, these cases cannot be considered pathological, cannot instantiate the concept of abnormality employed by Krafft-Ebing, Moll, and others. I think that what we ought to conclude, given the logic of Freud's argument and his radically new conceptualization in this paragraph, is precisely that cases of inversion can no longer be considered pathologically abnormal.

In light of these remarks, I think that we can conclude further that Freud

operates with a concept of the sexual instinct different from that of his contemporaries, or, better yet, that he does not employ the concept of the sexual instinct in his theory of sexuality. What is at issue here is not Freud's
choice of words. Commentators are forever remarking that English-reading
readers of Freud are led astray by the translation of *Trieb* as "instinct," since
Trieb is better translated by "drive," reserving "instinct" for *Instinkt*.[30] However, since many of Freud's contemporaries, among them Krafft-Ebing,
used *Trieb*, Freud's terminology did not constitute a break with previously
established terminology. It is not the introduction of a new word that sig-
nals Freud's originality but rather the fact that *Sexualtrieb* is not the same
concept as that of the sexual instinct. We can see this, to reiterate my main
point, by recognizing that Freud's conclusion is explicitly and directly opposed to any conclusion that could be drawn by using the concept of the
sexual instinct. The relationship between the concepts of *sexual instinct* and
sexual object found in nineteenth-century texts, a rule of combination partially constitutive of the concept of the sexual instinct, was completely un-
dermined by Freud, and as a consequence of this cutting away of old foundations, inversion could not be thought of as an unnatural functional
deviation of the sexual instinct. That *Sexualtrieb* is not the same as sexual
instinct is shown by the fact that the concept of sexual instinct played a
very specific role in a highly structured, rule-governed, conceptual space, a
space within which psychiatric theories of sexuality had operated since
about 1870.

If Freud's conclusions are as radical as I have made them out to be, if his
conclusions really do overturn the conceptual structure of nineteenth-century theories of sexual psychopathology, then we might well wonder what
prepared the way for these conclusions. I think that we can point to an *attitude* that prepared the way for Freud, even though there is a very large gap
between this attitude and the new conclusions Freud drew. Freud himself
tells us in a footnote the source of his attitude, and the fact that he mentions it only in passing should not lead us to underestimate the depth of its
significance: "The pathological approach to the study of inversion has been
displaced by the anthropological. The merit for bringing about this change
is due to Bloch" (*T*, p. 139, n. 2). In 1902–3, Iwan Bloch published a two-
volume book, *Beiträge zur Aetiologie der Psychopathia Sexualis,* which was
central in establishing the inadequacy of the degeneracy explanation of perversion. This work is exhaustive in cataloging the utter pervasiveness of

sexual aberrations, which, according to Bloch, have appeared in all historical periods, all races, and all cultures. His attitude toward these facts is surprising and, one might say, potentially revolutionary, although his work
lacks the conceptual rearticulation that was a precondition of any radical
conclusions.

In the introduction to the first volume of his work, Bloch announces that
he intends to show that "the purely medical view of the sexual anomalies,
which has been stated so well by Casper, von Krafft-Ebing, A. Eulenburg,
A. Moll, von Schrenck-Notzing, [and] Havelock Ellis, . . . [does not suf-
fice] for a fundamental explanation of the phenomena in this field," and he
then opposes to the "clinico-pathological theory" of the sexual aberrations
his own "anthropologic-ethnologic concept of the facts of so-called *psychopathia sexualis.*"[31] He claims that he will show that "this general concept of
the sexual anomalies as universal human, ubiquitous phenomena makes it
necessary to recognize as physiologic much that previously has been regarded as pathologic" (*AS*, p. 6). (Bloch follows a standard nineteenth-century medical convention of often using the contrast physiologic/pathologic
instead of normal/pathologic.) Given his "anthropologic" attitude, Bloch
finds no difficulty in making statements such as the following:

> We find minor deviations from the norm of *vita sexualis* quite gen-
> eral. There are few persons who have not somewhere touched the nar-
> row boundary between normal and pathological indulgence. (*AS*,
> pp. 165–66)

> There can be no doubt that a normal individual can accustom himself to
> the various sexual aberrations so that these come to be "perversions,"
> which deviations appear in the same form in sound persons as well as in
> diseased.[32]

The narrow boundary between the normal and the pathological, the fact
that sexual aberrations are a universal human phenomenon, was the primary evidence for Bloch that nervous degeneracy was not an accurate explanatory or diagnostic rubric under which perversion could be placed.
And his attitude about sexual aberrations was distinctively different—less
unequivocal, less psychiatric—from that of the authors with whom he was
engaged in debate. But this attitude toward inversion and toward the other
perversions, however different it was from the purely medical view and

however unstable it often seemed, never led Bloch to throw into doubt the concept of the sexual instinct that made possible the classification of these phenomena as deviant (and that therefore required some alternative explanation of their status as pathological). Freud might have taken Bloch's anthropological observations, in conjunction with the other clinical evidence he cites, to show merely that inversion, if only in a rudimentary or shadow form, was much more widespread than many psychiatrists had believed. This claim would still have allowed a conceptual priority to the "uniformity of the normal picture." Freud might then have advanced with this conclusion to blur the boundary between the normal and the pathological even further, thereby providing yet one more attack on the idea that a distinctive class of degenerate individuals suffered from inversion. But rather than drawing this limited, though significant, conclusion, Freud went to the core of the matter and decisively replaced the concept of the sexual instinct with that of a sexual drive "in the first instance independent of its object." This was a conceptual innovation worthy of the name of genius—although genius need not be conscious of itself as such, as we shall see if we turn to the next section of the first essay, entitled "Deviations in Respect of the Sexual Aim."

Freud defines perversions as

> sexual activities which either (a) extend, in an anatomical sense, beyond the regions of the body that are designed for sexual union, or (b) linger over the intermediate relations to the sexual object which should normally be traversed rapidly on the path towards the final sexual aim. (T, p. 150)

This definition of perversion is explained by the fact that, as Freud puts it,

> the normal sexual aim is regarded as being the union of the genitals in the act known as copulation, which leads to a release of the sexual tension and a temporary extinction of the sexual instinct—a satisfaction analogous to the sating of hunger. (T, p. 149)

So since the normal sexual aim is copulation and the anatomical region appropriate to this aim is the genitals, two main kinds of perverse deviations in respect of the sexual aim are possible. Under the heading of anatomical extensions, Freud discusses oral-genital sexual activities, anal-genital sexual activities, kissing, and fetishism, recognizing that the last might also have been classified as a deviation in respect of the sexual object. Under fixations of preliminary sexual aims, Freud discusses touching and looking, and sadism and masochism. Since I cannot discuss each of these examples here, let me focus on a few representative ones.

Sexual use of the mucous membrane of the lips and mouths of two persons, otherwise known as kissing, is, strictly speaking, a perversion, since, as Freud says, "the parts of the body involved do not form part of the sexual apparatus but constitute the entrance to the digestive tract" (*T*, p. 150). But when the mucous membranes of the lips of two persons come together, we are not in the habit of classifying the anatomical extension or resulting aim as a perversion. Indeed, Freud notes that we hold kissing in "high sexual esteem" and he goes on to claim that kissing is "the point of contact with what is normal" (*T*, pp. 150–151). So given kissing's technical status as a perversion and our refusal to classify it as such, those who claim oral-genital and anal-genital activities are perversions must be "giving way to an unmistakable feeling of *disgust,* which protects them from accepting sexual aims of this kind" (*T*, p. 151). Freud immediately adds that "the limits of such disgust are, however, often *purely conventional*" (*T*, p. 151; my emphasis).[33]

In discussing the kind of looking that has a sexual tinge to it, Freud acknowledges that most normal people linger to some extent over this form of pleasure, so he gives a number of conditions under which this pleasure in looking, usually called scopophilia, becomes a perversion. The most important of these conditions is when "instead of being *preparatory* to the normal sexual aim, it [pleasure in looking] supplants it." And Freud goes on to remark that "the force which opposes scopophilia, but which may be overridden by it (in a manner parallel to what we have previously seen in the case of disgust), is *shame*" (*T*, p. 157). Similarly, when the aggressive component of the sexual instinct "has usurped the leading position" so that sexual satisfaction "is entirely conditional on the humiliation and maltreatment of the object," we are faced with the perversion of sadism (*T*, p. 158). Shame and disgust are the two "most prominent" forces that keep the sexual instinct "within the limits that are regarded as normal" (*T*, p. 162), but Freud also lists pain, horror, and aesthetic and moral ideals as other normalizing restraints.[34]

In the conclusion to the third section, after mentioning the importance of such restraints, Freud insists that since these perversions admit of analysis, that is, since they "can be taken to pieces," they must be of a "composite nature":

> This gives us a hint that perhaps the sexual instinct itself may be no simple thing, but put together from components which have come apart again in the perversions. If this is so, the clinical observation of these abnormalities will have drawn our attention to amalgamations which have been lost to view in the uniform behaviour of normal people. (*T*, p. 162)

This passage introduces the concept of component instincts, a notion that will assume its full role in Freud's conception of sexuality only when he later connects it with the further idea of pregenital libidinal organizations. Some of these component instincts are specified by their source in an erotogenic zone, a zone of the body capable of sexual excitation—examples are oral and anal component instincts (see esp. *T*, pp. 167–169).[35] Other component instincts are specified by their aim, independent of any erotogenic zone—examples are the component instincts of scopophilia and cruelty (see *T*, pp. 191–193).

In the 1905 edition, the first edition, of the *Three Essays*, the component instincts are thought to function anarchically until the primacy of the genital zone is established. In his 1913 article, "The Disposition to Obsessional Neurosis," Freud introduces the concept of pregenital organization, recognizing that there is an anal organization of the libido. In the 1915 edition of the *Three Essays*, Freud recognizes an oral organization of the libido, and, finally, in his 1923 article, "The Infantile Genital Organization," he describes a phallic organization of it. All of these pregenital organizations are theoretically incorporated into the 1924 edition of the *Three Essays* in the section of the second essay entitled "The Phases of Development of the Sexual Organization." Though we should not undervalue the importance of the notion of pregenital organizations of the libido, it was Freud's articulation of the concept of component instincts that constituted another one of his major conceptual innovations (without which the notion of pregenital organizations would have made no sense). The concept of component instincts made it possible for Freud to say, to quote from his concluding summary of the *Three Essays*, that "the sexual instinct itself must be something put together from various factors, and that in the perversions it falls apart, as it were, into its components" (*T*, p. 231).

The idea that the sexual instinct is made up of components, that it so combines a multiplicity of erotogenic zones and aims, is a further radical break with the nineteenth-century medical conceptualization of the sexual instinct. Freud's argument, his structure of concepts, leads to the claim that neither the erotogenic zone of the genitals nor the aim of copulation bears any privileged connection to the sexual instinct. The "normal" aim of the sexual instinct, genital intercourse, is not part of the content of the instinct; or, to put it another way, recurring to Freud's previous conclusions about the sexual object, the sexual instinct and sexual aim are merely soldered together. If there is no natural aim to the sexual instinct, no given aim internal to this instinct, then deviations from the aim of genital intercourse appear to lose their status as genuine perversions, as pathological aberrations whose status outstrips any supposed statistical abnormality. If the structure of Freud's argument here, in conjunction with his argument in the previous section, is to show that neither a specific aim nor a specific object has any constitutive bond with the sexual instinct, and if the previously shared concept of the sexual instinct is thus effectively dismantled, then it is difficult to see how any conceptual foothold could remain for the concept of unnatural functional deviations of this instinct. In the case of both sexual aim and sexual object, it is only the apparent uniformity of normal behavior that directs us to think otherwise. But this apparently well-entrenched uniformity actually masks the operations of the sexual instinct, operations which, *when conceptualized by Freud,* show us that the idea of the natural function of the instinct has no basis whatsoever.[36] We ought to conclude from what Freud says here that there are no true perversions. The conceptual space within which the concept of perversion functions and has a stable role has been thoroughly displaced—and displaced in a way that requires a new set of concepts for understanding sexuality and a new mode of reasoning about it.

This is the place, obviously enough, at which someone might retreat to Freud's discussion of disgust and shame, claiming that these reactions can provide an independent criterion for classifying certain sexual phenomena as perversions. But however we are to understand the role of these reactions, it is absolutely clear from Freud's remarks that even though he believes that some of these phenomena are such that "we cannot avoid pronouncing them 'pathological'" (*T,* p. 161), these pronouncements, our shame, disgust, and moral and aesthetic ideals, cannot provide an appropri-

ate criterion of perversion. The tone of his example that we may be dis-
gusted at the idea of using someone else's toothbrush, which follows his
claim that these reactions are "often purely conventional," permits no other
intelligible reading (see *T,* pp. 151–152). And, of course, it almost goes without saying that such a last-ditch attempt to save the concept of perversion
would be at odds with the structure of the *Three Essays* as a whole and
would make most of its content completely beside the point.

Even if Freud's conclusions in effect overturn the conceptual apparatus
of perversion, it is well known that he did not embrace these conclusions unambiguously or unhesitatingly. The language of Freud's discussion
sometimes reads as if he is unaware of the conceptual innovations he has
wrought, as if nineteenth-century theories of sexual psychopathology can
remain secure in their conceptual underpinnings. In the section of the
third essay entitled "The Primacy of the Genital Zones and Fore-Pleasure,"
Freud can be found referring to "the appropriate [*geeignete*] stimulation of
an erotogenic zone (the genital zone itself, in the glans penis) by the appropriate [*geeignetste*] object (the mucous membrane of the vagina)" (*T,*
p. 161). But the whole point of Freud's argument in the first essay has been
that no particular zone of the body and no particular object is specially
suitable to, or qualified for, stimulation. The notion of appropriateness has
lost all of its conceptual plausibility because the concept of the sexual drive
is detached from that of a natural object and aim. And whatever transformations of puberty Freud may want to sketch in the third essay, these
transformations cannot reinstate the old concept of the sexual instinct, the
concept which gives a place to the notions of appropriate object and stimulation. The uneasy attitude of Freud's discussion is highlighted again in the
next section of the third essay, "Dangers of Fore-Pleasure" *(Gefahren der
Vorlust),* where Freud talks of the "normal sexual aim" as being "endangered
by the mechanism in which fore-pleasure is involved." The danger in question consists in the fact that one may become fixated on the pleasure of the
preparatory acts of the sexual process, and these acts may then take the
place of the normal sexual aim. Such displacement, Freud tells us, is the
"mechanism of many perversions" (*T,* p. 211). But again this is dangerous,
in the sense of pathogenic, only if it exhibits some kind of unnatural deviation from the normal aim of the sexual instinct;[37] and given Freud's previous argument, he cannot maintain this latter claim. He dimly indicates his
awareness of this fact when he introduces the distinction between fore-

pleasure and end-pleasure. The first is the "kind of pleasure due to the excitation of erotogenic zones," while the second is the kind of pleasure "due to
discharge of the sexual substances" (*T*, p. 210). Since no conceptual space
remains for the distinction between, as it were, natural and unnatural pleasure, or normal and abnormal pleasure, Freud is left merely with the difference between two kinds or degrees of pleasure, shorn of any pathological
implications. This is not the only place where Freud hesitates to believe
what he has said.

Let me focus on just a few more passages that will reinforce still further
the complexity of this problem. The first passage comes from Freud's discussion of "The Perversions in General" in the first essay, and I want to notice especially the attitude embodied in this passage.

> If a perversion, instead of appearing merely *alongside* the normal sexual
> aim and object, and only when circumstances are unfavorable to *them*,
> and favorable to *it*—if, instead of this, it ousts them completely and takes
> their place in all circumstances—if, in short, a perversion has the charac-
> teristics of exclusiveness and fixation—then we shall usually be justified
> in regarding it as a pathological symptom.   (*T*, p. 161)[38]

The phrase "we shall usually be justified in regarding it as a pathological
symptom" shows that we find here the attitude of, let us say, a pathologist,
apparently the very same kind of medical attitude found in Krafft-Ebing,
Moll, and their fellow-travelers. The rhetoric of this passage emphasizes
the characteristics of exclusiveness and fixation, as though perversions are
harmless until they become exclusive and fixed, as though this is the real
criterion of pathology. But it is clear enough that the tendency toward exclusiveness and fixation on genital activity is not only nonpathological but
a central component of Freud's conception of normal, healthy sexuality. It
is only when sexual activity is divorced from the normal sexual aim and object that it can become a perversion and so qualify for pathological status.
The moment the concept of perversion is introduced, with its corresponding concepts of normal aim and object, we are prepared for the attitude
that treats perversion as pathological. The crucial move, the moment that
makes the medicalizing attitude inevitable, is not the explicit listing of
characteristics that make perversions pathological, but the use of the concept in the first place.

Freud's problematization of perversion is shown by the fact that in the first essay the words "normal," "pathological," and "perversion" often appear in scare quotes or qualified by a phrase like "what we would describe as"; as we move through the other essays, the scare quotes become scarcer and the qualifications less emphatic, until, in the concluding summary of the book, these terms appear *simpliciter*. Indeed, in the paragraph preceding the one I have just quoted, "pathological" does appear in scare quotes, but by the end of the next paragraph the fact that we regard perversions as pathological is something which is unqualified and justified.

Although I could discuss the only later, detailed passage of the *Three Essays* in which Freud returns to inversion, as opposed to perversion, a passage where the same questions of attitude arise (see *T,* pp. 229–130), it will be more useful, I think, to concentrate on a remarkable passage in the concluding summary to the book. The passage appears during Freud's discussion of the various factors that can interfere with the development of a normal sexual instinct.

> Writers on the subject, for instance, have asserted that the necessary precondition of a whole number of perverse fixations lies in an innate weakness of the sexual instinct. In this form the view seems to me untenable. It makes sense, however, if what is meant is a constitutional weakness of one particular factor in the sexual instinct, namely the genital zone—a zone which takes over the function of combining the separate sexual activities for the purposes of reproduction. For if the genital zone is weak, this combination, which is required to take place at puberty, is bound to fail, and the strongest of the other components of sexuality will continue its activity as a perversion. (*T,* p. 237)[39]

We find in the writings of both Moll and Ellis the claim that an innate weakness of the sexual instinct is often responsible for the failure of normal heterosexual development, with perversion being the manifest result. In fact many writers before Freud used the terms "sexual instinct" and "genital instinct" interchangeably, as if the latter were simply a more precise name for the former. This identification was not in the least bit arbitrary, since the sexual instinct was conceived of as psychically expressing itself in an attraction for members of the opposite sex, with genital intercourse as the ultimate aim of this attraction. And since these features specified the natural operation of the sexual instinct, the common use of the alternative phrase "genital instinct" was not conceptually misplaced. But once Freud reconceived the sexual instinct as having no natural operation, once any specific aim and object of the drive were thought to be merely soldered to it, the genital zone lost the conceptual primacy that was a precondition of its principled identification with the instinct itself. When the sexual instinct is conceived of as an amalgamation of components, the genital zone being one such component but without any natural privilege, then to single out this zone as Freud does in this passage, to claim that a constitutional weakness of it is responsible for the perversion, is to maintain an attitude toward genitality that is no longer appropriate. Freud in effect reintroduces, behind his own back, an identification that he has shown to be untenable. His claim that these writers are mistaken in asserting that an innate weakness of the sexual instinct is responsible for perversion, but that their assertions would make sense "if what is meant is a constitutional weakness of one particular factor in the sexual instinct, namely the genital zone," is astonishing, since this is, of course, exactly what they meant, and had to mean, given their conception of the sexual instinct. It is Freud who cannot mean to say that the absence of this particular factor, the primacy of the genital zone, is a condition of perversion. The last sentence of this paragraph reads, "For if the genital zone is weak, this combination, which is required to take place at puberty, is bound to fail, and the strongest of the other components of sexuality will continue its activity as a perversion." But the system of concepts Freud has been working with in the first essay requires a slightly different conclusion, one whose subtle modulation from Freud's actual conclusion must be emphasized. The appropriate formulation of the conclusion should read, "For if the genital zone is weak, this combination, which often takes place at puberty, will fail, and the strongest of the other components of sexuality will continue its activity." The differences between these two formulations represent what I have been calling Freud's attitude.

Although it is a central feature of commentary that it can go on indefinitely, I want to stop and return in conclusion to issues of historiographical orientation. I should perhaps first describe the sense in which I think that my reading of the *Three Essays* is a history of psychoanalysis without names. It is not, of course, that I have refused to invoke Freud's name, or the names of Bloch, Moll, and others. It is rather that I have treated their names as, so to speak, place-holders for certain sets of concepts and the way these concepts fit together to constitute a conceptual space. We see that the concept of perversion in nineteenth-century psychiatry was part of a conceptual space in which, for example, the concept of the sexual instinct combined, according to definite rules, with those of sexual object, sexual aim, unnatural functional deviation, and so on. It was this conceptual space, itself a nineteenth-century invention, that made it possible for psychiatrists to make the statements about perversion that so dominated the period. These statements were thus set within a shared discursive practice. Freud's *Three Essays on the Theory of Sexuality* provided the resources to overturn this conceptual space by fundamentally altering the rules of combination for concepts such as sexual instinct, sexual object, sexual aim—with the consequence that these shared concepts, among others, were destroyed. The conclusion forced upon us is that perversion is no longer a legitimate concept, that the conceptual preconditions for its employment no longer exist in Freud's text. So that if Freud, despite himself, said that such and such phenomena were perversions, he could not have meant what Krafft-Ebing, or Moll, or Charcot had meant. We will not be able to arrive at this conclusion if we focus simply on whom Freud read, on who before him used what words in which contexts. We must turn rather to the issue of conceptual articulation, to reconstructing nineteenth-century and Freudian concepts of sexuality and determining their points of contact and dissociation. Many writers before Freud possessed bits and pieces of his terminology and exhibited an inchoate, unself-possessed grappling with the problems brought to light by the *Three Essays*. But it was Freud who ascended to the level of concepts, who systematically and lucidly thought what had previously remained in a kind of precognitive blockage, who turned what had been, at most, a creeping anxiety into a conceptual mutation.

Yet we know that Freud continued to use the idea of perversion, as if he failed to grasp the real import of his own work. And so now we must directly invoke Freud's name, and wonder about the accessibility of his achievement to Freud himself. I have said that what prepared the way for Freud's achievement was a certain attitude, one that was most clearly appropriated from the writings of Bloch but that could no doubt be found in other authors as well. This attitude allowed a sort of opening so that perversions might no longer be treated as unambiguously pathological. This notion of attitude, which I cannot elaborate theoretically here, is one component of the concept of *mentalité,* a concept that has been put to extraordinarily fertile use by recent historians, especially in France.[40] A mentality includes, among other constituents, a set of mental habits or automatisms that characterize the collective understanding and representations of a population. Bloch's *Beiträge zur Aetiologie der Psychopathia Sexualis* exhibits the tremors of a shift in mentality in which what was taken for granted begins to become dislodged. But this displacement could only be partial, and one was always in danger of falling back into the old mentality, precisely because there was no conceptual backing for this change of attitude. That Bloch never pushed this attitude into conceptual innovation starts to explain why his attitude was inherently unstable, why his work often reads like a kind of unsteady bridge between the old and new mentalities, a bridge always ready to collapse because still in need of completion.

Freud's genius consisted not simply in appropriating this attitude but in seizing and exploiting it. He provided a conceptual foundation for the newly emerging mentality that made it possible, once and for all, for us to change decisively our old mental habits. So why, one wonders, did Freud himself not so change his own mental habits, why did he exhibit an attitude virtually no less ambiguous and unstable than Bloch's? Any answer to this question is bound to be complicated, so in lieu of an answer let me provide the structure for what I take this answer to consist in. Automatisms of attitude have a durability, a slow temporality, which does not match the sometimes rapid change of conceptual mutation. Mental habits have a tendency toward inertia, and these habits resist change that, in retrospect, seems conceptually required. Such resistance can take place not only in a scientific community but even in the individual who is most responsible for the conceptual innovation. Freud was a product of the old mentality that regarded perversions as pathological, a mentality whose first real signs of disintegration can be found at the beginning of the twentieth century. Freud's *Three Essays* ought to have stabilized the new mentality, speeding up its entrenchment by providing it with a conceptual authorization. But given the divergent temporality of the emergence of new concepts and the formation of new mentalities, it is no surprise that Freud's mental habits never quite caught up with his conceptual articulations. The attitudes that comprise a mentality are sufficiently impervious to recognition, so much like natural dispositions, that many decades may intervene before habit and concept are aligned. However, without some appropriate conceptual backdrop, it is very unlikely that a new scientific mentality can genuinely displace an old one, since concepts, especially in science, are one fundamental habit-forming force, one force which, even if over a long span of time, makes possible a stable set of firm mental habits. Although social, cultural, institutional, and psychological factors may all delay the definitive formation of these new habits, it is conceptual innovation of the kind Freud produced that marks one place of genius. But we must remember that genius too has its habits, its inert tendencies, that create a form of friction between what could be said and what is said, so that genius is always ahead even of itself.

The hesitations and ambiguities of Freud's *Three Essays on the Theory of Sexuality* are not the result of some deconstructive indeterminacy or undecidability of the text but are rather the consequence of the dynamics of fundamental change. Mentality and concept are two different aspects of systems of thought, and we should not expect them to be coherently connected all at once, as if forms of experience could be dissolved and reconstituted overnight. Sidney Morgenbesser is said to have asked the following question on an exam at Columbia University: "Some people argue that Freud and Marx went too far. How far would you go?" Whether Freud went too far or not far enough, this is exactly the right range of question. How far can you go? How far will you go?

4

The Horror of Monsters

AS LATE AS 1941, Lucien Febvre, the great French historian, could complain that there was no history of love, pity, cruelty, or joy. He called for "a vast collective investigation to be opened on the fundamental sentiments of man and the forms they take."[1] Although Febvre did not explicitly invoke horror among the sentiments to be investigated, a history of horror can, as I hope to show, function as an irreducible resource in uncovering our forms of subjectivity.[2] Moreover, when horror is coupled to monsters, we have the opportunity to study systems of thought that are concerned with the relation between the orders of morality and of nature. I will concentrate here on those monsters that seem to call into question, to problematize, the boundary between humans and other animals. In some historical periods, it was precisely this boundary that, under certain specific conditions that I shall describe, operated as one major locus of the experience of horror. Our horror at certain kinds of monsters reflects back to us a horror at, or of, humanity, so that our horror of monsters can provide both a history of human will and subjectivity and a history of scientific classifications.

The history of horror, like the history of other emotions, raises extraordinarily difficult philosophical issues. When Febvre's call was answered, mainly by his French colleagues who practiced the so-called history of mentalities, historians quickly recognized that a host of historiographical and methodological problems would have to be faced. No one has faced these problems more directly, and with more profound results, than Jean Delumeau in his monumental two-volume history of fear.[3] But these are issues to which we must continually return. What will be required to write the history of an emotion, a form of sensibility, or type of affectivity? Any such history would require an investigation of gestures, images, attitudes, beliefs, language, values, and concepts. Furthermore, the problem quickly arose as to how one should understand the relationship between elite and popular culture, how, for example, the concepts and language of an elite would come to be appropriated and transformed by a collective mentality.[4] This problem is especially acute for the horror of monsters, since so many of the concepts I discuss which are necessary to our understanding of monsters come from high culture—scientific, philosophical, and theological texts. To what extent is the experience of horror, when expressed in a collective mentality, given form by these concepts? Without even attempting to answer these questions here, I want to insist that a history of horror, at the level of both elite concepts and collective mentality, must emphasize the fundamental role of description. We must describe, in much more detail than is usually done, the concepts, attitudes, and values required by and manifested in the reaction of horror. And it is not enough to describe these components piecemeal; we must attempt to retrieve their coherence, to situate them in the structures of which they are a part.[5] At the level of concepts, this demand requires that we reconstruct the rules that govern the relationships between concepts; thus we will be able to discern the highly structured, rule-governed conceptual spaces that are overlooked if concepts are examined only one at a time.[6] At the level of mentality, we are required to place each attitude, belief, and emotion in the context of the specific collective consciousness of which it forms part.[7] At both levels, we will have to go beyond what is said or expressed in order to recover the conceptual spaces and mental equipment without which the historical texts will lose their real significance.

In 1523, Martin Luther and Phillip Melancthon published a pamphlet entitled *Deuttung der czwo grewlichen Figuren, Bapstesels czu Rom und Munchkalbs czu Freyerbeg ijnn Meysszen funden.*[8] It was enormously influential and was translated into French, with John Calvin's endorsement, in 1557, and into English in 1579 under the title *Of two wonderful popish mon-*

FIGURE 4.1 The pope-ass.

sters. The pamphlet consisted of a detailed interpretation of two monsters: a pope-ass, discussed mainly by Melancthon, supposedly left on the banks of the Tiber River in 1496, and a monk-calf, interpreted by Luther, that was born on December 8, 1522, in Freiburg (Figures 4.1, 4.2). Both of these monsters were interpreted within the context of a polemic against the Ro-

FIGURE 4.2 The monk-calf.

man church. They were prodigies, signs of God's wrath against the Church which prophesied its imminent ruin. There were two dimensions to the Lutheran exegesis of these monsters.[9] On the one hand, there is a prophetic or eschatological dimension, only diffidently mentioned in this pamphlet, in which monsters and prodigies, as a general phenomenon, were taken to be signs of fundamental changes about to affect the world. Often these signs were interpreted as nothing less than an announcement that the end of the world was at hand, and support for this prophetic interpretation was adduced by citing the Book of Daniel, a biblical text invoked by both Melancthon and Luther. The other dimension, which, following Jean Céard, we can call allegorical, is the one with which this pamphlet is most preoccupied. The allegorical exegesis of these monsters is intended to show that each monster has a very specific interpretation that can be grasped because, in one way or another, it is represented before our eyes in the constitution of the monster itself; each monster is a divine hieroglyphic, exhibiting a particular feature of God's wrath. So, for instance, the pope-ass, according to Melancthon, is the image of the Church of Rome; and just as it is awful that a human body should have the head of an ass, so it is likewise horrible that the Bishop of Rome should be the head of the Church. Similarly, the overly large ears of the calf-monk exhibit God's denouncement of the practice of hearing confessions, so important to the monks, while the hanging tongue shows that their doctrine is nothing but frivolous prattle.

A useful study could be made of the adjectives that appear in this text; in lieu of such a study, let me just note that "horrible" and "abominable" occur frequently in both Luther's and Melancthon's discussions, often modifying "monster." The mood of these adjectives is accurately conveyed in the translator's introduction to the 1579 English translation of the text. It begins:

> Among all the things that are to be seen under the heavens (good Christian reader) there is nothing can stir up the mind of man, and which can engender more fear unto the creatures than the horrible monsters, which are brought forth daily contrary to the works of Nature. The which the most times do note and demonstrate unto us the ire and wrath of God against us for our sins and wickedness, that we have and do daily commit against him.[10]

The translator, John Brooke, goes on to tell us that his motive for translating this pamphlet is the better "to move the hearts of every good Christian to fear and tremble at the sight of such prodigious monsters,"[11] and he warns his readers not to interpret these two monsters as if they were but fables. He closes his preface with the hope that, after reading this pamphlet, we shall "repent in time from the bottom of our hearts of our sins, and desire him [God] to be merciful unto us, and ever to keep and defend us from such horrible monsters."[12] He concludes with a few more specific remarks about the pope-ass and calf-monk addressed, and we should not overlook the form of the address, "unto all which fear the Lord."

In order to better understand the preoccupation and fascination with monsters during the sixteenth century, a fascination fastened onto by Luther and Melancthon, whose text is fully representative of an entire genre, we must place these discussions within a wider context. As Jean Delumeau has argued in the second volume of his history of fear, it is within "the framework of a global pessimistic judgment on a time of extreme wickedness that one must place the copious literature dedicated to monsters and prodigies between the end of the fifteenth century and the beginning of the seventeenth."[13] Sinfulness was so great that the sins of men extended to nature itself, which, with God's permission and for the instruction of sinners, seemed to have been seized by a strange madness; the resulting monsters were to be understood as illustrations of these sins. Heresy and monsters were frequently linked during this period, by reformers and Catholics alike. Not only were prodigies specific punishments for particular sins but they also announced greater punishments to come—war, famine, and perhaps even the end of the world. This proliferation of monsters presaged a dark future explained by God's wrath at the increase of wickedness on earth.[14] François Belleforest summarized the shared sensibility: "The present time is more monstrous than natural."[15]

To make as clear as possible the relationship between horror and monsters, I am going to focus primarily on one text, Ambroise Paré's *Des monstres et prodiges,* originally published in 1573 and frequently reprinted after that.[16] Since I am going to set the conceptual context for my discussion of Paré in a rather unconventional way, I want to state explicitly that a full comprehension of this treatise requires that it be placed in relation to other learned and popular treatises on monsters that both preceded and followed it. We are fortunate in this respect to have Céard's thorough treatment of Paré in his brilliant *La Nature et les prodiges* and in the notes to his critical edition of *Des monstres et prodiges;*[17] moreover, in the best English-language treatment of monsters, Katharine Park and Lorraine Daston have provided a three-stage periodization—monsters as divine prodigies, as natural wonders, and as medical examples for comparative anatomy and embryology—that is indispensable in helping us to understand shifts in the conceptualization and treatment of monsters from the Middle Ages to the eighteenth century.[18] Rather than summarizing the work of these scholars, I am going to turn to a different kind of text to prepare my discussion of Paré, namely, Thomas Aquinas' *Summa Theologica*.

Aquinas' *Summa* is not only the greatest work of genius produced by medieval moral theology but also a profound synthesis of previous work, coherently connecting doctrines, ideas, and arguments whose relationships had never been made very clear; moreover, the *Summa* also made conceptually determinate notions that had had a deep and wide-ranging significance in the Middle Ages but that had not really been approached with sufficient analytical precision. I am going to use one portion of the *Summa* as representative of medieval attitudes, attitudes that have lasted, in one form or another, for many subsequent centuries. I shall not address the question of the *Summa*'s originality in this area; suffice it to say that I believe that this is one place in which Aquinas gave a conceptually powerful formulation to a set of ideas that had been essential, even if not very precise, to most of medieval moral theology.

Part II of Part II, Questions 153 and 154, of the *Summa Theologica* deal with lust and the parts of lust, respectively. Aquinas begins, in Article 2 of Question 153, by considering the question of whether the venereal act can be without sin. He argues as follows: if the dictate of reason makes use of certain things in a fitting manner and order for the end to which they are adapted, and if this end is truly good, then the use of these things in such a fitting manner and order will not be a sin. Now the preservation of the bodily nature of an individual is a true good, and the use of food is directed to the preservation of life in the individual. Similarly, the preservation of the nature of the human species is a very great good, and the use of the venereal act is directed to the preservation of the whole human race. Therefore, Aquinas concludes,

> wherefore just as the use of food can be without sin, if it be taken in due manner and order, as required for the welfare of the body, so also the use of venereal acts can be without sin, provided they be performed in due manner and order, in keeping with the end of human procreation.[19]

He proceeds in the first article of Question 154 to differentiate six species of lust—simple fornication, adultery, incest, seduction, rape, and the vice contrary to nature—all of which are discussed in the remaining articles.

My concern is with the vices contrary to nature, which are discussed in Articles 11 and 12. In Article 11, he argues that this type of vice is a distinct species of lust, since it involves a special kind of deformity; vices contrary to nature are not only contrary to right reason, as are all the lustful vices, but are also "contrary to the natural order of the venereal act as becoming to the human race," which order has as its end the generation of children.[20] Aquinas distinguishes four categories of vice contrary to nature—bestiality, sodomy, which he interprets as male/male or female/female copulation, the sin of self-abuse, and not observing the natural manner of copulation. It is difficult to determine exactly what falls under this last category, but it is clear from II-II, Question 154, Article 12, Reply to Objection 4, that male/female anal and oral copulation are two of the most grievous ways of not observing the right manner of copulation.

In Article 12, Aquinas rank-orders, from worst to least worst, all of the lustful vices. He claims, first, that all four categories of vice contrary to nature are worse than any of the other vices of lust; so that bestiality, sodomy, not observing the natural manner of copulation, and self-abuse are worse, because of their special deformity, than adultery, rape of a virgin, incest, and so on.[21] Vices contrary to nature are worse in kind and not merely in degree than other lustful vices. Aquinas then goes on to rank-order the vices contrary to nature. The least bad of these vices is self-abuse, since the "gravity of a sin depends more on the abuse of a thing than on the omission of the right use."[22] Next worse is the sin of not observing the right manner of copulation, and this sin is more grievous if the abuse concerns the right vessel than if it affects the manner of copulation in respect of other circumstances. Third worse is sodomy, since use of the right sex is not observed. Finally, the most grievous of all the vices contrary to nature, and so the most grievous of any lustful vice, is bestiality, since the use of the due species is not observed; moreover, in this instance, Aquinas explicitly cites a biblical text as support.[23] One final remark of Aquinas' must be mentioned before I turn to Paré. About the vices contrary to nature, from masturbation to bestiality, Aquinas writes,

> just as the ordering of right reason proceeds from men, so the order of nature is from God Himself: wherefore in sins contrary to nature, whereby the very order of nature is violated, an injury is done to God, the Author of nature.[24]

To act contrary to nature is nothing less than to act directly contrary to the will of God.

One may understandably be wondering how this discussion of Aquinas is relevant to the treatment of monsters, so let me turn immediately to Paré's *Des monstres et prodiges*. The preface to his book begins as follows:

> Monsters are things that appear outside the course of Nature (and are usually signs of some forthcoming misfortune), such as a child who is born with one arm, another who will have two heads, and additional members over and above the ordinary.
>
> Prodigies are things which happen that are completely against Nature, as when a woman will give birth to a serpent, or to a dog, or some other thing that is totally against Nature, as we shall show hereafter through several examples of said monsters and prodigies.[25]

Ceárd has argued that Paré was somewhat indifferent to the problem of precisely how one should distinguish monsters from prodigies. Monsters and prodigies did not constitute absolutely separate classes and during the successive editions of his book, Ceárd thinks Paré became more and more convinced that the term "monster" was sufficient to designate all of these phenomena.[26] But however imprecise and unarticulated this distinction might appear, the idea that there was a separate class of phenomena, prodigies, that were completely against nature affected the language, attitude, and conceptualization with which Paré approached his examples.

In the first chapter of *Des monstres et prodiges,* Paré distinguishes thirteen causes of monsters, which causes, although not completely exhaustive, are all the ones he is able to adduce with assurance. Ten of these causes are straightforwardly natural causes; two, the glory of God and the wrath of God, are straightforwardly supernatural causes; and one, demons and devils, has a long and complicated classificatory history.[27] Briefly, to classify the products of demons and devils as a result of supernatural causes was to threaten to place the devil on a par with God, granting him the same powers to overturn the natural order that God possessed. The possibility of such a theologically untenable position led to detailed discussions concerning the status of demonic causation; and as we can see from Chapters 26 to 34, Paré fit squarely into these discussions, concerned both to grant the reality of the devil and yet to limit his powers. Of the two straightforwardly supernatural causes, Paré's treatment of the first, the glory of God, is exhausted by one example, the restoration of a blind man's sight by Jesus Christ, an example literally copied from Pierre Boaistuau's *Histoires prodigieuses*, first published in 1560.[28]

The other supernatural cause, the wrath of God, is far more interesting for my purposes; most of the examples produced by Paré to illustrate this category are of the same kind, and they are closely linked to the natural cause of the mixture or mingling of seed. I want to discuss these examples in detail in order to support some claims about the history of horror. But I should make one more preliminary remark. Paré, like virtually every writer during this period, had no intellectual difficulty in referring to both supernatural and natural causes; he felt no incompatibility in discussing these two types of cause together. Yet although God was always in the background of *Des monstres et prodiges*, by far the most space is devoted to natural causes, with God's explicit appearances being relatively few. This contrasts, for instance, with Jacob Rueff's *De conceptu et generatione hominis*, a book known to Paré, published in 1554 and for a long time the classic work on the problems of generation. Rueff also discussed supernatural and natural causes together, but in Book V of *De conceptu*, when he discusses monstrous births, Rueff considers them all as divine punishment, and their physical causes, however active, are almost ignored in favor of the evidence of the judgments of God. In Rueff's text, whatever the physical or natural causes of the production of monsters, monsters are first of all punishments inflicted by God on sinners.[29] So Paré's book already demonstrates a shift of emphasis that makes his treatment of supernatural causes all the more interesting.

Paré's chapter on the wrath of God opens with these words:

> There are other creatures which astonish us doubly because they do not proceed from the above mentioned causes, but from a fusing together of strange species, which render the creature not only monstrous but prodigious, that is to say, which is completely abhorrent and against Nature. . . .
>
> It is certain that most often these monstrous and prodigious creatures proceed from the judgment of God, who permits fathers and mothers to produce such abominations from the disorder that they make in copulation, like brutish beasts. . . . Similarly, Moses forbids such coupling in Leviticus (Chapter 16).[30]   (Figure 4.3)

FIGURE 4.3 A colt with a man's head.

The creatures discussed in this chapter are produced by the natural cause of the fusing together of strange species, but, more important, their, so to speak, first cause is God's wrath at the copulation between human beings and other species, a practice that is explicitly forbidden in Leviticus. The result is not only a monster but a prodigy, a creature that is contrary to nature and that is described as completely abhorrent.

If we turn to the chapter that treats the natural cause of the mixture or mingling of seed, we find Paré endorsing the principle that nature always strives to create its likeness; since nature always preserves its kind and species, when two animals of different species copulate, the result will be a creature that combines the form of both of the species.[31] The kind of naturalistic explanation exhibited in this chapter is, however, framed by crucial opening and closing paragraphs, which I quote at length. The chapter begins with this statement:

> There are monsters that are born with a form that is half-animal and half-human . . . which are produced by sodomists and atheists who join together, and break out of their bounds contrary to nature, with animals, and from this are born several monsters that are hideous and very scandalous to look at or speak about. Yet the disgrace lies in the deed and not

FIGURE 4.4 A monstrous lamb.

in words; and it is, when it is done, a very unfortunate and abominable thing, and a great horror for a man or woman to mix with and copulate with brute animals; and as a result some are born half-men and half-animals.[32]   (Figures 4.4, 4.5)

The chapter closes with this:

Now I shall refrain from writing here about several other monsters engendered from such grist, together with their portraits, which are so hideous and abominable, not only to see, but also to hear tell of, that, due to their great loathsomeness I have neither wanted to relate them nor have them portrayed. For (as Boaistuau says, after having related several sacred and

FIGURE 4.5 A child, half dog.

profane stories, which are all filled with grievous punishments for lechers) what can atheists and sodomisis expect, who (as I said above) couple against God and Nature with brute animals?"[33]

What I want to isolate is the conjunction of God's wrath at human disobedience of his laws (a supernatural cause) with the production of a creature contrary to nature, a prodigy, the reaction to which is horror; and, finally, I want to emphasize that the prime example for Paré of such human disobedience is bestiality. These features are in effect Paré's analogue to Aquinas' discussion in the *Summa Theologica*. For Thomas, there is a distinct category of lust, worse in kind than other species of lust, namely, lust contrary to nature (remember that prodigies, being completely against nature, are worse in kind than monsters, being only outside the course of nature), the most grievous example of which is bestiality; moreover, when such sins are committed, an injury is done to God. Paré physicalizes this framework of concepts by exhibiting the consequence of such an injury to God; the resulting bestial creature is a symbolic representation of God's wrath, and the reaction of horror we have to such hideous creatures is intended to remind us of, and to impress upon us, the horror of the sin itself. Thus the special viciousness of sins contrary to nature extends to the creatures produced by these sins. Paré reserves his most charged language—horror, horrible, hideous, loathsome, abominable—for these creatures and the sins they represent.

The link between moral disorder and the disorder of nature was a constant theme during this period. It was widely believed that evil committed on earth could leave its mark on the structure of the human body.[34] And the way in which the physical form of the body gave rise to moral and theological questions went far beyond the case of prodigies. The issue of monstrous births as a whole raised practical problems for priests, since they had to decide whether any particular monstrous child was human, and so whether it should be baptized or not. There were, of course, disagreements about how to make these determinations, but the form of the body served as a guide to theological resolution. The kind of reasoning employed is well represented by Guido of Mont Rocher's *Manipulus Curatorum Officia Sacerdotus* of 1480:

> But what if there is a single monster which has two bodies joined together: ought it to be baptized as one person or as two? I say that since baptism is made according to the soul and not according to the body, howsoever there be two bodies, if there is only one soul, then it ought to be baptized as one person. But if there are two souls, it ought to be baptized as two persons. But how is it to be known if there be one or two? I say that if there be two bodies, there are two souls. But if there is one body, there is one soul. And for this reason it may be supposed that if

there be two chests and two heads there are two souls. If, however, there be one chest and one head, however much the other members be doubled, there is only one soul.[35]

I mention this example to indicate that Paré's use of the body as a moral and theological cipher is only a special instance, and not an entirely distinctive one, of a much more general mentalité.

What is most remarkable about Paré's book is that when he confines himself to purely natural causes, he employs the concept of monster exclusively (phenomena outside the course of nature) and not the concept of prodigy. Furthermore, the experience of horror is absent from his descriptions. Horror is appropriate only if occasioned by a normative cause, the violation of some norm, as when the human will acts contrary to the divine will. The chapter that immediately follows Paré's discussion of the wrath of God concerns monsters caused by too great a quantity of seed. Compare its opening language with the language of the previous chapter already quoted.

> On the generation of monsters, Hippocrates says that if there is too great an abundance of matter, multiple births will occur, or else a monstrous child having superfluous and useless parts, such as two heads, four arms, four legs, six digits on the hands and feet, or other things. And on the contrary, if the seed is lacking in quantity, some member will be lacking, [such] as feet or head, or [having] some other part missing.[36]   (Figures 4.6, 4.7)

Even Paré's discussion of hermaphrodites in Chapter 6 bears no trace of horror, and we see that their formation is due entirely to natural causes, with no admixture of willful violation of a norm (Figure 4.8). Hermaphrodites are monsters, not prodigies, naturally explicable and normatively neutral.

If we read Paré's treatise chapter by chapter, we find that horror is a normative reaction, a reaction engendered by a violation of a specific kind of norm. When causal knowledge, that is, knowledge of the natural causes, is produced to explain a monster, the effect of such explanation is to displace horror, to alter our experiences of the phenomenon with which we are confronted. Horror is linked to Paré's discussion of supernatural causes because the issue in these discussions is always the normative relation between the

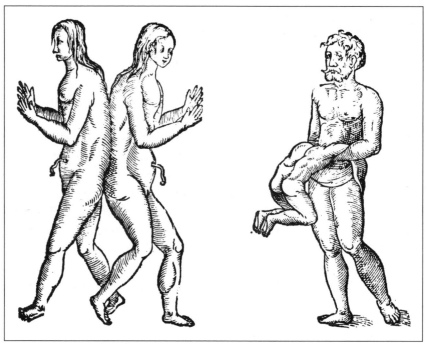

FIGURE 4.6 Examples of too great a quantity of seed.

divine and human wills. A horrible prodigy is produced when the human will acts contrary to nature, contrary to the divine will, and so when this contrariness (as Aquinas makes conceptually articulate and as is reflected in Paré) involves the thwarting of a very particular kind of norm. I see no reason to doubt the accuracy of Paré's descriptions, of where and when he experienced horror, especially because this kind of description is confirmed in so many other treatises.[37] It strikes me as no odder that Paré and his contemporaries would experience horror only when confronted by a prodigy, by some especially vicious normative violation, than that the Israelites of the Old Testament would come to experience horror at the seemingly heterogeneous group of phenomena called "abominations." And the inverse relationship between horror and causal explanation is the other side of the similar relationship between wonder and causal explanation. A sense of wonder was the appropriate reaction to the production of a miracle, just as horror was the appropriate reaction to the production of a prodigy. Lorraine Daston has argued, in examining the decline of miracles and the sen-

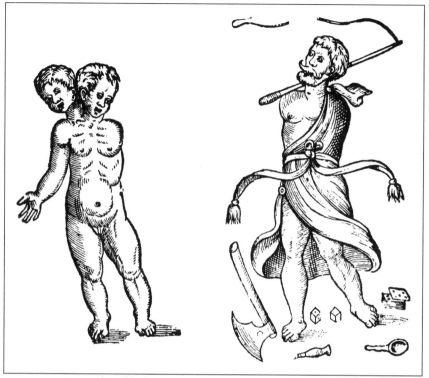

FIGURE 4.7 Examples of lack in the quantity of seed.

sibility of wonder, that "it was axiomatic in the psychology of miracles that causal knowledge drove out wonder, and in the seventeenth century the converse was also emphasized: wonder drove out causal knowledge."[38] The psychology of miracles and the psychology of prodigies were phenomenologically and analytically akin to each other.

In his chapter on the mixing and mingling of seed and the hideous monsters that result from bestiality (Figure 4.9), Paré describes a man-pig, a creature born in Brussels in 1564, having a man's face, arms, and hands, and so representing humanity above the shoulders, and having the hind legs and hindquarters of a swine and the genitals of a sow (Figure 4.10). This man-pig was one of a litter of six pigs and, according to Paré, "it nursed like the others and lived two days: then it was killed along with the sow on account of the horror the people had of it."[39] As one would expect from what I have argued, horror was in fact the reaction triggered by this man-

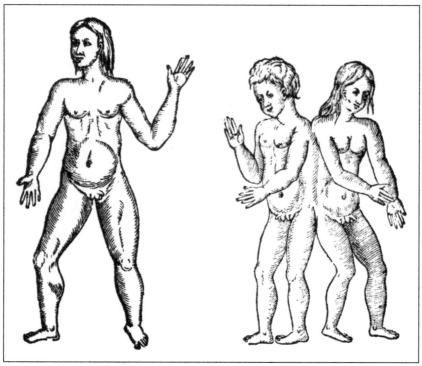

FIGURE 4.8 Hermaphrodites.

pig, and it was so consuming as to push the people to kill both the sow and her monstrous offspring.

In 1699, Edward Tyson, a fellow of the Royal Society and Royal College of Physicians, communicated a report, published in the *Philosophical Transactions of the Royal Society*, entitled "A Relation of two Monstrous Pigs, with the Resemblance of Human Faces, and two young Turkeys joined by the Breast." Tyson announces his intention at the start:

> By the description of the following monsters I design to prove that the distortion of the parts of a fetus may occasion it to represent the figure of different animals, without any real coition betwixt the two species.[40]

He proceeds to describe, in much detail, a so-called man-pig, discovered at Staffordshire in 1699. His article contains no evidence of horror, disgust, dread, or any related emotion. As he continues, it becomes clear that his description of the seemingly human face of the pig is meant to show that it

FIGURE 4.9 A monster, half man and half swine.

FIGURE 4.10 A pig having the head, feet, and hands of a man and the remainder of a pig.

is the result of some depression of the pig's face, caused by a compression of the womb or by the pressure of the other pigs in the same part of the womb. No reference to bestiality is necessary to understand the production of this creature, and no horror is, or should be, occasioned by it. Tyson mentions the case of a man-pig reported by Paré, the very case I have quoted, and is content to point out some differences between Paré's case and his, for example, that his man-pig did not possess human hands. Tyson is cautious about whether recourse to bestiality is ever required to explain such monsters, but the main thrust of his article is to show that causal explanations of the kind he has produced have a much greater explanatory relevance than has often been recognized. His attitude stands at a great distance from Paré's, and it is exemplified by his remark, made when discussing other reported cases of monstrous pigs, "I believe either fiction, or want of observation has made more monsters than nature ever produced"[41]—sometimes almost employing the concept of monster as if monsters were thought to be creatures contrary to nature, whereas the whole point of his communication has been to show that they result from abnormal deformations due to natural causes.

The displacement of horror as a result of causal explanation, as though knowing the cause of a monster calms the horror we might feel, can also be seen in the case of John Merrick, the so-called Elephant Man, and such displacement operates in one and the same individual, namely, Merrick's physician, Frederick Treves (Figures 4.11, 4.12). In the medical reports submitted to the Pathological Society of London, words such as "deformity," "abnormality," "remarkable," "extraordinary," and "grossly" describe Merrick's condition. The reports do not convey an experience of horror but rather an impression of how extreme Merrick's deformities are, and, because of that extremity, they indicate the immense medical interest of his condition. However, when we read Treves's memoir and he describes his and others' first encounters with the Elephant Man, the mood is completely different. Here we find words and phrases such as "repellent," "fright," "aversion," "a frightful creature that could only have been possible in a nightmare," "the most disgusting specimen of humanity that I have ever seen," "the loathing insinuation of a man being changed into an animal," and "everyone he met confronted him with a look of horror and disgust."[42] (See Figure 4.13.) It is as though we can describe Treves's emotional history by saying that when he attends to the complicated causal etiology

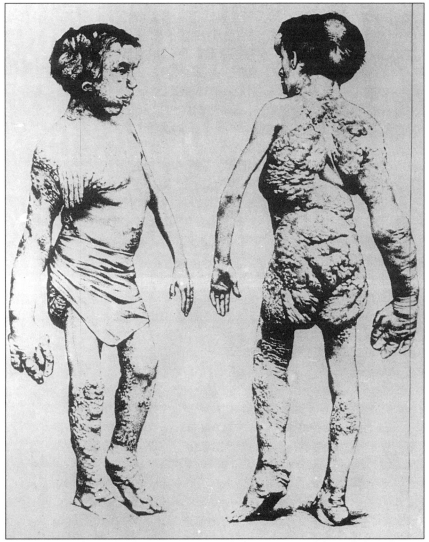

FIGURE 4.11 John Merrick, 1884–85. From *The Transactions of the Pathological Society of London,* vol. 36, 1885.

of Merrick's condition, he can transform his own reaction from one of horror and disgust to pity and, eventually, sympathy. We often assume that the appellation "Elephant Man" derives from the fact that Merrick was covered with papillomatous growths, a derivation of this name reported in one of the medical communications. And certainly this appearance could have ac-

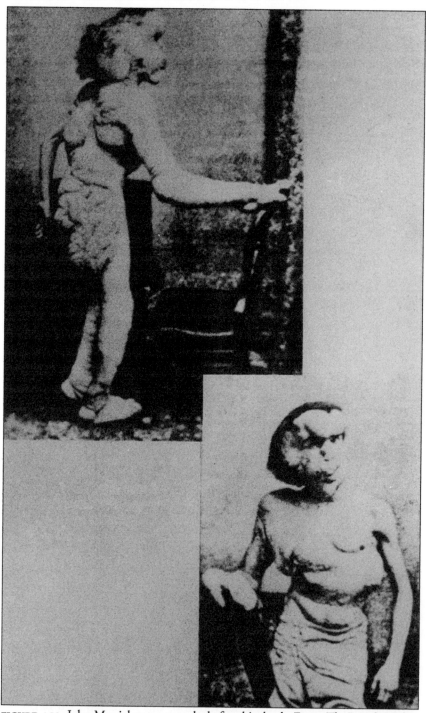

FIGURE 4.12 John Merrick some months before his death. From *The British Medical Journal,* vol. 1, 1890.

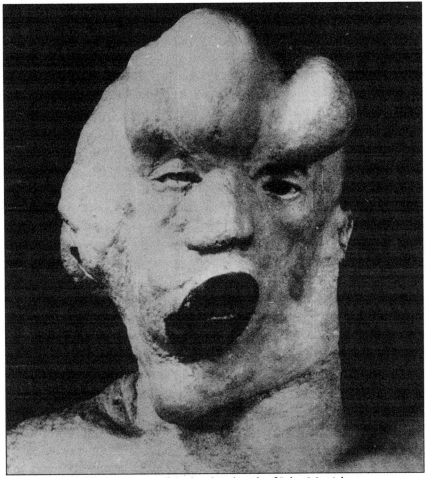

FIGURE 4.13 Postmortem cast of the head and neck of John Merrick.

counted for that title. But it is easy to forget that this is not the official reason that Merrick himself gave for his being called the Elephant Man. He reported that shortly before his birth, his mother was knocked down by a circus elephant and that this accident, with its horrifying consequences, was the source of the label "Elephant Man." It is perfectly evident that this story conceals, and not very well, the fantasy of bestiality, and it is exactly this fantasy that is embedded in Treves's memoir when he speaks of "the loathing insinuation of a man being changed into an animal."

Although the adjective "abominable" occurs frequently in discussions of

monsters and prodigies, I will not insist here on the obvious differences between this use of the term and the concept of abomination in the Old Testament. The use of "abominable" to describe prodigies remains inextricably
linked to horror, as I have argued; but the doctrine of natural law, absent
from the Old Testament, decisively alters one feature of the biblical conception. A study of the relevant biblical passages would show that it is primarily one uniquely specified people who, because of their special relation
to God, feel horror at abominations. But in the texts I have discussed, it is
rather as though the horror of sins contrary to nature, and of the products
that result from them, is experienced by all human beings qua rational beings. For the use of natural reason alone is sufficient to grasp the viciousness of sins contrary to nature, and bestiality, for example, is a violation of
natural law, which requires no special act of divine revelation to be known
but is nothing else than the rational creature's participation in God's eternal
law.[43] So every human being ought to experience horror at that which he
knows, as a rational being, to be contrary to nature. In this context, the
doctrine of natural law helped to conceal the recognition that horror is a
cultural and historical product and not demanded by reason alone, a fact
that is more easily recognized in the pertinent biblical texts. Since horror
came to be enmeshed in the framework of natural law and natural reason,
prodigies, and the wrath of God, could be described in a way that was intended to represent the experience of every human being, not simply the
experience of a culturally specific group. Objects of horror could now directly appear to be naturally horrifying.

As I have already shown, bestiality, the worst of the sins contrary to nature, exhibited its viciousness in the very structure of the human body itself, in the creatures produced by the willful violation of God's natural law.
But this configuration, whereby a certain kind of undermining of norms
was exhibited in the effects of physical pathology, was not restricted only to
this one form of lust contrary to nature. Eighteenth- and early–nineteenth-
century treatises on onanism reproduce this same pattern of concepts; self-
abuse, another one of Aquinas' sins contrary to nature, ravages the physical
structure of the body, producing, among its effects, acute stomach pains;
habitual vomiting that resists all remedies during the time this vicious habit
is continued; a dry cough; a hoarse, weak voice; a great loss of strength;
paleness; sometimes a light but continuous yellowness; pimples, particularly on the forehead, temples, and near the nose; considerable emaciation;
an astonishing sensibility to changes in the weather; an enfeeblement of

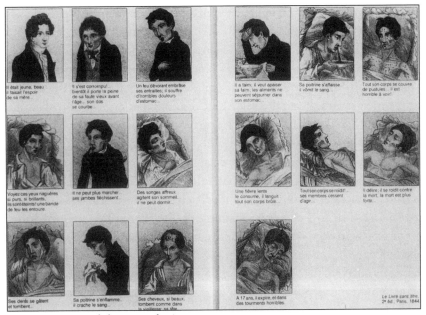

FIGURE 4.14 Death by masturbation.

sight sometimes leading to blindness; a considerable diminution of all mental faculties often culminating in insanity; and even death (Figure 4.14).[44] Indeed, this relationship between the viciousness of the sin and the pathology of the body even gave rise to a genre of autopsy report, in which the autopsy of a masturbator would reveal that the effects of this loathsome habit had penetrated within the body itself, affecting the internal organs no less than the external appearance.[45] In Samuel Tissot's *L'Onanisme: Dissertation sur les maladies produites par la masturbation,* we find the same kind of terminology and sensibility that accompanies Renaissance descriptions of prodigies. Tissot opens his discussion of cases, with which he has had firsthand experience, with the following preamble:

> My first case presents a scene which is dreadful. I was myself frightened the first time I saw the unfortunate patient who is its subject. I then felt, more than I ever had before, the necessity of showing young people all the horrors of the abyss into which they voluntarily plunge themselves.[46]

And he invokes the idea of masturbation as contrary to nature in strategically central passages.[47]

It is often said that Tissot's treatise is the first scientific study of masturbation, and his book is engulfed by medical terminology and punctuated by attempts to give physiological explanations of the pathological effects provoked by masturbation. But it is just as evident that his book remains firmly placed within a tradition of moral theology, which begins with a conception of masturbation as an especially vicious kind of lust. It produces mental and physical disease and disorder, but even in the scientific treatments inaugurated by Tissot, it remains a vicious habit, not itself a disease but a moral crime against God and nature. Tissot begins his book with the claim, which he says that physicians of all ages unanimously believe, that the loss of one ounce of seminal fluid enfeebles one more than the loss of forty ounces of blood.[48] He immediately recognizes that he must then explain why the loss of a great quantity of seminal fluid by masturbation, by means contrary to nature, produces diseases so much more terrible than the loss of an equal quantity of seminal fluid by natural intercourse. When he offers an explanation, in Article II, Section 8 of his book, he attempts to frame it in terms of purely physical causes, the mechanical laws of the body and of its union with the mind. But try as he might, he cannot help but conclude this section by reintroducing the claim that masturbators "find themselves guilty of a crime for which divine justice cannot suspend punishment."[49]

Theorists of sodomy also exploited this same kind of connection between normative taint and physical deformation. The normative origin of attitudes toward sodomy is contained not only in the very word, with its reference to the episode of Sodom and Gomorrah in Genesis, but also in the emergence of other words to refer to the same practices. For instance, buggery derives from the French *bougrerie,* a word that refers to a Manichaean sect that arose at Constantinople in the ninth century, and that recognized a sort of pontiff who resided in Bulgaria. Thus to be a *bougre* meant that one was a participant in heresy, and there is no reason to believe that this heretical sect had any special proclivity toward sodomy. However, eventually, the accusation of *bougrerie* came to be identified with an accusation of sodomy, and the link to heresy became submerged.[50] Moreover, in French, the phrase "change of religion" could be used to describe pederasty; to become a pederast was to change religion *(changer de religion).*[51] Both sex and religion have their orthodoxies, their heresies, their apostasies—their normative paths and deviations.

Even when the theological underpinnings of the concept of sodomy receded into the background, its normative content and origin was always close at hand. Ambroise Tardieu, whose enormously influential *Étude médico-légale sur les attentats aux moeurs* was first published in 1857, devotes about one-third of this book to a discussion of pederasty and sodomy. Tardieu restricts the term "pederasty" to the love of young boys, whereas the more general term "sodomy" is reserved for "acts contrary to nature, considered in themselves, and without reference to the sex of the individuals between whom the culpable relations are established."[52] Most of the cases of sodomy Tardieu describes concern either male/male anal intercourse or male/female anal intercourse. The fact that he repeatedly characterizes these acts as contrary to nature indicates the normative tradition into which his work fits. Although Tardieu acknowledges that madness may accompany pederasty and sodomy, he wishes to make certain that these acts escape "neither the responsibility of conscience, the just severity of law, nor, above all, the contempt of decent people."[53] He is aware that the "shame and disgust"[54] that these acts inspire have often constrained the reports of observers, and his book is intended to remedy this lack, and in extraordinary detail.

Much of Tardieu's discussion of pederasty and sodomy is concerned with the physical signs that permit one to recognize that these activities have transpired, with the material traces left by these vices in the structure of the organs. Tardieu believed that an exhaustive discussion of these signs is necessary if legal medicine was going to be able to determine with assurance whether such acts contrary to nature and public morality had taken place. He describes the deformations of the anus that result from the habit of passive sodomy, a topic that had already received much discussion in the French and German medicolegal literature. But he goes on to describe the signs of active pederasty, signs left on the viril member itself, which he claims have been completely ignored in previous treatises. Changes in the dimension and form of the penis are the most reliable indications of active sodomy and pederasty. The active sodomist has a penis that is either very thin or very voluminous. The excessively voluminous penis is analogized to "the snout of certain animals,"[55] while Tardieu describes the much more common, excessively thin penis of active sodomists in the following remarkable way:

> In the case where it is small and thin, it grows considerably thinner from the base to the tip, which is very tapered, like the finger of a glove, and recalls completely the *canum more*.[56]

To confirm his general observations, he reports the physical conformation of the penises of many active sodomists; about one, he says,

> Having made him completely undress, we can verify that the viril member, very long and voluminous, presents at its tip a characteristic elongation and tapering that gives to the gland the almost pointed form of the penis of a dog.[57]

Another of Tardieu's active sodomists has a penis that "simulates exactly the form of the penis of a pure-bred dog."[58] As if to confirm that sodomy is contrary to nature and God, the relevant parts of the human body are transformed by this activity so that they come to resemble the bodily parts of a dog. What could be more horrifying than the moral and physical transformation of the human into a beast, a man-dog produced no longer by bestiality but by the disgusting practice of sodomy. Long after the classical discussions of prodigies, the category of the contrary to nature continued to mark out one fundamental domain of horror.

By the late nineteenth century, the experiences provoked by so-called freak shows already contrasted with the horror of the contrary to nature. Rather than exhibiting the physical consequences of normative deviation, the freaks exhibited in sideshows and circuses were intended to amuse, entertain, and divert their audiences. In general,

> the urban workers who came to stare at freaks were by and large an unsophisticated audience in search of cheap and simple entertainment. . . . In the early 1870s William Cameron Coup had introduced a two-ring concept while working with Barnum and by 1885 most shows revolved around a multiple ring system. The result was a drift toward glamour and spectacle as the basic product of the big shows. The tendency was well developed by the early nineties and brought specific changes to the exhibits. Contrasts of scale—fat ladies and living skeletons, giants and dwarfs—and exhibits involving internal contrasts—bearded ladies, hermaphroditic men and ladies toying with snakes—began to displace the more repulsive exhibits. As the shows were freighted with fewer mutilated horrors they became less emotionally loaded and less complex as experiences.[59]

It should be noted that part of the purpose of the multiple-ring circus would have been defeated by the displaying of horrors. For if having more than one ring was intended to get the spectators to look from exhibit to ex-

FIGURE 4.15 Avery Childs, the Frog Boy.

hibit, to gaze periodically and repeatedly at each of the rings, to experience the circus in all of its diversity, then the exhibition of a horrifying object would have tended to thwart this experience. The experience of horror disposes us to fix on its object, unable to avert our gaze, fascinated as well as repulsed, blocking out virtually everything but the object before our eyes. Thus, horror is incompatible with the glamour, spectacle, and variety that is inherent in the multiple-ring circus. The modern circus had to be set up so that no single exhibit so predominated that the many rings were, in effect, reduced to one.

Even if we put aside the fact that the categories of freaks and prodigies were by no means composed of the same specimens, we can see how different this experience of freaks was by examining photographs of them. Charles Eisenmann was a Bowery photographer who took many portraits of freaks during the late nineteenth century. Some of these photographs represent characters that are half-human and half-animal and so, at least in this respect, can be thought of as successors to the medieval and Renaissance prodigies produced by bestiality. But these photographs exhibit no indication of horror. Avery Childs, the Frog Boy, is evocative and amus-

FIGURE 4.16 Fred Wilson, the Lobster Boy.

FIGURE 4.17 Jo Jo, the Russian Dog-Face Boy.

ingly photographed but no more horrifying than a contortionist, his slippers emphasizing that he is more human than frog (Figure 4.15). Indeed, these photographs insist on the humanity of their subjects, precisely the opposite of Paré's discussions, which highlight the bestiality of prodigies. Fred Wilson, the Lobster Boy, suffers from a serious congenital deformity, but dressed in his Sunday best, with his hair neatly combed, one is drawn as much to his human face as to his supposed lobster claws (Figure 4.16). And even Jo Jo, the Russian Dog-Face Boy, one of Barnum's most famous attractions, wears a fringed velour suit and sports that great symbol of Western civilization, the watch chain (Figure 4.17). Furthermore, his right hand bears a ring, and his left hand is neatly placed on his knee. And he poses with a gun, as if to suggest that he is not an animal to be hunted but can himself participate in the all too human activity of the hunt. Horror at the prodigious, amusement by the freak—the history of monsters encodes a complicated and changing history of emotion, one that helps to reveal to us the structures and limits of the human community.

5

Styles of Reasoning: From the History of Art to the Epistemology of Science

SOMEONE ATTEMPTING TO WRITE a history of recent history and philosophy of science might approach this enterprise by organizing such a history around the various uses of certain prominent methodological and historiographical terms. Indeed, someone faced with this critical historiographical terminology might initially feel overwhelmed by the task of sorting out the employment of, to take some examples, Gaston Bachelard's epistemological obstacles, Thomas Kuhn's paradigms, Paul Feyerabend's incommensurability, Gerald Holton's themata, or Michel Foucault's epistemes. Most recently we have seen many more occurrences of the notion of style, both in the invocation of the general notion of a style of reasoning or thinking in the sciences, and in the more specific notions of national styles in medicine, physics, mathematics, and biology. The particular fate of each of these methodological-historiographical terms has been rather different, but I think the general impression is widespread, both within and outside of the discipline of the history and philosophy of science, that nothing of great consequence turns on which of these terms one employs. After all, a quick reading of the relevant literature reveals that, for instance, the ideas of paradigm, incommensurability and episteme are often used more or less interchangeably. Furthermore, one would be hard pressed to determine the exact content of any of these notions, since they have been appropriated and stretched in ways that have resulted in their having very little determinate usage whatsoever.

The use of the idea of style, a notion that is already employed in other disciplines, threatens to leave us in a similar situation—a very suggestive idea, namely that science and the sciences can be understood as exhibiting styles, seems to be able to be put to whatever uses the peculiarities of a particular author demand. In many of its occurrences, the notion of a style of reasoning appears to be wholly metaphorical, and it is not even an especially lucid metaphor, since, more often than not, one would have difficulty specifying what, if anything, is *specifically* implied by the use of this term. Such circumstances have left the notion of a style of reasoning far more obscure, and so of far less utility, than it need be. If nothing specific is to be gained by adding yet another historiographical term to an already crowded array, then we would be prudent to dispense with the notion of a style of reasoning altogether, thereby forestalling the inevitable confusions that would otherwise ensue. However, if we think that the idea of styles of reasoning really does do specific methodological work, and does something different from that done by the seemingly competing notions I have already adduced, then one's first task is to say *exactly* what one means by a style of reasoning. It is with this task that this essay will be primarily concerned.

Each of the historiographical notions I have mentioned has been used to address a distinct, even if sometimes overlapping, problem or set of problems. One way to understand better the differences among these terms is to demarcate very precisely the problem to which each of them is intended to respond. So let me begin by articulating, as clearly as I can at the start of this essay, the set of problems in relation to which I will invoke the notion of a style of reasoning. The fundamental problem on which I will focus is: What are the conditions under which various kinds of statements come to be comprehensible? Not everything is comprehensible at all times, either for individuals or for entire historical periods. In a previous series of essays, I have examined the conditions under which a specific corpus of statements, statements that make up part of the discipline of psychiatry, became comprehensible. I have implicitly, and sometimes explicitly, employed the notion of a style of reasoning in my historical work, although without tak-

ing up this notion with the philosophical detail required for its fully legitimate employment.[1] As will be obvious, the set of historiographical and
epistemological issues that has most concerned me can be raised with respect to any of the sciences. To be more precise, I am interested, in the first
instance, in one particular form of this problem of comprehensibility,
namely, under what conditions can one comprehend various kinds of statements as being either true-or-false? Not every statement claims the status of
being either true-or-false; but those statements that claim a scientific status
do claim to be part of the domain of truth-and-falsehood. So the primary
problem I will address is: Under what conditions do statements come to be
possible candidates of truth-or-falsehood in such a way as to claim the
comprehensibility of a science?

Before I begin to specify how I understand the notion of style in styles of
reasoning, and how I understand the intimately related notions of a conceptual space and its history, I should first explain that certain connota-
tions of the notion of style will be intentionally left aside in my account of
it. There is a sense of "style," quite common in popular discussions, which
links style to individual personality, even idiosyncrasy. It is this sense of the
word that is implied by the last line of J. L. Austin's review of Gilbert Ryle's
The Concept of Mind—"Le style, c'est Ryle."[2] This use of "style" has perhaps its most natural home in discussions of fashion. Yet, despite its intrinsic interest, this use of "style" is not helpful in trying to characterize styles
of reasoning in the sciences. In discussing styles of reasoning in what follows, I shall make almost no reference to differences of individual temperament. Indeed, it is perhaps a peculiarity of my understanding of a style of
reasoning that proper names function almost as place-holders for certain
central concepts, so that a style of reasoning is primarily concerned not
with the ideas of individuals, but rather with a set of concepts and the way
that they fit together. As much as style in fashion is linked to individuals,
so is it divorced from specific personalities when we come to consider styles
of reasoning.[3]

In beginning to characterize styles of reasoning, I want to start, so to
speak, inside out. Rather than commencing with recent Anglo-American
history and philosophy of science, I want to start with what for us is its
somewhat more philosophically alien French analogue. Specifically, I want
to consider some suggestions of Michel Foucault, who stands in a line of
distinguished French epistemologists of science, beginning with Gaston

Bachelard and running through Georges Canguilhem before it reaches Foucault. At the end of an interview, "Truth and Power," given in the late seventies, Foucault makes two suggestions:

> "Truth" is to be understood as a system of ordered procedures for the production, regulation, distribution, circulation and operation of statements.

> "Truth" is linked in a circular relation with systems of power which produce and sustain it, and to effects of power which it induces and which extend it. A "regime" of truth.[4]

Since Foucault was usually his own best interpreter, I like to think of this first suggestion as his own succinct retrospective interpretation of his archeological method, while the second suggestion is his equally succinct interpretation of his genealogical method. In attempting to understand both the notions of styles of reasoning and of conceptual spaces and their history, I shall take some clues from Foucault, concentrating on the first suggestion, which he called the method of "archeology."

If truth is understood as a system of ordered procedures for the production, regulation, distribution, circulation, and operation of statements, and if what is part of the domain of truth is itself variable throughout history, then it should not be surprising that Foucault undertook to write a history of truth. Of course, one might respond that it is one thing to write a history of truth and quite another to claim that, as Foucault's colleague at the Collège de France Paul Veyne has put it, there is no other truth than that of successive historical productions.[5] Foucault did not believe that there can be an epistemologically useful theory of truth divorced from the variable historical conditions under which statements become candidates for the status of truth. Combining, in his own way, some lessons from Foucault with some from A. C. Crombie, Ian Hacking has given us the most philosophically promising characterization of styles of reasoning to date. At the end of his paper "Language, Truth, and Reason," Hacking makes some assertions and draws some inferences from them that he admits are all in need of clarification. But I shall quote all five of his claims here, since they provide part of the background for what I want to say about styles of reasoning:

(1) There are different styles of reasoning. Many of these are discernible in our own history. They emerge at definite points

and have distinct trajectories of maturation. Some die out, others are still going strong.

(2) Propositions of the sort that necessarily require reasoning to be substantiated have a positivity, a being true-or-false, only in consequence of the style of reasoning in which they occur.

(3) Hence many categories of possibility, of what may be true or false, are contingent upon historical events, namely the development of certain styles of reasoning.

(4) It may then be inferred that there are other categories of possibility than have emerged in our tradition.

(5) We cannot reason as to whether alternative systems of reasoning are better or worse than ours, because the propositions to which we reason get their sense only from the method of reasoning employed. The propositions have no existence independent of the ways of reasoning towards them.[6]

For my purposes here, the most important claims that Hacking makes are that there are different styles of reasoning and that these styles determine what statements are possible candidates of truth-and-falsehood (with the exception of those statements which require no style of reasoning at all). As new styles of reasoning develop, they bring with them new categories of possible true-and-false statements. To take an example from Hacking,[7] consider the following statement that you might find in a Renaissance medical textbook: "mercury salve is good for syphilis because mercury is signed by the planet Mercury which signs the marketplace, where syphilis is contracted." Hacking argues, correctly I think, that our best description of this statement is not as false or as incommensurable with current medical reasoning, but rather as not even a possible candidate for truth-or-falsehood, given our currently accepted styles of reasoning. But a style of reasoning central to the Renaissance, based on the concepts of resemblance and similitude, brings with it the candidacy of such a statement for the status of true-or-false. Categories of statements get their status as true-or-false vis-à-vis historically specifiable styles of reasoning.

If we take Hacking as having given us a preliminary characterization of styles of reasoning, where are we to look for further clarification? The most difficult problem, as I have said, is precisely that of more fully cashing out the notion of style, and the most obvious place to look for help is to characterizations of style in art history. A reading of Meyer Schapiro's well-known essay "Style" makes it evident that there is as little agreement among art historians about the notion of style as there is among philosophers about the notions of knowledge or truth.[8] So there is no question of my applying some commonly agreed upon conception of style in art to scientific reasoning. Rather, I will appropriate that notion of style in art-historical writings that I have found most useful for my concerns about the scientific comprehensibility of psychiatry. This is, of course, not to claim that my characterization of style is the only one, or even that it is the most useful one for other purposes. The problem is to articulate some plausible conception of style that will help us to think about styles of reasoning. Schapiro clearly sets forth many of the problems that surround the idea of style in the uses made of it in art history. I have no doubt that further problems are created by transferring this idea from art to reasoning. But, to emphasize what I have previously said, if we cannot make any sense of "style" in styles of reasoning, then we ought to give up the notion, instead of pretending that it serves a fruitful methodological purpose. I do think that some sense can be made of it, and I also think that art history provides a good, even if not perfect, guide.

Many art-historical discussions about style focus on the notion of expression or expressive quality, and since I will say nothing directly about expressive quality here, I want simply to indicate what some of its theoretical problems are. Perhaps the most significant difficulty is one of understanding how expressive qualities correspond to formal and structural elements in art, and to the way in which these elements are combined.[9] In his famous discussion in *Words and Pictures* of frontal and profile modes of representation in art, Meyer Schapiro shows how, in medieval art, presenting figures either in profile or frontally has different effects as "expressive means."[10] He documents, for instance, that a conservative thirteenth-century cleric objected to representations of the Virgin Mary in profile, since the frontal form was seen as both more sacred and more beautiful.[11] Moreover,

> In other arts besides the medieval Christian, profile and frontal are often
> coupled in the same work as carriers of opposed qualities. One of the pair
> is the vehicle of the higher value and the other, by contrast, marks the
> lesser. The opposition is reinforced in turn by differences in size, posture,

costume, place, and physiognomy as attributes of the polarized individuals. The duality of the frontal and profile can signify then the distinction between good and evil, the sacred and the less sacred or profane, the noble and the plebian, the active and the passive, the engaged and the unengaged, the living and the dead, the real person and the image. The matching of these qualities and states with the frontal and profile varies in different cultures, but common is the notion of a polarity expressed through the contrasted positions.[12]

In discussing Egyptian reliefs and painting, Greek vase paintings, and the paintings in medieval Arabic illuminated manuscripts, Schapiro shows that the profile is sometimes reserved for the lesser figure in a pair and sometimes for the nobler figure. He concludes, and this is crucial for my account to follow, that "the contrast as such is more essential than a fixed value of each term in the pair."[13] I also believe that it is certain contrasts in modes of representation that are essential to an account of style, and I further believe that the problem of expressive quality or value, although certainly important, has a derivative or secondary role. Whatever else may be the case about expressive quality, it is at least partially a function of formal or structural elements, and until we are clearer about the role these latter elements play in characterizing style, we are unlikely to make any headway with the problematic notion of expressive value. As Heinrich Wölfflin advises, "Instead of asking 'How do these works affect me, the modern man?' and estimating their expressional content by that standard, the historian must realise what choices of formal possibilities the epoch had at its disposal. An essentially different interpretation will then result."[14] In what follows, I shall take Wölfflin's advice, and so shall have little more to say about expressional content.

Indeed, it is Wölfflin's *Principles of Art History: The Problem of the Development of Style in Later Art* that will provide my guide in characterizing the notion of style in styles of reasoning. Although I am not unaware of the problems in Wölfflin's account, I am less concerned with the adequacy of its details than with its methodological procedure. Despite the objections one might bring to bear on this account as a whole, his procedure is highly instructive in helping us to understand the idea of a style of reasoning.[15] Wölfflin argues that the difference between the classic and baroque style is best characterized in terms of five pairs of polar categories or concepts.

Moreover, he argues that "there can be discovered in the history of style a substratum of concepts referring to representation as such, and one could envisage a history of the development of occidental seeing, for which the variations in individual and national characteristics would cease to have any importance."[16] That is, Wölfflin wants to write a history of the visual possibilities to which artists are bound. Thus he will argue, to take a typical example, that the impression of reserve and dignity found in Raphael's paintings is "not entirely to be attributed to an intention born of a state of mind: it is rather a question of a representational form of his epoch which he only perfected in a certain way and used for his own ends."[17] Wölfflin's procedure in writing his history of style is, as is well known, to set forth the determining concepts of classic and baroque art in terms of five pairs of opposed concepts. His five major chapters discuss the linear and the painterly, plane and recession, closed and open form, multiplicity and unity, and clearness and unclearness. The first of each of these pairs of concepts makes up the classic style, and the second of each of the pairs makes up the baroque style. Since I cannot even begin to do justice to the richness of Wölfflin's account in this essay, I will let a quotation from the conclusion to his book serve as a summary:

> In its breadth, the whole process of the transformation of the imagination has been reduced to five pairs of concepts. We can call them categories of beholding without danger of confusion with Kant's categories . . . It is possible that still other categories could be set up—I could not discover them—and those given here are not so closely related that they could not be imagined in a partly different combination. For all that, to a certain extent they involve each other and, provided we do not take the expression literally, we could call them five different views of one and the same thing. The linear-plastic is connected with the compact space-strata of the plane-style, just as the tectonically self-contained has a natural affinity with the independence of the component parts and perfected clarity. On the other hand, incomplete clarity of form and the unity of effect with depreciated component parts will of itself combine with the a-tectonic flux and find its place best in the impressionist-painterly conception. And if it looks as though the recessional style did not necessarily belong to the same family, we can reply that its recessional tensions are exclusively based on visual effects which appeal to the eye only and not to plastic feeling.

We can make the test. Among the reproductions illustrated there is hardly one which could not be utilised from any of the other points of view.[18]

This summary gives some indication of Wölfflin's procedure in the book. He discusses in detail each of the five pairs of polar concepts, showing how they are exemplified in a wide variety of painting, drawing, sculpture, and architecture. He also shows how the concepts are linked together to constitute what we might think of as two opposed visual spaces, that of the classic and that of the baroque. In this way we get a determinate conception of classic and baroque style, framed in terms of their contrasted modes of representation. A similar methodological procedure in characterizing style is applied to architecture in an early book written by Wölfflin's former student, Paul Frankl. Frankl argues that the differences between the Renaissance (classic) and baroque styles of architecture can be understood in terms of four polar concepts, spatial addition and spatial division, center of force and channel of force, one image and many images, and freedom and constraint.[19] Although his four pairs of polarities differ considerably from Wölfflin's, it is his methodological agreement with Wölfflin in characterizing distinct styles that interests me.

Given his understanding of the opposition between classic and baroque style, Wölfflin can formulate his famous thesis that "even the most original talent cannot proceed beyond certain limits which are fixed for it by the date of its birth. Not everything is possible at all times, and certain thoughts can only be thought at certain stages of the development."[20] Something like this claim could just as easily have been found in a book by Foucault, since he too is concerned to show the possibilities to which our distinct historical periods bind us. And we should not be surprised to discover something akin to those discontinuities for which Foucault is famous appearing in Wölfflin when he writes,

> False judgments enter art history if we judge from the impression which pictures of different epochs, placed side by side, make on us. We must not interpret their various types of expression merely in terms of *stimmung*. They speak a different language. Thus it is false to attempt an immediate comparison of a Bramante with a Bernini in architecture from the point of view of *stimmung*. Bramante does not only incorporate a different ideal: his *mode of thought* is from the outset *differently organized* from Bernini's.[21]

It is this conceptualization of style, with its polar categories, realms of limited possibilities, and breaks and discontinuities, that I believe needs to be adopted in trying to understand historically the change in styles of reasoning that gave rise, for instance, to the emergence of psychiatric comprehensibility.[22]

I want explicitly to dissociate Wölfflin's view of the development of style from his account of the structure of style. Wölfflin's, in my opinion, philosophically defective conception of stylistic change and development has done much to obscure what is of permanent value in his discussion of the concept of style. By separating his concept of style from his teleological schema of development, I hope to reopen, to revive, some methodological issues that extend far beyond the domain of art history. I fully recognize, and the irony is duly noted, that many of the theoretically most significant recent works of art history are united by a common opposition to giving historiographical prominence to the concept of style. Whatever benefits such an opposition may have had in recent art history, I nevertheless want to insist that the structure of Wölfflin's account has unexploited and unexplored power when applied to reasoning in the sciences.

Although in what follows I want to focus on the idea of a conceptual space, I should at least mention some other components of style, related to those I have already discussed, which I will only touch on indirectly, but which any complete discussion of style would have to take into account. These components are most thoroughly and most interestingly discussed in Michael Baxandall's *Painting and Experience in Fifteenth Century Italy*.[23] Baxandall wants to reconstruct what he calls "Quattrocento cognitive style," especially as it relates to Quattrocento pictorial style. He hopes to offer "insight into what it was like, intellectually and sensibly, to be a Quattrocento person,"[24] what it was like to think and see in a Quattrocento style. He takes a cognitive style to consist of the interpreting skills, categories, model patterns, and the habits of inference and analogy that one possesses.[25] He then examines fifteenth-century Italian painting and society to exhibit the details of each of these components of Quattrocento cognitive style. If I were going to try to exhibit exhaustively the style of reasoning that made, for example, the statements of psychiatry possible, I would have to say something about all of the elements of style that Baxandall refers to. For example, I would have to discuss the habits of inference and analogy used by psychiatrists, and to show their distinctiveness from previous habits of inference and analogy. I would also have to examine the interpreting skills that are part of psychiatry, especially its diagnostic skills, and to show the differences between these diagnostic skills and those of earlier times. And I would also hope to be able to show all of the changes in examples of diseases from neurological to psychiatric textbooks. But in my historical writing on the emergence of psychiatric reasoning I have left some of these important factors aside so as to concentrate on what I take to be the fundamental element of style, namely, the categories or concepts and the way they combine with one another to constitute a style.

It is, I think, no accident that in his inaugural lecture to the Collège de France, *L'Inventaire des différences*, Paul Veyne links the work of Wölfflin and Foucault when he discusses two slightly different ideas whose conjunction, he tells us, bears the name "structuralism":

> On the one hand, all social reality is objectively limited; on the other, all social reality is confused in our representation and it is up to us to conceptualise it and to see it clearly.[26]

Veyne goes on to remind us that the limitations which historical agents undergo, the fact that "artists submit to the conventions, the pictorial 'discourse' of their epoch," led Wölfflin to conclude that "every painting has two authors, the artist and his period."[27] These conventions, to which the artist submits "purely and simply", limit or distort his expression without his knowledge, so that "the signifier is no longer everywhere glued to the signified."[28] According to Veyne, Wölfflin and Foucault have "simply recalled that man is not entirely active, and that it comes to pass that he submit."[29] For Veyne this no more requires the assassination of the human than does the teaching of Catholic theology that the actions of a just person who receives cooperating grace have two authors, God and him, or that when a just person undergoes operating grace, it is God who acts through him.[30]

Moreover, Veyne claims, I believe correctly, that when, for instance, we are at the Louvre in front of a painting, Wölfflin's ten fundamental concepts enable us "to have more ideas about the painting, to be more conscious of its originality and, literally, to see it better."[31] And he concludes,

> One is wrong to oppose the apprehension of individualities, in all their richness, to conceptualisation, which would be a much too general bab-

bling; quite the contrary, each concept that we conquer refines and en-riches our perception of the world; without concepts one sees nothing.[32]

These considerations are the background for Veyne's later claim that "historical facts are organized not by periods or by peoples, but by notions; they do not have to be replaced in their time, but under their concept. Then, at the same time, facts no longer have individuality except relative to this concept."[33] It is such an understanding of the epistemological role of concepts, differently articulated by Wölfflin and Foucault in their respective domains, that constitutes the core of my notion of a style of reasoning.

In applying the Wölfflinian conception of styles of reasoning, we encounter a number of significant epistemological and methodological problems created by moving from perception and vision to reasoning and argumentation. But rather than turning to these problems, I want to give at least some indication of how I have (implicitly) employed the idea of styles of reasoning in my historical and historiographical practice. Just as Wölfflin wanted to reconstitute a specific visual space through a set of interrelated categories—for example, the categories of the linear, plane, closed form, multiplicity, and clearness constituted classical space—so a particular style of reasoning is centrally constituted by a set of interrelated or linked concepts. These concepts are linked together by specifiable rules to form what we might think of as a determinate conceptual space, a space that determines what statements can and cannot be made with the concepts. I have tried to show that starting around 1870 a new psychiatric style of reasoning about diseases emerges, one that makes possible, among other things, statements about sexual perversion—about homosexuality, masochism, sadism, and fetishism—that then quickly become commonplace in discussions of "sexuality." The appearance and proliferation of these statements were a direct consequence of this new style of reasoning, which we could also think of, in Foucault's terms, as the birth of a new discursive practice. So to write a history of the birth of nineteenth-century psychiatry by way of the notion of a style of reasoning requires writing a history of the emergence of a new system of concepts and showing how these concepts are internally related by a set of rules to form a structured conceptual space. One wants to see what concepts, connected in what particular ways, allowed statements about sexual perversions that had never been made before, and ultimately permitted, so I have argued, the very constitution of the sexual perversions.[34]

Furthermore, a crucial part of my historical account has been to demonstrate that this psychiatric style of reasoning is to be contrasted with the anatomical style of reasoning about diseases. In the arena of the sexual, the anatomical style of reasoning took *sex* as its object of investigation and concerned itself with diseases of structural abnormality, with pathological changes that resulted from some macroscopic or microscopic anatomical change. The pathology of hermaphroditism most visibly exemplifies this style of reasoning. In the psychiatric style of reasoning, on the other hand, it is not sex but *sexuality* that is the relevant domain of investigation. Thus it is not hermaphroditism but homosexuality that is elevated to the status of an exemplary disease. If we study the history of pathological anatomy, neurology, and psychiatry in the nineteenth century, we can begin to reconstruct some of the polar concepts that make up the two opposed styles of reasoning. We are presented, for instance, with the polarities between sex and sexuality, organ and instinct, structure and function, and anatomical defect and perversion. The first of each of these pairs of concepts partially makes up the anatomical style of reasoning about disease, while the second of each of these pairs helps to constitute the psychiatric style of reasoning. These polarities analytically differentiate two conceptual modes of representation, two conceptual spaces, methodologically parallel to Wölfflin's polarities that distinguish two visual modes of representation. By figuring out exactly how these concepts combine with one another in determinate ways to form possible true-or-false statements, and by enumerating the kinds of inference, analogy, evidence, verification, and explanation that are associated with these conceptual combinations, we can reconstitute a full-fledged style of reasoning.

One conclusion I have drawn from my attempt to reconstitute the psychiatric style of reasoning about sexuality is that the very concept of perversion (as well as the experience of being a pervert) did not exist before the latter part of the nineteenth century.[35] By seeing that and how the concept of perversion was part of a style of reasoning, one sees that and how it required a whole set of related concepts, the entire ensemble of which was linked together in specifiable ways. The concept of perversion demanded a whole new conceptual space embedded in a new style of reasoning.

When I first made these claims, over a decade ago, I remember all too distinctly the incredulity with which they were greeted by certain Anglo-American historians of philosophy, committed, as they were, to a historical methodology whose basic assumptions were rarely examined in detail.

Thus I was asked rhetorically, as though the question answered itself, did not Augustine frequently invoke the idea of perversion, and wasn't the fact that he used this idea a clear refutation of my conclusions? The question was as profoundly naive as it was methodologically important. I do not want to begin to unravel the rhetoric of this question without emphasizing that I have developed the notion of a style of reasoning here to apply to scientific reasoning, to be of historiographical use in the history of science. One cannot simply take this notion and apply it whole cloth to systems of philosophical thought, as though the differences between science and philosophy could be ignored. But for my specific purpose now, abstracting from these differences, I will allow that there are some systems of philosophical thought that possess sufficient conceptual structure to permit the comparison of their concepts with the concepts employed in styles of scientific reasoning. However, in making such a comparison one must not be content with vague parallels, with aligning words or phrases or isolated formulas. Rather, one must compare *conceptual structures,* which Pierre Hadot has defined as "group[s] of notions that mutually imply one another in a given philosophical system."[36] In his great two-volume work on Porphyry and Victorinus, Hadot has shown that in the theological works of Marius Victorinus we can discover the influence of a lost Neoplatonic source, which Hadot has identified as the work of Porphyry. Hadot was able to recognize, reconstruct, and identify this source by showing that there were Neoplatonic conceptual structures in Victorinus' work that coincided with characteristically Porphyrean themes. He emphasized that "it is important that the conceptual structure is not reconstructed by making appeal to phrases or words separated from their context and drawn from the most disparate places";[37] a conceptual structure requires conceptual and literary unity. Although Hadot was dealing primarily with the reconstruction of a lost source, his brilliant methodological procedures are directly relevant to making the kind of comparisons necessary to answer the question about Augustine that I have just reported. We must compare not words or isolated formulas, but whole conceptual structures; otherwise our comparisons will be misleading, indeed pointless.

In a too little known but extraordinary paper, Mino Bergamo, a historian of seventeenth-century French mysticism, has shown that Ignatius of Loyola's use of the word "indiferente" and François de Sales's use of the word "indifference" in fact imply opposite conceptual structures, so that there is a "discontinuity . . . dissimulated under the veil of a lexical permanence."[38] Thus Bergamo finds that although seventeenth-century French mystics often make use of traditional religious elements, they never do so without transforming these elements, "without imposing on such elements a re-elaboration that sometimes enriches them, and sometimes inverts their meaning."[39] And he concludes that one can, simultaneously, repeat the same thing while saying something else, that "repetition is the site in which, more than in any other, difference is articulated."[40] Something similar, again abstracting from the otherwise significant dissimilarities, could be said about Augustine's use of the term "perversion" and the nineteenth-century psychiatric use of this term. Lexical continuity hides radical conceptual discontinuity. When Augustine concludes his recounting of his own adolescent theft of pears in Book II of the *Confessions,* he writes, "In their perverted way all humanity imitates you [God]" ("perverse te imitantur omnes"), and he speaks, more specifically, of our perversely imitating divine omnipotence.[41] In Book XII of *The City of God,* Augustine argues that pride "is a defect of the soul that perversely loves its own power while it despises the more righteous power of a higher Power. Hence whoever perversely loves the good of any natural being, even if he should obtain it, becomes evil himself through this good as well as wretched by the loss of a higher good."[42] (The adverb in both sentences is "perverse.") And when he gives his account of the nature of Adam's transgression in Book XIV of *The City of God,* Augustine writes:

> "pride is the start of all sin." Moreover, what is pride but a craving for perverse elevation? [Quid est autem superbia nisi perversae celesitudinis appetitus?] For it is perverse elevation to forsake the ground in which the mind ought to be rooted, and to become and be, in a sense, grounded in oneself. This happens when a man is too well pleased with himself, and such a one is thus pleased when he falls away from that unchangeable good with which he ought rather to have been pleased than with himself. Now this falling away is voluntary, for if the will had remained steadfast in love of the higher unchangeable good that provided it with light to see and kindled it with fire to love, it would not have been diverted from this love to follow its own pleasure.[43]

Even without undertaking any detailed textual exegesis, it is evident that Augustine's use of the notion of "perversion" inhabits a conceptual structure not only distinct from but opposed to that of the psychiatric style of reasoning. For Augustine perversion is a deficiency of the will, a voluntary defection from the immutable good of God. It is an inversion of the hierarchy of value, substituting a lower good for a higher one. The opposite of perversion is conversion, a turning toward God and an adhering to Him.[44] In the psychiatric style of reasoning, perversion is located outside of the boundaries of the will. It is a disease of the sexual instinct, psychobiologically embedded in one's personality, and not legitimately the object of moral approbation or disapprobation. The opposite of perversion is normal sexual desires or appetites, which are similarly independent of volition. Indeed, one of the main functions of this concept of sexual perversion is precisely to separate this phenomenon from the domain of vice.[45] The fact that Augustine also uses the term "perversion" does not by itself settle any issue at all.

A careful analysis of his use of the notion of "perversion" shows that Augustine's concept of perversion does not share the same conceptual space as the nineteenth-century psychiatric concept, indeed that the same word hides two radically different concepts, two radically different conceptual structures. Rather than undermining my conclusions, Augustine's use of "perversion" confirms them. We shall not understand the *concept* of perversion until we examine its rule-governed behavior with other concepts to see what kinds of statements can be made with it. It is no mere surface phenomenon that Augustine's statements diverge so markedly from those of nineteenth-century psychiatric discourse. The examination of his texts underscores the specificity, and novelty, of this latter discourse.

As Bergamo has said elsewhere, a series of recurrences of the same phrase can correspond to a multiplicity of different statements. Even the identical sentence need not constitute the same statement. A statement is defined by a "field of stabilization" ("un campo di stabilizzazione"), which is constituted by the rules of usage and the relations that connect the statement to other statements.[46] This field of stabilization assures the possibility of the repeatability of statements, but also imposes particularly exacting restrictions on this repeatability, thus distinguishing the statement from the virtually infinitely repeatable phrase.[47] In order for a *new statement* to emerge under the appearance of an identical phrase or sentence it is necessary that a *new field of stabilization* be organized, which provides "new schemes of utilization and new series of relations, and that, in short, transforms the conditions of inscription of the phrase."[48] In my terminology, the same word, virtually infinitely repeatable, may express different concepts. Our concepts are stabilized by a conceptual space, a style of reasoning that specifies the rules of usage of these concepts. What at first might appear identical may in fact be radically different, depending on the precise way in which the concept enunciated is stabilized. Since the same word or phrase can be stabilized in diverse, even opposite ways, we will literally not comprehend what is being said unless we understand the style of reasoning that provides the conditions of inscription of the words. Styles of reasoning give systematicity, structure, and identity to our thought; they are, as it were, the glue that holds our thoughts together. As Wölfflin knew, without concepts one sees nothing; and, as should be even more evident, without concepts one says nothing. It is for these reasons, above all, that we cannot do without the idea of styles of reasoning.

6

The Epistemology of Distorted Evidence: Problems around Carlo Ginzburg's Historiography

Le strade del giudice e quelle dello storico, coincidenti per un tratto, divergono poi inevitabilmente. Chi tenta di ridurre lo storico a giudice semplifica e impoverisce la conoscenza storiografica; ma chi tenta di ridurre il giudice a storico inquina irrimediabilmente l'esercizio della giustizia.

—CARLO GINZBURG, *Il giudice e lo storico*

I

THE EPIGRAPH TO THIS ESSAY—"The ways of the judge and those of the historian coincident for a while then inevitably diverge. Whoever attempts to reduce the historian to a judge simplifies and impoverishes historiographical knowledge; but whoever attempts to reduce the judge to a historian irremediably pollutes the exercise of justice"—is taken from Carlo Ginzburg's recently published book, *Il giudice e lo storico.*[1]

This book provides the most recent extended basis for Ginzburg's reflections on the topic of evidence and related concepts, and the epigraph I
have chosen highlights his attempt to chart both the initial convergences
and ultimate divergences between the tasks of the judge and the historian,
as well as their philosophical underpinnings. Ginzburg's historical work has
been so significant and powerful that it is all too easy to overlook the fundamental contribution of his historiographical considerations; these latter
considerations, although spread out over a wide range of books and articles, when taken together provide a compelling framework of questions, issues, and theoretical conclusions that ought to inform how our histories—
intellectual, cultural, and social—are constructed and written.[2]

II

Ginzburg shows that in the classical tradition both the historian and the
lawyer were "expected to make a convincing argument by communicating
the illusion of reality, not by exhibiting proofs collected either by himself
or by others." Following Arnaldo Momigliano, he argues that until the
mid-eighteenth century collecting proofs was "an activity practiced by anti-
quarians and erudites, not by historians" ("CE," p. 291). In "Montrer et
citer" he traces the historiographical role and fate of the ancient concept of
enargeia, of the idea that the historian must produce accounts that are clear
and palpable, that are living narratives conveying an impression of life that
will move and convince their readers.[3] The requirement of *enargeia* was
linked to a rhetorical tradition in which the orator made some nonexistent
object visible to his audience by "the almost magical force of his words"
("MC," p. 47). *Enargeia* was always associated with the sphere of direct experience, with a witnessing by the historian that allowed him to put an invisible reality before the eyes of his readers. "*Enargeia* was an instrument
appropriate to communicating *autopsia,* in other words, a direct view, by
the force of style" ("MC," p. 47). And annals were contrasted with history
by ancient and medieval writers; history recounted events in which the nar-
rator had taken part, which he had himself viewed, while annals were concerned with a more remote past that was not directly present to the historian and his generation (see "MC," secs. 9–10). Moreover, by the sixteenth
century, the dullness of style found in annals and their absence of true narrative structure were sometimes praised in comparison with the rhetorically

seductive images offered by history, as though the fragmentary and rough features of the former were better sources of evidence than the smooth, almost self-cohering pictures of the latter (see "MC," p. 51).

The ways in which the notion of *enargeia* gave way to the notions of evidence and proof furnish a crucial chapter in the history of the emergence of modern historiography. Treatises such as Henri Griffet's 1769 *Traité des différents sortes de preuves qui servent à établir la vérité de l'histoire* explicitly compared the historian to a judge who tested the reliability of witnesses and evaluated the claims of proofs.[4] Ginzburg writes that Griffet's work expressed "a still-unaddressed intellectual need" ("CE," p. 291), and I understand him to have expressed this need in his own words when he writes that we believe that

> historians must be ready to support their considerations by proofs of one kind or another. Or, if you prefer a descriptive proposition rather than a normative one: we at least believe (the neo-skeptics included, I suppose) that historians (neo-skeptics included) can only produce an "effect of truth" by linking their observations to some sort of proof. Citation (direct or indirect) has supplanted *enargeia*.   ("MC," p. 53)

Ginzburg is, of course, fully aware of the fact that the judicial model of historiography has also emphasized the judge's sentence, that it can lead to a "moralistic historiography" based on "moral and political court-speeches, followed by condemnations or acquittals" ("CE," pp. 293, 292). And as Ginzburg remarks, insisting on the ultimate divergences between the tasks of the historian and the judge, "moral certainty does not have the value [*non ha valore*] of proof."[5] A "deleterious model of judicial summations pronounced by an outmoded political historiography" is not the only model available to the historian who is committed to the notion of proof.[6] Moreover, I have not yet even mentioned the more subtle effects, enumerated by Ginzburg, of the judicial model, those seen, for example, in his claim that "on the one hand, it urges historians to focus on events (political, military, diplomatic) that could be easily ascribed to specific actions performed by one or more individuals; on the other, it disregards those phenomena (like social life, *mentalités,* and so on) that resist an approach based on this explanatory framework." Ginzburg acknowledges "the diminished prestige of this kind of historiography . . . as a positive phenomenon" ("CE," pp. 292–293, 293).[7] But such an acknowledgment does not require, as some historians appear to have believed, that we simply dismiss the notion of proof, as if history without evidence were the royal road to historiographical satisfaction. Whatever theoretical impatience, or even embarrassment, might today surround the notion of proof, what is called for is a more detailed investigation of the legitimate roles of proof, evidence, and truth in historical writing *as opposed to* legal and judicial argumentation and judgment. There is not some one notion of proof and evidence applicable by both the judge and the historian to their respective domains. But just as we must be careful not to pollute the exercise of justice, we must be vigilant in not simplifying historiographical knowledge. Jettisoning proof, evidence, and truth from our consciousness is an impoverishment hardly distinguishable from abject poverty.

III

Perhaps the most pervasive underlying distinctions between the judge and the historian revolve around the different ideals that regulate their tasks. The judge must render a just sentence; the historian must provide a truthful account. As John Rawls has precisely and unforgettably formulated this claim, at the beginning of the first section of *A Theory of Justice*, "Justice is the first virtue of social institutions, as truth is of systems of thought. A theory however elegant and economical must be rejected or revised if it is untrue; likewise laws and institutions no matter how efficient and well-arranged must be reformed or abolished if they are unjust."[8] Both judges and historians invoke the notions of evidence and proof, but their respective regulative ideals of justice and truth decisively contribute to the understanding of what is to count as a piece of evidence, what is to count as a proof. Legal evidence and historical evidence may overlap, but the former is in the service of establishing a just verdict, while the latter is relevant for securing a truthful account of events, whether they be individual or social, long or short term. What is evidence for some purposes may be beside the point for others. Obviously enough, the *concepts* of justice and truth are compatible with a diversity of conflicting *conceptions* of justice and truth; or, to put it another way, the regulative ideals of justice and truth are open to divergent interpretations of these ideals.[9] But the fact that there are substantive disagreements about which particular conception of justice or truth is most defensible does not imply that a judge's deliberations should not be shaped by the ideal of justice or that a historian's reconstructions can ignore the demands of truth.[10] Ginzburg recognizes this fact in his use of the phrase "effect of truth" that I have already cited. He says that he has used the phrase "effect of truth" rather than "truth"

> in order to emphasize that different cultures have given different interpretations of the concept of truth. But as far as I know the distinction between false and true statements—and at first sight through their connection to the facts—has always been an essential element of historical knowledge, of whatever kind, everywhere that one has cultivated, up to the present, historical knowledge as a form of social activity. ("MC," p. 53)

In mentioning, even in passing, the regulative ideal of justice with respect to the judge, I cannot forbear invoking, in this context, an extraordinary book by Natalia Ginzburg, which takes up issues of evidence, proof, truth, law, and, ultimately, justice. *Serena Cruz o la vera giustizia* discusses a celebrated Italian case of adoption, of a baby named Serena Cruz, involving claims and counterevidence and finally culminating in a judicial verdict that decided the fate of the young child. At the very end of her discussion, Ginzburg quotes an Italian citation of an American Supreme Court judge, who responded to a lawyer's invocation of justice by saying, "I am not here to render justice [*per fare giustizia*] but to apply the law."[11] Ginzburg writes that she cannot understand these words, that they seem to her "devoid of meaning." She argues not only that justice and the law should be one, but that since the laws are made to defend justice, when the two part ways, when the laws are defective, judges should "turn somersaults to apply it [the law] as justly as possible" (*SC*, pp. 95, 96). And the last two lines of her book insist on the regulative role of the ideal of justice in the most unambiguous terms: "Might something exist that is more important than justice in the government of countries, in the relations with human events and aspirations? But nothing exists that is more important than justice" (*SC*, p. 96). In his discussion of the Sofri case Carlo Ginzburg shows, in effect, that if one displaces the principle *in dubio pro re* (according to which the accused can be convicted only if one is absolutely certain of his guilt) from its regulative role in judicial proceedings, one may well be led to misuse completely the notion of proof, sliding tacitly from the plane of mere possibility to that of the assertion of fact. By making logical compatibility function as if it were equivalent to actual verification, one could well convict an innocent person. This might be acceptable if one's regulative ideal were *in dubio pro re publica*—for instance, the will of *il Duce*—but reasons of state ought to have no regulative role in the halls of justice.[12] The judge, insofar as he is governed by justice, must make use of specific conceptions of evidence and proof, forged by the ideals to which his role commits him.

Shifting briefly to the regulative ideal of truth in historical inquiry, we can see some of the distortions, the epistemological deficiencies, that result from an attempt to ignore it by looking at Ginzburg's recent debate with Hayden White. I want to insist, first of all, that it is an arduous undertaking for a historian to try to proceed consistently without the concept of truth. Indeed, in many of these debates, a given historian will employ the rhetoric of truth, arguing as though he is doing nothing more than advocating a specific conception of truth different from that of his interlocutors. But a short analysis will show that his specific conception of so-called truth has no philosophical plausibility whatsoever as an interpretation of the concept of truth and that it is only the demands of the regulative ideal of truth, exerting themselves despite attempts to ignore them, that account for the rhetoric employed, a rhetoric that, in this context, wears its emptiness virtually on its surface. It is no accident that some of the starkest instances of these issues can be found in discussions of the "revisionist" interpretation of the Holocaust. Taking up White's objections to Pierre Vidal-Naquet's conclusions about the Robert Faurisson affair, Ginzburg, quoting White, summarizes as follows:

> The Zionist historical interpretation of the Holocaust, White says, is not a *contre-vérité* (as has been suggested by Vidal-Naquet) but a truth: "its truth, as a historical interpretation, consists precisely in its *effectiveness* [Ginzburg's italics] in justifying a wide range of current Israeli political policies that, from the standpoint of those who articulate them, are crucial to the security and indeed the very existence of the Jewish people." In the same way, "the effort of the Palestinian people to mount a politically *effective* [Ginzburg's italics] response to Israeli policies entails the production of a similarly *effective* [Ginzburg's italics] ideology, complete with an interpretation of their history capable of endowing it with a meaning that it has hitherto lacked."

Ginzburg's next sentence conveys his own philosophical stance: "We can conclude that if Faurisson's narrative were ever to prove *effective*, it would be regarded by White as true as well."[13]

Ginzburg's remark is, I think, meant as a kind of *reductio ad absurdum* of the identification of political effectiveness and truth. He implies that an interpretation or conception of truth that makes it equivalent to political effectiveness falls outside of the boundaries, however flexible, of our understanding of the concept of truth. It is to give up the very concept of truth, as shown by the fact that however effective Faurisson's account might be (it is, as Vidal-Naquet has shown, not very effective, and we should even wonder how effective it could be), we would not conclude that it was a true account. I suppose that someone might respond by claiming that White is doing nothing more epistemologically vicious than proposing a pragmatist conception of truth. But I would argue, though I shall not undertake this here, that a survey of the history of philosophy as well as an analysis of philosophical debates about the nature of truth would show that in no way is this even a defensible construal of the pragmatist notion of truth, that the pragmatists wanted to provide an interpretation of truth that did much more than brutely force its identification with political effectiveness.[14]

Someone might, I guess, respond further that whether we call a historical account true or effective is a matter of words, up to us to choose according to our interests. If it serves our purposes to call an account true because it is effective, then nothing forbids us from doing so, nothing compels us to withhold the label "true." But whether someone possesses the concept of truth is not up to us to so decide; it is not a matter of legislative decree, as though possessing a concept were like being granted the right to vote.[15] Neither declaration nor rhetorical convolution is sufficient to show that someone who understands political effectiveness *by that very fact* possesses the concept of truth. And Ginzburg's claim against White is, first, that White's response to Vidal-Naquet forgoes the concept of truth and, second, that this concept regulates the enquiries of the historian. From these claims, it does follow that Faurisson's narrative does not count as history; and this strikes me as precisely the appropriate standpoint to have.

In the preface to the reprinting of his brilliant essay "Un Eichmann de papier," one of the most powerful contributions to the problem of historical evidence I know, Vidal-Naquet expresses the point of view that is implied by the essential intertwining of history and the regulative ideal of truth. It is a point of view that I believe he shares with Ginzburg, and in both cases it is a consequence of some of their basic historiographical claims, claims that converge around the roles that each ascribes to evidence, proof, and truth:

What is at stake here is not feeling but truth. . . . A dialogue between two parties, even if they are adversaries, presupposes a common ground, a common respect—in this case for truth. But with the "revisionists," such ground does not exist. Could one conceive of an astrophysicist entering into dialogue with a "researcher" claiming that the moon is made of Roquefort cheese? Such is the level at which the parties would have to be situated. And, of course, no more than there is an absolute truth is there an absolute lie, even though the "revisionists" have made valiant efforts to attain that ideal. By which I mean that were it to be determined that the passengers of a rocket or a spaceship had left a few grams of Roquefort on the moon, there would be no point in denying their presence. Until now, the contribution of the "revisionists" to our knowledge may be compared to the correction, in a long text, of a few typographical errors. That does not justify a dialogue, since they have above all amplified beyond measure the register of falsehood.[16]

IV

After Ginzburg's discussion of White at the conference "Nazism and the 'Final Solution,'" I heard several audience members complain that Ginzburg, in his defense of evidence, truth, and proof, was just a conservative positivist. Passing over the fact that there were left-wing as well as right-wing versions of positivism, I found these murmurings incoherent after thinking about Ginzburg's own historical writings and procedures. As Ginzburg clearly states in "Checking the Evidence," a certain positivistic conception of the relationship between evidence and reality must be "unequivocally rejected." Evidence is not a "transparent medium . . . an open window that gives us direct access to reality." But neither is evidence "a wall, which by definition precludes any access to reality." As Ginzburg correctly diagnoses it, "this extreme antipositivistic attitude . . . turns out to be a sort of inverted positivism" ("CE," p. 294).

In examining the history of positivism and antipositivism in twentieth-century history and philosophy of science, Peter Galison has recently argued that in light of their obvious differences, the latter being a reaction against the former, we must be careful not to overlook the fact that these positivisms and antipositivisms are "flip-side versions of one another" and that "in their mirror reflections there is a good deal of similarity." Each has a "privileged vantage point"—whether the observational foundation from which the positivist builds up or the paradigm or conceptual scheme from which the antipositivist looks down—that carries similar historiographical consequences.[17] A common picture of both scientific unity and periodization can be found running through the issues that divided positivist and antipositivist history and philosophy of science.[18] Indeed, I would add that it is part of the cultural dominance of this common picture that *we* are led to believe that if someone rejects positivist foundationalism and observational transparency, then he or she must be an antipositivist, who considers "all referential assumptions as a theoretical naiveté" since discourse (or theory, or narrative tropes) constitutes the objects that it pretends to describe realistically ("CE," p. 294).[19] This structuring of the alternatives—either the direct, virtually unmediated access to reality dreamed of by positivism or the self-sustaining, walled-in antipositivist discourse that precludes access to reality—makes it extraordinarily difficult to see how there could be any other possibility. The common structure of these mirror images threatens to exhaust the space of epistemological options. His detailed historical studies have allowed Galison to propose a conceptualization of the dynamics of scientific theory, experimentation, and instrumentation that stands outside the purview of the common picture, thus also allowing him to throw into relief the historiographical burdens of the traditional positivism/antipositivism debates.[20] If we examine Ginzburg's historical practice, we will see that although he is not an antipositivist, one who rejects the historiographical legitimacy of notions like evidence and proof, neither is he a positivist, who takes these notions as given, as though they involve an unproblematic relation with truth and reality.

Ginzburg's essay "The Inquisitor as Anthropologist" is one of our clearest and most profound discussions of the problems with positivist interpretations of evidence and truth. Ginzburg recognizes an unsettling analogy between inquisitors, anthropologists, and historians, an analogy that manifests a fundamental epistemological difficulty with certain forms of evidence and especially with those forms of evidence employed by Ginzburg himself in *The Night Battles* and *The Cheese and the Worms*:

> The elusive evidence that inquisitors were trying to elicit from defendants was not so different, after all, from our own objectives; what was different, of course, were their means and ultimate ends. . . . The inquisitors' urge for truth (their own truth, of course) has produced for us extremely

rich evidence—deeply distorted, however, by the psychological and physical pressures which played such a powerful role in witchcraft trials. Suggestive questioning was especially apparent in inquisitors' interrogations related to the witches' sabbat, the very essence of witchcraft, according to demonologists. When this occurred, defendants echoed, more or less spontaneously, the inquisitorial stereotypes which were diffused throughout Europe by preachers, theologians, and jurists. . . . Similarly, the comparison between inquisitorial trials and anthropological field notes could have, from the historian's point of view, a negative implication: the presence of those long-ago anthropologists would be so obtrusive as to prevent us from knowing the beliefs and thoughts of the unhappy natives brought before them.[21]

Rather than drawing a completely pessimistic conclusion from the presence of this epistemological problem (as many antipositivists do), Ginzburg insists on the importance of the fact that historians never have direct access to reality. As he puts it in "Checking the Evidence":

A piece of historical evidence can be either involuntary (a skull, a footprint, a food relic) or voluntary (a chronicle, a notarial act, a fork). But in both cases a specific interpretative framework is needed, which must be related (in the latter case) to the specific code according to which the evidence has been constructed. Evidence of both kinds could be compared to a distorted glass. Without a thorough analysis of its inherent distortions (the codes according to which it has been constructed and/or it must be perceived), a sound historical reconstruction is impossible. ("CE," p. 295)

Evidence is mediated by codes, and an adequate historiography must attend to the heterogeneous procedures by which we encode evidence. According to Ginzburg, there are no neutral documents: "even a notarial inventory implies a code, which we must decipher." And the evidence gathered from inquisitorial trials certainly does not "convey to us 'objective' information" ("IA," pp. 161, 160). But these codes are not prisons in which we find ourselves forever confined. We must understand the processes of encoding, of different kinds of evidential distortion, in order to interpret the evidence, to assess its reliability or unreliability, to know what it is evidence of. Codes that seemed impenetrable can eventually be deciphered, and new evidence, encoded in new ways, can shed light on old evidence, changing our interpretations of codes we had believed were unambiguous. Ginzburg's remarks about inquisitorial evidence should be applied, *mutatis mutandis,* to a whole range of historical evidence:

> In order to decipher them [the documents of inquisitors], we must learn to catch, behind the smooth surface of the text, a subtle interplay of threats and fears, of attacks and withdrawals. We must learn to disentangle the different threads which form the textual fabric of these dialogues. ("IA," pp. 160–61)

There is no formalizable set of rules that tells us how to decipher historical evidence (here the analogy with a code is loosened), but there are truly great historical works whose power partly resides in the ability of a historian to read the evidence, to show us how to enter into the codes of evidence in order to see *what* the evidence *is,* what it shows us about the phenomena we are interested in, what the phenomena are.

Let me now briefly turn to Ginzburg's groundbreaking contribution in this area. In the prefaces to the English and Italian editions of his book *The Night Battles,* Ginzburg stresses that the exceptional nature of the documents he used lies in "the gap between the questions of the judges and the confessions of the accused which was gradually reduced only in the course of decades."[22] Many historians had come to believe that all of the confessions of those accused of witchcraft were the consequences of torture and suggestive questioning on the part of the judges, that these confessions possessed no spontaneity or independence and were therefore evidence of the judges' beliefs, providing no access to the practices or beliefs of the witches. Ginzburg's Friulian sources, when critically decoded, allowed him to conclude that "the Friuli diabolical witchcraft grew out of the deformation of a preceding agrarian cult" (*NB,* pp. xx–xxi).[23] That is, Ginzburg's reading of the sources showed a gap, what he called "a clash between different, even conflicting voices," or, following Mikhail Bakhtin, a dialogue ("IA," p. 160), and it was this subtle but significant gap that made it possible for Ginzburg to reconstruct the process that revealed

> how a cult with such obviously popular characteristics as that of the benandanti gradually was transformed under inquisitorial pressure, ending up with the distinctive features of traditional witchcraft. But this dis-

crepancy, this gap between the image underlying the interrogations of the judges and the actual testimony of the accused, permits us to reach a genuinely popular stratum of beliefs which was later deformed, and then expunged by the superimposition of the schema of the educated classes. Because of this discrepancy, which endured over several decades, the benandanti trials constitute a precious source for the reconstruction of the peasant mentality of this period. (*NB*, p. xviii)[24]

Ultimately, the nocturnal gatherings of the *benandanti*, which were intended to induce fertility, were transformed into the devil's sabbat, with the storms and destruction that followed (see *NB*, p. xx). However, the lack of communication between judges and accused allowed "the emergence of a real dialogue—in the Bakhtinian sense of an unresolved clash of conflicting voices" ("IA," p. 164). Ginzburg's readings of these dialogues permitted him (and us) to see the existence of a "deep cultural layer which was totally foreign to the inquisitors." As he notes, "the very word benandante was unknown to them: . . . was it a synonym of 'witch' or, on the contrary, 'counterwitch'?" ("IA," p. 160). The meaning of this word was one of the stakes in the struggle between the *benandanti* and inquisitors. Although power settled the semantic dispute in favor of the inquisitors, and *benandanti* became witches, the miscommunications and struggles provided evidence about the *benandanti* not otherwise available (see "IA," p. 160). Ginzburg's historiographical exploitation of these gaps, his extraordinary ability to read the codes, furnishes evidence for a set of phenomena that gives us a *more accurate* characterization of the *benandanti*. Whatever the distortions of the inquisitorial evidence, Ginzburg's procedure of reading the gaps does culminate in genuine evidence about a cultural reality that is no longer inaccessible to us.

In *The Cheese and the Worms*, again using inquisitorial documents, Ginzburg's reconstruction of the cosmology of Domenico Scandella, known as Menocchio, encounters similar problems concerning evidence and proof. Ginzburg's reading of these documents uses the gaps, miscommunications, resistances, and struggles as evidence of the existence of a peasant and oral culture that was "the patrimony not only of Menocchio but also of a vast segment of sixteenth-century society" (*CW*, p. xii). As in the case of the *benandanti*, only such a procedure of deciphering the documents will allow us to come to grips with the inherent distortions of the evidence created by the relationship of unequal power between Menocchio and his inquisitors. It is precisely the discrepancies and divergences in the documents that provide some of the most compelling evidence for Ginzburg's conclusions. But the case of Menocchio has its own particular difficulties:

> Here, too [as in the case of the *benandanti*], the fact that many of Menocchio's utterances cannot be reduced to familiar themes permits us to perceive a previously untapped level of popular beliefs, of obscure peasant mythologies. But what renders Menocchio's case that much more complicated is the fact that these obscure popular elements are grafted onto an extremely clear and logical complex of ideas, from religious radicalism, to a naturalism tending toward the scientific, to utopian aspirations of social reform.   (*CW,* p. xix)

The fact that although Menocchio's ideas seem to be derived from an "ancient oral tradition," they at the same time "recall a series of motifs worked out by humanistically educated heretical groups" should not lead us to exaggerate the importance of educated culture, as though Menocchio's ideas must really be derived from the latter, since ideas "originate *always and only* in educated circles" (*CW,* pp. xxii, 155). Ginzburg's reading of the documents, encoded as they are, exhibits "the gulf between the texts read by Menocchio and the way in which he understood them and reported them to the inquisitors," a gulf that indicates "a filter, a grill that Menocchio interposed unconsciously between himself and the texts" and that itself presupposed the peasant culture of which he was part (*CW,* pp. xxii, xii). The route to this peasant culture is hardly unproblematic, "given the fact that the documentation reflects the relationship of power between the classes of a given society" (*CW,* p. 155). Ginzburg's stunning achievement is to have used positively these distorted reflections in order to provide access to peasant, oral culture. What I have called his procedure of reading the gaps permits him to construct the evidence *more accurately,* so as to conclude that

> even if Menocchio had been in more or less indirect contact with educated circles, his statements in favor of religious tolerance and his desire for a radical renewal of society have an original stamp to them and do not appear to be the result of passively received outside influences. The roots of his utterances and of his aspirations were sunk in an obscure, almost unfathomable, layer of remote peasant traditions.   (*CW,* pp. xxii–xxiii)

One of the main aims of *The Cheese and the Worms* was to use the case of Menocchio in order to help demonstrate that "between the culture of the dominant classes and that of the subordinate classes there existed, in pre-industrial Europe, a circular relationship composed of reciprocal influences which traveled from low to high as well as from high to low" (*CW,* p. xii). But such a demonstration depends on the possibility of constructing the evidence so that one can have access to peasant culture, of not reducing this culture merely to a shadow of written culture. No "reciprocal movement between the two levels of culture" can be shown if there is no way to distinguish or disentangle the two levels or if it is assumed that there is no independence whatsoever to oral culture, since its ideas must ultimately be traced back to written culture (*CW,* p. xiv). Contrary to Paola Zambelli's interpretation, Ginzburg did not want to establish "'the absolute autonomy of peasant culture,'" which would have defeated his goal of trying to show that "we are in the presence of two cultures, linked, however—and this is the point—by circular (reciprocal) relationships," relationships that, as Ginzburg acknowledges, have "to be analytically demonstrated case by case," as in the case of Menocchio (*CW,* pp. 154–155).[25] But he did need to establish the relative autonomy or independence of peasant culture, the existence of *two* cultures, and, given the distorted nature of the evidence, the fact that "the thoughts, beliefs, and the aspirations of the peasants and artisans of the past reach us (if and when they do) almost always through distorting viewpoints and intermediaries," the existence of these *two* cultures could not be taken for granted (*CW,* p. xv). Ginzburg needed to show how to decode the evidence in order to demonstrate that we were in fact in the presence of two cultures, while showing also that these two cultures were reciprocally linked. As he says, "The fact that a source is not 'objective' . . . does not mean that it is useless" (*CW,* p. xvii). Both *The Cheese and the Worms* and *The Night Battles* provide extraordinary examples of how a nonobjective source can be useful, supply us with concrete lessons in how we might decipher a nonobjective source so that it can be seen to have evidentiary value. Ginzburg's historiographical commitment consists in not rejecting a distorted source outright just because it is distorted. And his historical practice consists in allowing us to see precisely those procedures of reading and interpretation that produce compelling evidence on the basis of nonobjective sources, thereby demonstrating that although the relationship between evidence and reality is problematic, it is not hopeless.

Before concluding this section, I want to mention a set of examples that comes from the history of psychiatry and psychology and that raises problems of evidence, proof, and reality as acute as those of Ginzburg's inquisitors. In his already-classic paper "Making Up People," Ian Hacking describes a philosophical notion that he calls dynamic nominalism, a notion that he applies to his own account of the invention of split personality and to my account of the invention of the homosexual:

> The claim of dynamic nominalism is . . . that a kind of person came into being at the same time as the kind itself was being invented. In some cases, that is, our classifications and our classes conspire to emerge hand in hand, each egging the other on. . . . Dynamic nominalism remains an intriguing doctrine, arguing that numerous kinds of human beings and human acts come into being hand in hand with our own invention of the categories labeling them. It is for me the only intelligible species of nominalism, the only one that can even gesture at an account of how common names and the named could so tidily fit together.[26]

Leaving aside the general epistemological complexities of dynamic nominalism, I want to focus on some questions of evidence that are analogous to those raised by Ginzburg's work on inquisitorial documents. My own account of the history of perversion and perverts has been a heavily top-down account, emphasizing the role of psychiatric concepts and categories in creating the reality of homosexuality, masochism, and sadism. I have argued that we do not have evidence of the homosexual preexisting the concepts and categories of nineteenth-century psychiatry, that this supposed evidence is actually evidence of sodomy, and that it was only retrospectively (mis)interpreted as evidence of homosexuality after the concept of the homosexual was well entrenched in psychiatric theory and practice.[27] Hacking's early work on multiple personality also emphasized the top-down aspects of the creation of the multiple, but his more recent work has also carefully considered another vector, the vector that comes from below, that comes from, so to speak, nonexpert culture.[28] Hacking recognized the existence of these two vectors right from the beginning of his work. He wrote:

> I do not believe there is a general story to be told about making up people. Each category has its own history. If we wish to present a partial

framework in which to describe such events, we might think of two vectors. One is the vector of labeling from above, from a community of experts who create a "reality" that some people make their own. Different from this is the vector of the autonomous behavior of the person so labeled, which presses from below, creating a reality every expert must face. ("MP," p. 234)

The evidential problem related to these two vectors stems from the fact that virtually all of the early-nineteenth-century evidence we have comes from above, that the case reports encode the evidence in terms of the concepts and categories of psychiatry, and that we have, at best, very marginal access to any vector from below. Perhaps we are faced here with some examples, limited though they are, in which we start with only *one* culture, the culture of medicine, which creates a reality that then becomes relatively autonomous over time. It might well be that beginning with the creation of the homosexual by psychiatry, homosexual culture only gradually evolved a life of its own that exerted greater and greater autonomy with respect to the concepts, categories, and practices that created it. But it might also be the case that, like many historians of witchcraft, we have failed to read the evidence correctly; we have neglected to exploit the gaps, miscommunications, and resistances, and so we have failed to see the existence, from the beginning, of a partially autonomous reality from below. Ginzburg's procedure of reading the gaps in distorted evidence may help us to correct conclusions that have been too hastily drawn from unexamined historiographical assumptions. Without assuming that evidence concerning homosexuality, multiple personality, and other psychiatric disease categories will yield identical conclusions, I want to look at one such piece of evidence, while heeding the lessons of Ginzburg's historical practice.

The piece of evidence I have in mind is reproduced by Hacking in "Making Up People" and comes from an 1886 article by Pierre Janet. Hacking adduces it as "one all-too-tidy example of how a new person can be made up" ("MP," p. 224).[29] Janet is speaking to Lucie, who, having the habit of automatic writing, is responding to him in writing, without her normal self's awareness:

Janet. Do you understand me?
Lucie (writes). No.
  J. But to reply you must understand me!

L. Oh yes, absolutely.

J. Then what are you doing?

L. Don't know.

J. It is certain that someone is understanding me.

L. Yes.

J. Who is that?

L. Somebody besides Lucie.

J. Aha! Another person. Would you like to give her a name?

L. No.

J. Yes. It would be far easier that way.

L. Oh well. If you want: Adrienne.

J. Then, Adrienne, do you understand me?

L. Yes.

("MP," pp. 224–225)

When I first read this exchange, I, in effect, took it as evidence not only of the dominance of medical culture in making up people but as exhibiting the absence of evidence of any competing or conflicting cultural reality. But after studying Ginzburg's procedures of reading distorted evidence, I wonder whether I was not too quick in my implicit conclusions. For this exchange, brief as it is, is full of gaps, miscommunications, and resistances. Lucie's alternating "yes" and "no," her initial refusal to provide another name, followed by her "Oh well. If you want: Adrienne," show, if not a full-fledged Bakhtinian clash of conflicting voices, at least the existence of a real gap. Janet does not have to exert much force to create Adrienne out of Lucie, but Lucie's resistances could be evidence of another level of reality, one quite foreign to Janet. If we had pages and pages of such dialogue, as Ginzburg had of his inquisitorial dialogues, then it would be easier to read the gaps, to know whether we could exploit them as evidence of a partially autonomous culture from below, a cultural reality that is systematically distorted by an unequal power relationship. That the distortions could be so great as to make the evidence unrecoverable goes without saying. But that even this brief, highly distorted exchange between Janet and Lucie exhibits visible gaps, if only one knows how to look for them, should give us cause for historiographical reflection. We must follow Ginzburg's lead in this area and not let inherent distortion of the evidence pass us by, as it so easily can, without further examination. We must look patiently for dialogic discrepancies, divergences, and misunderstandings, attending detectivelike to the always encoded evidence we do have, learning, as Ginzburg has taught us, "to catch, behind the smooth surface of the text, a subtle interplay of threats and fears, of attacks and withdrawals" ("IA," p. 161).

V

Reading the entire corpus of Ginzburg's historiographical writings, I have noticed the occurrence, again and again, of the concept of integration (l'integrazione). In this final section, I want to use Ginzburg's remarks about integration to present a more general historiographical schema, one that will, I hope, help bring together some of the issues I have already touched on. Ginzburg's pinpointing and descriptions of problems of integration single out what seems to me to be one of the most significant and fruitful directions of future historiographical research.

Ginzburg cites the beginning of Natalie Davis' *The Return of Martin Guerre,* where she writes:

> In the absence of the full testimony from the trial (all such records for criminal cases before 1600 are missing from the Parlement of Toulouse), I have worked through the registers of Parlementary sentences to find out more about the affair and about the practice and attitude of the judges. In pursuit of my rural actors, I have searched through notarial contracts in villages all over the dioceses of Rieux and Lombez. When I could not find my individual men or women in Hendaye, in Artiget, in Sajas, or in Burgos, then I did my best through other sources from the period and place to discover the world they would have seen and the reactions they might have had.[30]

Commenting that debates about the guilt or innocence of Bertrande de Rols, the wife of Martin Guerre, seem to him a "bit off the mark," Ginzburg adds,

> The specific aim of this kind of historical research should be, I think, the reconstruction of the *relationship* (about which we know so little) between individual lives and the contexts in which they unfold . . . The context, seen as a space of historical possibilities, gives the historian the possibility to integrate the evidence, often consisting only of scattered fragments, about an individual's life.[31]   ("CE," p. 301)

He writes elsewhere that an investigation can be deepened by "uniting the specific case to the context, here understood as the realm of historically determined possibility";[32] and it is this process of uniting that constitutes one of the central aspects of integration. The case of Menocchio is as significant as that of Martin Guerre in calling for a reconstruction of the relationship between individual lives and the contexts in which they occur. Describing the distinctiveness of Menocchio, Ginzburg emphasizes that, nevertheless, this distinctiveness unfolds within very definite limits:

> As with language, culture offers to the individual a horizon of latent possibilities—a flexible and invisible cage in which he can exercise his own conditional liberty. With rare clarity and understanding, Menocchio articulated the language that history put at his disposal . . . [The case of Menocchio] permits us to define the latent possibilities of something (popular culture) otherwise known to us only through fragmentary and distorted documents, almost all of which originate in the "archives of the repression." (*CW*, pp. xx–xxi)

The relationship between the individual and his or her context constitutes the core of the problem of integration. But from the standpoint of theory, I want to argue, there are at least three distinct dimensions to the problem of integration, each with its own specific issues and difficulties. Although the three dimensions are interconnected in any historical account, they are analytically distinct, and it will further our understanding to begin with their distinctive features.

I will call the first dimension the epistemologico-ontological dimension of integration, since at this level certain very general, but rather decisive, philosophical issues are raised. Some of these issues are discussed by Giovanni Levi in his "Les Usages de la biographie,"[33] but rather than trying to give an exhaustive enumeration of these problems, I will highlight a few representative examples. As Levi notes, one of the questions about the relationship of the individual to his context concerns the kind of rationality that one imputes to historical actors.[34] The construction of an entirely rational actor, with full access to the relevant aspects of his or her context, possessing more or less complete information about his or her possibilities, and using this information, always in a socially uniform way, to make epistemologically well-grounded decisions, hardly withstands philosophical critique. But, as Levi shows, many historical reconstructions rely on exactly this picture of individual rationality, and on the unstated assumption that the individual's relationship to his context is one of epistemological transparency, allowing knowledge of the context to provide the basis, in conjunction with stable cognitive dispositions, for entirely rational decisions. Levi suggests that if one studies biographies, one will discern a more accurate conception of individual rationality, which he calls "selective rationality."[35] In this conception, as I understand it, we do not assume that an individual has full access to the context in which his actions and life take place, or that all individuals have identical access to the contexts of their actions. Moreover, the uses made by individuals of information that we can demonstrate is available to them is not socially uniform, since social or class position may affect not only what information is available, but also how it is used. Finally, we cannot proceed as if individuals' cognitive dispositions obey rigid mechanisms that are invariant over persons and time. Levi believes that the reading of biographies throws into relief the ways in which individual rationality does work, showing us the cognitive mechanisms by which individuals make decisions, their uses of information, and their access, or lack of it, to their possibilities and cultural contexts. More generally, biography can underscore what is at stake in our integration of the relationship between an individual and his context, from the point of view of considerations of rationality.

A second aspect of the epistemologico-ontological dimension of integration revolves around issues of liberty and power. Recently, too many historians have set about reconstructing the cultural context in such a way that it virtually determines the actions of the individual, representing him as deprived of any ability to integrate himself into the context in an active, perhaps even interventionist, mode. It is as though the discovery of the crucial importance of context, and the need to reconstruct it, takes place at the cost of the negligence, if not disappearance, of the domain of individual liberty, so that individuals are depicted as reacting to the dynamics of cultural power, rather than as being in reciprocal interaction with them. As Levi claims, no normative system, one central component of cultural context, is so fully structured

as to eliminate every possibility of conscious choice, of manipulation or of interpretation of the rules, of negotiations. It seems to me that biography constitutes, for this reason, the ideal place to verify the interstitial—

and nevertheless important—character of the liberty that agents have at their command . . . the unequal distribution of power, as great and as coercive as it is, is not without the offer of a certain margin of maneuver to the dominated: these latter can then impose on the dominating non-negligible changes.[36]

Ginzburg's model of the circular exchange between the cultures of the dominant and subordinate classes and, more abstractly, an analytics of power that does not conceptually oppose cultural domination and individual resistance are philosophically necessary correctives to a conception that swallows the individual up into the context, not so much integrating him as absorbing him entirely. Biography can return the face of the individual to its necessary place in an often impersonal cultural and social context, allowing us better to conceptualize how context and individual should be integrated in a particular historical reconstruction.

Levi is reacting against various recent theoretical accounts that, by insisting too exclusively on deterministic and unconscious structures that make up the cultural context, reduce the individual to a mere function of his contextual determinations. These accounts, emphasizing structure, social habitus, and context, present so unbalanced a reconstruction of the relationship between the individual and his context, putting so much weight on the latter, that the individual becomes little more than an illustrative node, thus making impossible certain forms of integration of context and individual. These accounts are paralleled by those prosographical biographies that, rather than treating the individual as a singular person, view him as focusing and condensing all of the significant characteristics of a group.[37]

Furthermore, when the context is reconstructed in this deterministic, rigid, and epistemically unproblematic fashion, there are serious consequences for how an apparently singular individual can be treated. Such individuals, as they fall outside the context, are viewed as limit-cases that have lost all links with normal society.[38] They escape the mechanistic gears of contextual determination only to be relegated to an "absolute extraneousness" that is "prior to culture"(*CW*, p. xix). Nothing can be said about these individuals, given that their singularity consists in their exteriority and imperviousness to the cultural context so reconstructed; there is no possibility of integration, since singularity is tantamount to unintegrability. So, as Ginzburg says, "the only legitimate reactions that remain are 'astonishment' and 'silence'" (*CW,* p. xviii).[39]

Both those reconstructions that treat singular individuals as extraneous to their cultural context and those that evacuate the individual by reference to his contextual determinations operate with a highly suspect notion of context. Although historians today take it as given that a context undergoes transformations over time, as Levi points out, they also often take for granted that at any specific historical moment the context is "fully coherent, transparent, stable."[40] They fail to examine the incoherencies within the context itself, ignore the fact that the context is never free from contradictions, and overlook the crucial point that there is not a single, cohesive context, one whose solidity and durability extends over the individual, depriving him of his specificity as a result of its homogeneous all-encompassing constraints.[41] The nature of a context is no more theoretically given than is the extent of individual liberty. The integration of context and individual requires not only a defensible analysis of individual rationality and a plausible dynamics of social domination and individual action, but also a conceptualization of context that is much more sensitive to its complexities and heterogeneities.

Let me turn now to the second dimension of integration, what I will call the historiographical dimension. This dimension includes all of the issues of evidence and proof that I have discussed in section IV of this paper. We are faced here with problems of marshaling evidence, of constructing proofs, of decoding distortions, and of integrating this material: such integration must take account of evidence issuing from the standpoint of the individual and of evidence derived from his cultural context and his space of historical possibilities. The procedures of historiographical integration will interact closely with the third dimension of integration that I shall discuss shortly—namely the dimension of literary presentation—but for the moment, I want to pry apart, somewhat artificially, the historiographical questions of integrating evidence about individual and context from the issue of its literary presentation.

In discussing these historiographical problems, I want to indicate the importance, in Ginzburg's thinking, of Arsenio Frugoni's *Arnaldo da Brescia nelle fonti del secolo XII,* originally published in 1954. The target of

Frugoni's account is the "philological-combinatory method," a method that combines evidence derived from different sources, perspectives, and contexts into a homogenous unity, as if the integration of evidence can only take the form of the "perfect weave of a mosaic," as if a benevolent providence always justifies the historian's infinite confidence that all evidence fits together in a complementary, systematic, and cohesive fashion.[42] The philological-combinatory method treats pieces of evidence and their contexts as though they were all fragments of a systematic treatise, or of a complete and unified picture, so that the task of the historian consists in finding the appropriate connectives to bring the whole treatise into view, to reconstruct its systematicity and unity, thus reproducing the integrity of the original mosaic.[43] In treating Arnaldo da Brescia from the standpoint of very diverse twelfth-century sources, Frugoni wanted to treat each source on its own, as it was written, from its own perspective and with its own specific commitments, without assuming that complementarity would be found between one source and another.[44] One did not start from the premise of a necessary fit between the sources, a fit that would culminate in the reconstruction of a systematic whole, but rather, as Frugoni put it elsewhere, one attempted to understand each source, each statement, *"by, first of all, keeping in mind the particular circumstances that determined it."*[45] By first treating each source as an individual, separate testimony, what emerged from the writings of Saint Bernard, Otto of Frisinga, Gerhoh of Reichersberg, and other sources, both anonymous and named, was not a perfect weave, but, to use Ginzburg's words, "various portraits of Arnaldo of Brescia, gleaned from diverse visual perspectives."[46] Only an unwarranted historiographical assumption could lead one to conclude that the variety of these portraits was a defect of integration, that a single picture must emerge through historical reconstruction. Since the testimony about Arnaldo da Brescia was encoded in different ways, since it was derived from diverse contexts, and underwent a variety of distortions, a historical reconstruction that reproduced a unified picture of Arnaldo could itself be judged to be the product of a defective integration, an integration that imposed historiographically indefensible constraints.

Ginzburg's use of inquisitorial documents in *The Night Battles* and *The Cheese and the Worms* decodes the dialogical exchanges in these documents in order to show the conflict of individual perspectives and cultural contexts between the accused and the inquisitors. Rather than attempting to reconstruct a unified picture, as had so often been done in the past, Ginzburg had to exploit the "anomalies" and "cracks" in documentation he acknowledged to be highly distorted so as to exhibit a variety of portraits, to demonstrate the reciprocal interactions between two cultures—peasant and learned—that were not unified, not cohesive, not fragments of the same systematic whole.[47] Unification only came about later through the attempted imposition of the inquisitorial schema on the beliefs, attitudes, and practices of the accused. It would have been easy, even natural, to overlook the conflicts, to have seen a false cohesiveness, and Ginzburg's extraordinary skills were manifested in the precise ways in which he deciphered the distortions, in which he took an apparently impenetrable code of inquisitorial distortion and allowed peasant beliefs and culture to emerge from it. Fortunately, and contrary to first appearances, the documents were not a perfect weave; but to see their imperfections required both the overcoming of old historiographical commitments and the deployment of the interpretive skills I have already described. One of the central issues in this dimension of historiographical integration turns on how to use and decode evidence, without assuming either the transparency of the evidence or the existence of, as it were, a single super-code that is the master key to understanding all of the evidence. We have to learn how to *integrate* evidence, in part by figuring out how to decipher it, by distinguishing between different procedures of encoding evidence and by preserving those distinctions, by looking not for undistorted evidence but for specific kinds of distortions, and by aiming at integration, which is not necessarily unification.

These problems of deciphering evidence are, obviously enough, not limited to the encoding of judicial testimony. Evidence may be encoded in literary forms that impose their own peculiar distortions, distortions that, historiographically, we do not see because we take the evidence as more transparent than it is, overlooking the weight of the literary structure as well as its historical determinateness. To consider some examples very briefly, since at least the time of the publication of Ernest Renan's study of Marcus Aurelius, many readers and writers have assumed that Marcus' *Meditations* were "a personal diary of his inner states." Scholars have found throughout the *Meditations* evidence of Marcus' pessimism, of his bitterness and disgust with human life, and some of them have even concluded that Marcus' personality resulted from a gastric ulcer or even from opium addiction. But as Pierre Hadot has emphasized, Marcus tells us almost nothing about himself in the *Meditations*.

> It is too facile for us to imagine that like many modern authors, ancient writers write in order directly to communicate information, or the emotions they happened to be feeling. We assume, for instance, that Marcus' *Meditations* are intended to transmit his everyday feelings to us; that Lucretius is himself an anxious person, and used his poem *On the Nature of Things* to try to combat his anxiousness; that Augustine is really confessing himself in his *Confessions*.[48]

As Hadot has convincingly argued, Marcus' declarations and statements are not expressions of his own pessimism toward or disillusionment with life; they are rather a "means he employs in order to change his way of evaluating the events and objects of human existence."[49] Marcus' *Meditations* exhibit Stoic spiritual exercises, which aim to transform one's way of thinking and living so as to allow one to live in conformity with Reason. These exercises obey rigorous, codified, and systematic rules, and Hadot has shown, in great detail, that the key to understanding Marcus' spiritual exercises is to be found in the works of Epictetus. Marcus is attempting, in accordance with Stoic doctrines, to liberate himself from the conventional anthropomorphic view of the world and of human activities; he wants to view things as they are in themselves, which requires the arduous spiritual work of self-transformation. So, for instance, "when Marcus speaks of the monotony of human existence, it is not in order to express his own boredom, but in order to *persuade himself* that death will not deprive us of anything essential."[50] The striking formulations of the *Meditations* are in the service of the practice of these spiritual exercises and their goal of enabling one to live the philosophical way of life.

Furthermore, as Hadot says elsewhere, there are many constraints on ancient authors that the modern reader does not recognize: "Understanding a work of antiquity requires placing it in the group from which it emanates, in the tradition of its dogmas, its literary genre, and requires understanding its goals."[51] We must attend to the *topoi* of these works, that is, to "the formulas, images, and metaphors that forcibly impose themselves on the writer and the thinker in such a way that the use of these prefabricated models seems indispensable to them in order to be able to express their own thoughts."[52] And, as Philippe Lejeune has demonstrated in his studies of autobiography, there are historically specific constraints on modern autobiographies, forces that structure how they are written and read, so that we must not assume that all autobiographies are created identically, the diaphonous expression of their authors' wish to communicate his inner life to others. Even as apparently homogenous a genre as the post-Rousseauean autobiography exhibits a variety of implicit codes, irreducible to one another, through which the works are both produced and received.[53]

To treat one last example even more briefly, in recent work I have been doing on accounts of Saint Francis' receiving the stigmata, I have been surprised to discover how dependent many contemporary historians are on the early biographies of Francis written by Thomas of Celano and Saint Bonaventure. But I have been much more surprised by the ways in which these historians have treated the biographies, as though they presented unencoded evidence, written from a disinterested perspective, and conveyed in a literary form not in need of analysis. The features that these biographies are hagiographies, that they are written using a narrowly demarcated conception of evidence, that even this evidence is interpreted or encoded in very specific modes, and that the contexts from which they are written are very limited ones seem to have passed almost unnoticed, and certainly unproblematically, into contemporary accounts. Consider the following account of Saint Francis receiving the stigmata:

He saw the mountain covered by light, the heavens open, and a burning seraph swiftly descend. Light blazed everywhere. Every blade of grass was clear and distinct in the dazzling light.

Francis raised his eyes. The angel had his eyes open, his feet stretched out. He was nailed to a cross. A living cross with six flaming wings, two raised over his head, two covering his body, and two spread out in flight.

Then he was over Francis and rays darted from the wounds in his feet, his hands, his side, to pierce Francis' hands, feet, and heart. Francis' soul was caught up in a vortex of fire. An infinite joy filled him and also infinite pain. He raised his arms toward the living Cross, only to fall unconscious against the stone.

The whole mountain of La Verna seemed to be burning, as if the sun were high. Shepherds, taking their flocks to the pasture-lands of the sea, were awakened. Muleteers got up, thinking it was dawn, and set out on the road again.

They travelled on in what seemed bright daylight. And then they saw the immense light fade and vanish. Night returned, alive with stars.[54]

This narrative is taken not, as one might expect, from a thirteenth-century hagiography, but from Arnaldo Fortini's *Nova vita di San Francesco,* published in 1959 and still considered to be the most complete historical biography of Saint Francis we possess. I shall not here engage in a detailed historiographical and rhetorical analysis of this passage; let me simply point out that it reproduces, with some differences, the account of the stigmata in the Third Consideration of the *Fioretti,* written about one hundred years after Francis' death.[55] This latter account, in turn, reproduces, with some differences, the narrative found in Thomas of Celano's *The First Life of St. Francis,* probably completed in 1229, three years after Francis' death.[56] Since according to its Prologue, Thomas wrote his biography "at the command of our lord, the gloriously reigning Pope Gregory,"[57] we can hardly expect its evidence and context, and their integration, to be unproblematic, to be free from the requirements of careful and detailed decoding and analysis. Fortini's narrative, standing in absolute contiguity with a thirteenth-century biography, clearly shows the constraints that literary form can impose. As though mesmerized by the emotion, language, and structure of hagiographical biography, Fortini imports a historiographically naive conception of evidence and context into his historical reconstruction of the event of the stigmata.

Furthermore, when, in Volume II of his *Nova vita,* Fortini produces the historical documentation to support his literary narrative, his historiographical problems are hardly lessened. Fortini begins with the statement that "today history and science are all but unanimous in recognizing the marvel *(il prodigio)* of the Stigmata."[58] He then proceeds to list the most trustworthy testimonies to the stigmata, assuming that since these are ancient, and, in some cases, contemporary testimonies, their accuracy can be assured.[59] Among these accounts, Fortini counts three letters of Gregory IX, the pope who canonized Francis. Yet he fails to mention that Gregory himself seems at first to have had some doubts about certain aspects of the stigmata, as evidenced by the bulls of canonization of 1228. But Gregory did eventually come to insist on the reality of the stigmata; according to Saint Bonaventure, the dissipation of his doubts was the result of a nocturnal apparition of Saint Francis that came to Gregory and convinced him of the authenticity of the stigmata.[60] This does not seem to me adequate grounds to count Gregory among the most reliable witnesses to the stigmata. Moreover, Fortini mentions none of the doubts, equally ancient and contemporary with Francis, that could disrupt the hagiographical context of his narrative. As André Vauchez has definitively shown, battles about the authenticity or inauthenticity of Francis' stigmata were fought from the very start, and must be placed in a very complex context, a context that includes issues as general as that of changing conceptions of spirituality and saintliness in the thirteenth century.[61] Fortini's most general problem is a historiographical one. He writes his account completely from the standpoint of a hagiographical biography, as though the only relevant context is that of Saint Francis himself and his defenders. The context is so narrowly and so specifically construed that certain pieces of evidence must be ignored, and the resulting integration of context and evidence is so smoothly self-sustaining, so exaggeratedly without cracks and anomalies, that it virtually seals its own unbelievability. By contrast, Vauchez's integration of conflicting evidence and of diverse contexts, some narrow and others much wider, all requiring their own particular decoding, manifests none of the historiographical rigidity found in Fortini, and produces a much more adequate historical reconstruction.[62] The history of accounts of St. Francis receiving the stigmata raises very forcefully the issues of what counts as a relevant context in historical description, how one should compare contexts, and how context and evidential reliability are related. Concerning inquisitorial documents, Ginzburg has written, "We can test our interpretation in a comparative context which is much broader than the one available to inquisitors" ("IA," p. 164). I would add that, in this case too, we can test our interpretation in a comparative context that is much broader than the one available to hagiographers.

The entire question of how to compare and integrate contexts (and the evidence derived from them) is, in effect, a main topic of Ginzburg's *Ecstasies*, one of the great treatises on what I might call the methodology of comparative contextualization. Since discussion of that book should merit a separate treatment, I shall restrict myself here to a few additional remarks about how Ginzburg approaches the topic of integrating different contexts in his *The Enigma of Piero*.[63] In the preface to that book, Ginzburg indicates the insurmountable difficulties one encounters in trying to date Piero della Francesca's works on the basis of either stylistic or iconological evidence alone. Although he is concerned specifically to show the methodological problems with Roberto Longhi's attempt to date the Urbino *Flagellation,* his arguments have a much more general import. He argues both that evidence derived from the context of stylistic analysis and evidence derived from the context of iconological interpretation run the "very serious risk" of producing

> circular chains of interpretation, based entirely on conjecture. The chain relies on the reciprocal reinforcement of its various links, and the whole construction is suspended in a vacuum.[64]

Ginzburg hopes to move beyond the threatened vacuum by adding another context of evidence to the attempt to date Piero's work, a context originating in documentary research into the commissioning of these works. Such evidence, Ginzburg believes, has been insufficiently exploited; and when art historians have tried to reconstruct the commissioning of Piero's work, they have not done so "on the basis of documents in libraries or archives," but have chosen to use the evidence of the works themselves, specifically their iconography, thus creating a vicious circle whose evidentiary value is severely compromised.[65] By ignoring the context of documentary evidence, they have missed the opportunity to place a reliable control on their iconological interpretations, one external to a circle of interpretations always in danger of being self-perpetuating. Ginzburg wants to use iconography (he himself does not engage in stylistic analysis) in conjunction with documentary evidence about commissioning in order to confront problems of dating whose precise resolution requires different kinds of evidence derived from a variety of contexts. His aim is "to *bring together* the data derived from both sets of investigations"[66] (that is, documentation about commissioning and iconography), thereby producing a more adequate integration of evidence and context, an integration that makes clear how to construct, compare, and put together a range of contexts, resulting in broader and more compelling evidence about when Piero's paintings were produced. Even given the rather specific problems occasioned by the dating of Piero's works, Ginzburg's historiographical procedures here, as in the examples of his readings of inquisitorial trials, have much to teach us, whatever our more particular historical concerns, about how to face what I have called the historiographical dimension of integration.

One final example of the comparative integration of a range of contexts and their evidence will serve to lead me toward the third and final dimension of integration. Remaining for a moment at the historiographical level, I want to make a few remarks about Ginzburg's discussion of Eileen Power's *Medieval People.* In the course of his treatment of the historiographical advances made in that genre of historical writing that consists in "the mixture of imaginary biography and *documents authentiques*" ("CE," p. 297), Ginzburg takes up Power's attempt to reconstruct the life of the ordinary peasant Bodo. I want to consider three statements of Power and Ginzburg's comments on these statements from the point of view of the historiographical integration of context and evidence. Here are Power's statements:

> [1] Let us try and imagine a day in his life. On a fine spring morning towards the end of Charlemagne's reign Bodo gets up early . . . If you had followed behind Bodo when he broke his first furrow you would probably have seen him take out of his jerkin a little cake, baked for him by Ermentrude out of different kinds of meal, and you would have seen him stoop and lay it under the furrow and sing: "Earth, Earth, Earth! O Earth, our mother!" [This is followed by a text of an Anglo-Saxon charm.]
>
> [2] Bodo would certainly take a holiday and go to the fair.
>
> [3] Bodo goes whistling off in the cold.[67]

Ginzburg notes not only the legitimacy but the necessity of "the integration [*l'integrazione*] of the documentary lacunae, which is due to the poverty of the documentation, with elements drawn from the context."[68] But, as his next remarks indicate, not all contexts have equal status and the evidence derived from them needs to be evaluated differentially. Concerning [1], Ginzburg writes: "it is unlikely that Bodo, a dweller of the Ile-de-France, ever sang an Anglo-Saxon charm" ("CE," p. 299).[69] That is, given the context of Bodo's social and cultural environment, there is no reason to believe that he would have sung Anglo-Saxon charms. Perhaps Bodo's cultural context does not make this impossible, but in light of what we do know about the social environment of such peasants, we would need a very particular, rather precise piece of evidence to support Power's reconstruction of this aspect of Bodo's life. As regards [2], Ginzburg says that it is an integration of individual and context prompted by a judgment of historical compatibility.[70] Presumably many peasants like Bodo would take holidays and go to fairs. Although it is no more than a conjecture that Bodo himself went to such fairs while on holiday, there are specific historical facts about the existence of these fairs and the behavior of such peasants that could be used to support this conjecture, that could be evinced as contextual grounds on the basis of which Power's statement about Bodo would be acceptable. Finally, with respect to [3], Ginzburg points out that it would be naive to ask if it is based on a source *(una fonte)*,[71] as if one required a specific source to show that Bodo did in fact whistle. The integration found in [3] is prompted by a general consideration of plausibility: "peasants whistle today, they certainly also whistled in Charlemagne's time."[72] In order to be able to justify Power's claim that "Bodo goes off whistling in the cold," one does not need to be able to produce particular historical facts, such as one needs to support the claim in [2], but only more general features of cultural plausibility. As Ginzburg reminds us, however, general plausibility is not eternally fixed; what is generally plausible, even taking one's cultural parameters very broadly, is not indisputably plausible. As Ginzburg writes in "Checking the Evidence," "But human whistling, being a cultural practice, cannot be automatically projected into a society" ("CE," p. 299). And as he adds in *Il giudice e lo storico*, "men are not nightingales; their whistling is not a natural act."[73] In some contexts, the fact that so-and-so whistled may be highly implausible, and once we fully recognize that whistling is a cultural practice, we will also recognize that even integrations like those found in [3] cannot be treated as historiographically unproblematic. The question of when and how whistling became a cultural practice is, to my mind, a fascinating problem, and we should not overlook this type of problem by treating cultural plausibility, even of the most general kind, as if it were a concatenation of necessary facts.

Ginzburg's treatment of Power brings me directly to the third dimension of integration, what I shall call the literary dimension. This dimension concerns the literary presentation, by the historian, of his or her account of the relevant events and facts. That the "historian *writes*,"[74] and that his narratives require attention to the literary dimension of his writing, has led some historians to blur the distinction between history and fiction to the point that it becomes a distinction without a difference. Recent historiography has stressed what Ginzburg calls "the traceable fabulatory nucleus in narratives with scientific pretensions—beginning with historiographic ones"—and has not emphasized the "discernible cognitive nucleus" in narratives, both fictional and historiographical.[75] Ginzburg does not see the current theoretical situation so myopically. He declares that

> in opposition to these tendencies, it must be stressed that an increased awareness of a narrative dimension does not imply an attenuation of the cognitive possibilities of historiography but, on the contrary, their intensification. Indeed, it is exactly from this point that a radical critique of historiographic language, of which we now have only a hint, will have to commence.[76]

I understand Ginzburg to be stressing that although it is, of course, true that historical accounts are narratives, with their specific literary devices, it is also true that narratives have cognitive implications; these cognitive implications and possibilities stand in need of discussion and critique. The historian must pay careful attention to the various ways in which his own literary choices and presentations are loaded with determinate cognitive consequences and lead to specific, if not always explicitly formulated, inferences on the part of his readers. The literary integrations of historical writing do not annul the distinction between fiction and reality, but necessitate subtle and cognitively complex decisions on the part of the historian, just as do the literary integrations of the novelist. Consider again Power's statement, "Bodo would certainly take a holiday and go to the fair." This is an arguably defensible historiographical integration; however, as Ginzburg suggests, it is less successful as a literary integration: "The word 'certainly' here means 'presumably,' an often-recurring switch in the historian's language" ("CE," p. 299, n. 28).[77] The cognitive implications of "certainly" are, obviously enough, rather different from those of "presumably," and a literary accumulation of certainties instead of the required probabilities will inevitably lead the reader to draw false inferences, inferences that cannot be supported by the evidence. Here literary presentation is at odds with historical reconstruction. And how one presents an account will affect its cognitive reception no less than what one presents in the account.

Sometimes both historiographical integration and literary integration will be unacceptable, each mirroring the other's defects. In his remarks on Jonathan Spence's *Death of Woman Wang*, Ginzburg considers Spence's attempt to reconstruct what the poor peasant woman Wang was dreaming just prior to her violent death. Spence uses a series of fragments from the literary works of a seventeenth-century Chinese writer, P'u Sung-ling, combining some of the images in these fragments so as to "come near to expressing what might have been in the mind of woman Wang as she slept before death" ("CE," p. 302)." Ginzburg comments that although the dream is printed in italics, "to recreate the dream of a poor peasant woman through the words of a learned essayist and storyteller looks like a somewhat gratuitous exercise" ("CE," p. 302). Using the categories I have developed in this essay, I would interpret Ginzburg's comment as implying, first, that Spence's historiographical integration is defective. For Spence uses the context of a learned male essayist's works in order to derive evidence about a peasant woman's dreams, a context that is thoroughly implausible given what we know about cultural background and social relations in seventeenth-century China. There is no more reason to believe that such a context provides reliable evidence for reconstructing Wang's dreams than there is to believe that Bodo's cultural context included Anglo-Saxon charms. Second, since Spence utilizes "the words of a learned essayist" to reproduce the content of Wang's dream, we are also faced with a failure of literary integration. Spence's own historical narrative *incorporates* these words, with their many cognitive implications, thus identifying his own historical standpoint with a series of literary devices that cannot but distort the content of the dream. Spence's choice of words, combining the words of P'u Sung-ling, is a narratological failure that doubles his historiographical failure. His literary presentation may be enjoyable to read, but has cognitive consequences that will straightforwardly misdirect the reader. His exercise is, no doubt unintentionally, misleading as well as gratuitous.

An important part of the adequacy of a historian's literary integrations will consist in his ability to exhibit these integrations, to show, within his narrative, exactly how he is constructing his own literary presentation of the historical evidence. Ginzburg cites "an auto-critical footnote" to the thirty-first chapter of Edward Gibbon's *History of the Decline and Fall of the Roman Empire,* where Gibbon writes:

> I owe it to myself and to historic truth to declare that some *circumstances* in this paragraph are founded only on conjecture and analogy. The stubbornness of our language has sometimes forced me to deviate from the *conditional* to the *indicative* mood.[78]

Ginzburg insists on the significance of distinguishing between the indicative and conditional moods, as when he compares Davis favorably to Power since "instead of concealing within the indicative mood the integrations she made in order to fill up documentary gaps, Davis emphasizes them by using either a conditional mood or expressions like 'perhaps' and 'may have been'" ("CE," p. 301). And elsewhere he refers to "the swarm of expressions like 'perhaps,' 'bound to,' 'one can presume,' 'certainly' (which in the language of historians usually means only 'most probably'), and so on,"[79] which occur in her book *The Return of Martin Guerre,* all of which manifest attention to the procedures of literary integration. Ginzburg compares Davis' approach "to modern art-restoration techniques, like the so-called *rigatino,* in which the lacunae in the painted surface are emphasized by fine hatches instead of concealed by repainting, as they were in the past" ("CE," p. 301).[80] Rather than trying to hide her own literary integrations, a historian like Davis, conscious of the cognitive consequences and rhetorical force of these integrations, allows them to show themselves, and so permits the reader to distinguish correctly between the implications of a "certainly" and those of a "perhaps." She makes it possible for the reader to determine when she is filling in the lacunae that the documents themselves leave open concerning the individual. As Ginzburg says of Davis' work: "'True' and 'probable,' 'proofs' and 'possibilities' interlace, even as they remain rigorously distinct."[81] If space permitted, this would be the place to examine carefully Ginzburg's own literary integrations in, for instance, *The Cheese and the Worms.* I think that one would find that, despite his formidable literary talents, Ginzburg does not let his skills as a writer overtake the need to keep his own literary integrations constantly in view. For, contrary to Gibbon, it is not "the stubbornness of our language" that forces us to deviate from the conditional to the indicative mood, but, rather, a continually threatening deficiency of self-consciousness and methodological rigor, a self-consciousness it is all too easy for a historian to put aside if he or she is a superb writer. One great achievement of *The Cheese and the Worms* is that it remains cognizant of its own literary presentation of the life and trial of Menocchio, without sacrificing a literary eloquence and style that is wonderful to read.

In "Proofs and Possibilities," Ginzburg analyzes the relations between historiographical writing and the novel, showing, through a discussion of Daniel Defoe and Henry Fielding, "the dependence . . . of the English novel . . . on previous and contemporary historiography."[82] He then charts the ways in which "novelists little-by-little shed the fetters of their position of inferiority,"[83] culminating today in a situation where historians show "an increasing predilection for the themes and, in part, the expository forms once reserved for novelists."[84] Precisely because some of our best historians, including Ginzburg, have taken up the themes and expository forms once reserved for novelists, and because they are writing *history*, these historians must maintain a point of view with respect to their literary integrations distinct from that of fiction writers. Shared expository forms should not lead to identical literary integrations, as though the particular cognitive implications and possibilities of historical writing must be merged with those of the novel. One of the best pieces of historiographical and literary advice for contemporary historians, cited by Ginzburg in "Proofs and Possibilities," comes, perhaps unexpectedly, from Alessandro Manzoni's *Dal romanzo storico e, in genere, de' componimenti misti di storia e d'invenzione:*

> It might not be out of place to mention that history sometimes also uses the verisimilar, and can do so harmlessly if it uses it properly and presents it as such, thereby distinguishing it from the real . . . It is a characteristic of man's impoverished state that he can know only something of what has been, even in his own little world; and it is an aspect of his nobility and his power that he can conjecture beyond what he can actually know. When history turns to the verisimilar, it does nothing other than favor or promote this tendency. It stops narrating momentarily and uses, instead, inductive reasoning, because ordinary narrative is not the best instrument for this, and in adjusting to a different situation, it adopts a new purpose. In fact, all that is needed to clarify the relationship between the factual and the verisimilar is that the two appear distinct. History acts almost like someone who, when drawing a city map, renders in a distinctive color the streets, plazas and buildings planned for the future and who, while distinguishing the potential from the actual, lets us see the logic of the whole. History, at such moments, I would say, abandons narrative, but only in order to produce a better narrative. History aims to present reality, as much in conjecturing as in narrating; therein lies its unity.[85]

To present reality, while distinguishing the factual from the verisimilar and letting us see the logic of the whole, strikes me as presciently profound guidance for historians today.

As Ginzburg has underlined, current questions and problems about narration affect the category not only of historical narration, but of "narration *tout court.*"[86] We can use the dimension of literary integration in historical writing to approach the issue of the "variable relationships between historiographic narration and other types of narration,"[87] recognizing that different forms of writing will incorporate different kinds of literary integrations. The practices of historical narration and the cognitive status of literary presentations impose requirements on the historian that he cannot do without. Nor can he take refuge from these requirements in a false consciousness that his work presents just the facts, no more than the facts. Instead, he should develop a more acute self-consciousness about his own literary interventions, using the opportunities in his writing to help us investigate more thoroughly our own *fin-de-siècle* "relationship between the one who narrates and reality."[88]

7

Foucault and the Analysis of Concepts

IN TRYING TODAY to confront Foucault's procedures for analyzing concepts with those found in the conceptual analysis of Anglo-American analytic philosophy, I cannot help but remind myself of Foucault's remark, toward the beginning of his New York University lecture "Sexuality and Solitude":

> Let me announce once and for all that I am not a structuralist, and I confess, with the appropriate chagrin, that I am not an analytic philosopher. Nobody is perfect.[1]

I have, needless to say, no intention of turning Foucault into an analytic philosopher. But neither do I think that there is no useful relation that can be brought to bear between specific aspects of Foucault's work and the tradition of Anglo-American conceptual analysis. Hilary Putnam has described the interest in and influence of Foucault on both Ian Hacking and myself in the following way:

> what interested Hacking and Davidson was the idea that certain techniques of analytic philosophy can be combined with certain techniques of history. Instead of treating concepts as eternal objects, one could consider them as objects that come into existence, serve historically contingent

goals, die, without ceasing to be interested in the analytic question of knowing what is the proper way to analyze such and such a concept . . . this territory requires a double education as a historian and an analytic philosopher.[2]

It is precisely this combination of certain techniques for analyzing concepts and of certain techniques for writing their history that I want to place at the center of my considerations today.

You will recall that at the beginning of *L'Ordre du discours* Foucault considers the opposition between the true and the false as a "system of exclusion" side by side with those systems of exclusion constituted by "prohibition" and by "division" (le partage). But Foucault, recognizing what many will consider the dangers of such a proposal, himself asks how it can be reasonable to compare the constraint of truth with the historical contingencies of prohibition and division. And he replies to his own question:

Certainly, if one places oneself at the level of a proposition, within a discourse, the division between the true and the false is neither arbitrary, nor modifiable, nor institutional, nor violent. But if one places oneself at a different scale, if one poses the question of knowing what was, what is constantly, across our discourses, this will to truth that has traversed so many centuries of our history, or what is, in its very general form, the type of division that governs our will to know, then it is perhaps something like a system of exclusion (a system that is historical, modifiable, institutionally constraining) that one sees appearing.[3]

Notice that the characteristics that Foucault here ascribes to this system of exclusion are that it is historically contingent, modifiable, institutionally supported, and constraining. Thus the opposition between true and false discourse, considered as such a system, is, according to Foucault, a very specific kind of opposition, that is, an opposition that is organized around historical contingencies, subject to modifications, embodied in institutional supports, as well as one whose exercise produces constraints, an opposition, moreover, that masks our very will to truth. And this characterization is appropriate, even though, as Foucault himself admits, if one places oneself at the level of the propositions within the discourse, the opposition between the true and the false appears "neither arbitrary, nor modifiable, nor institutional, nor violent."

Foucault goes on to speak about certain "great scientific mutations" that can be read as "the appearance of new forms in the will to truth":

> There is without doubt a will to truth in the nineteenth century that does not coincide, either through the forms that it puts into play, or through the domains of objects to which it is directed, or through the techniques on which it relies, with the will to know that characterizes classical culture (la culture classique).[4]

In a series of essays inspired by Foucault's general methodological remarks and by *La Volonté de savoir,* I have tried to show that the psychiatric style of reasoning about sexuality is precisely one of these "new forms of the will to truth," containing new concepts, new objects of knowledge, new techniques and institutional supports. In short, I have tried to describe, in some historical detail, the "regime of truth" which governed psychiatric discourse about sexuality in the nineteenth century, concentrating especially on new concepts, like that of sexual perversion, and the way in which these new concepts were combined in determinate ways to produce a new realm of statements (énoncés) whose object was *sexuality.*[5] Thus I tried to take quite seriously Foucault's remark that

> by "truth" is to be understood a set of ordered procedures for the production, the legislation, the distribution, the circulation, and the functioning of statements.[6]

In undertaking this historical-analytical work, which I thought of as an analysis of the concept and, ultimately, of the experience of sexuality, I came to see that the procedures for the production of true discourses about sexuality were, indeed, very well ordered, while at the same time having a determinate historical origin. The particular opposition between truth and falsity exhibited by the psychiatric style of reasoning about sexuality was a very specific form of the will to know, which could not be read back into earlier forms of knowledge about sexual acts and behavior. I ended up understanding, by a route somewhat different from Foucault's, the *depth* of his claim about the Greeks and the Romans (and, I would add, as I think he would have, the early Christians), that

> our carving out of sexual behaviors into homo- and heterosexual is absolutely not relevant for the Greeks and the Romans. This means two

things: on the one hand, that they did not have the notion, the *concept,* of homo- and heterosexual; and, on the other hand, that they did not have the experience of them.[7]

I also came to see that the standard Anglo-American analyses of concepts like perversion failed utterly to take into account the historically determinate conditions of emergence of the psychiatric "will to truth" and the way in which these conditions of emergence determined what could be done with these concepts.[8] The history of this particular will to truth profoundly affected the structure of the knowledge (savoir) that was possible within it. As Ian Hacking has said with respect to a different domain, "the organization of our concepts and the difficulties that arise from them, sometimes have to do with their historical origins.[9] The analysis of *scientia sexualis* is one area in which one can fully agree with Jacques Bouveresse's formulation of Wittgenstein's view that "the historical connection is truly explanatory only to the extent that it can also be interpreted as a conceptual connection."[10] The historical origin and development of the psychiatric style of reasoning about sexuality could be recast in the form of a description of the conceptual connections between different statements within this style of reasoning.[11]

This type of historical analysis of concepts makes it very clear that concepts are neither self-identifying mental states nor free-standing objects. The concept of perversion, for example, must not be identified with some mental state that can be found by introspection to, so to speak, bear the label "perversion." Nor is the concept of perversion or sexuality to be identified with some self-subsistent object, whose content can be discovered by some kind of intellectual intuition. These concepts are to be identified by the uses that are made of them, by the connections that govern their employment and that allow them to enter into what Foucault thought of as specific "games of truth" (jeux de vérité). Since these uses, connections, and games of truth are not to be analyzed in metaphysical or transcendental terms, as if they were fixed and unrevisable, one should not be surprised to find those of us influenced by Foucault insisting that we must attend to "the history of the emergence of games of truth."[12]

One might have thought that Anglo-American philosophers would have learned from Wittgensten that concepts cannot be divorced from the practices of their employment. And one might have also thought that, extending this point of view, we would have realized that although conceptual articulations in the "games of truth" studied by Foucault have criteria and are governed by rules, these rules are not to be read as divine decrees, given once and for all (or, of course, as arbitrary impositions, based on individual decisions changeable at will). But many analytic philosophers, despite Wittgenstein, treat concepts exactly as if they existed prior to any employment whatsoever, as if their identification did not depend on their connections with one another, on what we can actually do with them. Thus we find analytic philosophers attempting to take the concept of perversion out of the style of reasoning that stabilizes it, out of its games of truth, and treating it as though it were a trans-historical object of analysis, neither modifiable nor constrained by particular rules of formation and combination.[13] These philosophers behave like the ethnologists criticized by Wittgenstein, about whom one can say, in Jacques Bouveresse's formulation,

> that the error of ethnologists is to behave too often like someone who "without knowing how to play chess . . . were to try and make out what the word 'mate' meant by close observation of the last move of some game of chess." "Roughly," wrote Wittgenstein, "understanding a sentence means understanding a language."[14]

One can also say, roughly speaking, that to understand a concept of the kind I have been discussing is to understand the style of reasoning of which it is part.

You will no doubt be surprised, perhaps even dismayed, to see me linking the names of Wittgenstein and Foucault. I have no evidence that Foucault ever studied Wittgenstein carefully, and it would be rather easy to set out the *many* differences that separate their motivations, perspectives, and claims. But at least in one respect, I want to try to make this conjunction seem more plausible. I will try to motivate this juxtaposition by first taking up one of the first, and still most significant, French essays written on Wittgenstein's later philosophy, published in 1960 by the great historian of ancient thought Pierre Hadot. After giving a careful explication of Wittgenstein's notion of "language games," Hadot says that he wants to show that "taken up again in an historical perspective that Wittgenstein moreover totally ignores, this notion of language games allows philosophy to understand certain aspects of its own history and consequently to better understand itself."[15] It is just such a use of Wittgenstein, taken up in a

historical perspective, that allows a certain angle of rapprochement between Wittgenstein and Foucault. According to Hadot, picking up on
Wittgenstein's idea that one must "break radically with the idea that language always functions in only one way and always for the same goal":

> One must also . . . break with the idea that philosophical language func-
> tions in a uniform way. The philosopher is always in a certain language
> game, that is to say, in a certain attitude, in a certain form of life, and it is
> impossible to give a meaning to the theses of philosophers without situat-
> ing them in their language game.[16]

Applying these remarks to the history of philosophy, Hadot goes on to say,

> With respect to this matter, one should consider as very different lan-
> guage games those literary genres, so profoundly diverse, of the dialogue,
> the exhortation or protreptic, the hymn or the prayer (for example, the
> *Confessions* of Saint Augustine), the manual, the exegetical commentary,
> the dogmatic treatise, the meditation. And one should likewise distin-
> guish the traditional attitudes from Antiquity—the dialectic of the *Topics,*
> properly rhetorical argumentation, logical reasoning, the properly didac-
> tic exposition. One would often see that the very fact of situating oneself
> in one of these traditions predetermines the very content of the doctrine
> that is expressed in this language game: the "commonplaces" are not as
> innocent as one might believe.[17]

Without stopping here to consider the way in which Hadot put this advice
into practice in, for example, his own groundbreaking work on Porphyry
and Victorinus, I want to cite at length an example he gives in "Jeux de
langage et philosophie," since it has uncanny resonances with some of
Foucault's remarks in *L'Archéologie du savoir.* Here is how Hadot explains
one of the lessons he draws from Wittgenstein:

> Let us suppose that a contemporary philosopher, arriving in a train sta-
> tion or an airport, surrounded by a swarm of journalists, makes the fol-
> lowing declaration to them: "God is dead." By itself this formula does not
> have a unique sense; it allows a plurality of meanings. For the Greeks who
> chanted in their processions "Kronos is dead" this liturgical acclamation
> had a ritual and mythical meaning. For the Christian who believes in the
> Incarnation, the formula also has a meaning: it means that one must re-

late the human action which is the death of Jesus to the eternal Word which is God. For Nietzsche, finally, this formula belongs neither to the language game of ritual acclamation, nor to the language game of theology, nor to the language game characteristic of historical affirmation. The formula is introduced in a parable, the parable of the madman who looks for God in the marketplace with a lantern and whom the people do not understand: "I come too soon, it is not yet my time. This enormous event is still on the way, it has not yet reached the ears of men." Under this symbolic form, it is a call that ultimately has a religious value, to the extent that the "no" to God must be a "yes" to the values that rest only on man. It is "a negation whose violence turns around into an affirmation," an overcoming of nihilism. The declaration of the philosopher to the journalists has a quite different meaning. It is obviously an allusion to Nietzsche, but it is no longer the prophetic and symbolic announcement of an "enormous event," but the recalling of a formula, a repetition; it is no longer an anguished call, but at most a knowing recapitulation of a historical situation. It is perhaps a program, but it takes on, in the language game of the interview, a meaning entirely different from that which Nietzsche aimed at through the same formula.[18]

I have quoted this long example because it allows one to see the force of Hadot's later claim that "theses only have a full meaning within the limits of a determinate 'discourse' and should not be separated from the general purpose of this 'discourse.'"[19] Hence his insistence, as a historian of philosophy, on placing philosophical theses within a "determinate discourse," and his warning against treating philosophical language as if it were articulated within "an ideal and absolute discourse."[20] If Hadot could understand how to invoke Wittgenstein to call for a "history of philosophical language games," it was in part because his study of the ancients had made him sensitive to the fact, and to the significance of the fact, that the *spoken* discourses of ancient philosophy, with their concrete use of rhetorical, pedagogical, and psychagogical elements, were not addressed to "man in himself."[21]

Let me now turn directly to a few passages from *L'Archéologie du savoir,* a book which may seem thoroughly un-Wittgensteinian indeed. But consider what Foucault says when he is concerned with the problem of the identity of a statement (énoncé):

The assertion that the earth is round or that species evolve does not constitute the same statement before and after Copernicus, before and after
Darwin . . . The sentence "dreams realize desires" can indeed be repeated
throughout the centuries; it is not at all the same statement in Plato and
in Freud.[22]

Foucault explicitly says that for formulations of this kind, it is not that the
meaning of the words has changed.[23] In considering the identity of the
statement rather than focusing on the problem of meaning, Foucault con-
centrates on the set of conditions that are imposed on the identity of a
statement by "the set of other statements in the midst of which it appears,
by the domain in which one can use it or employ it, by the role or the functions it has to play."[24] Hence Foucault, attempting to account for *both* the
repeatability of the statement and for the fact that it can be repeated only
under strict conditions, writes, in a series of remarks that contain extraordinary methodological value:

> The schemes of utilization, the rules of employment, the constellations in
> which they can play a role, their strategic potentialities constitute a *field of
> stabilization* for the statements that makes it possible, despite all the dif-
> ferences of enunciation, to repeat them in their identity; but the same
> field can also define, beneath the most manifest semantic, grammatical,
> or formal identities, a threshold from which there is no longer equiva-
> lence and one must indeed recognize the appearance of a new statement
> . . . The constancy of a statement, the maintenance of its identity through
> the singular events of enunciations, its doublings across the identity of
> forms, all of this is a function of the *field of utilization* in which it finds it-
> self invested.[25]

I might say, following Foucault, that the field of utilization of a statement
constitutes its field of stabilization, that a statement (or, in the case of my
work, a concept) gets its identity from the way in which it is stabilized.
When Foucault gives a crucial role to "the possibilities of utilization" of a
statement, when he says that "the identity of a statement is itself relative
and oscillates according to the use one makes of the statement and the
manner in which one manipulates it," he is insisting that we not treat a
statement as an ideal form that can be reactualized under any conditions
whatsoever.[26]

As Hadot has said with respect to conceptual structures, one cannot reconstruct such a structure

> by appealing to sentences or words separated from their context and drawn from the most disparate places . . . In other words, one should not separate the conceptual structures from the developments in which they are recognizable.[27]

A phrase such as "dreams realize desires" will be stabilized by a series of relations that connect it with other statements, and the field of stabilization that one discovers when this phrase is employed by Freud will be quite different from that found in Plato, leading us to recognize that the same phrase can be used in more than one statement. If one fails to reconstruct the field of stabilization, what I have sometimes called the style of reasoning, that confers an identity on the concept of perversion, one will not understand the difference between the nineteenth-century psychiatric invocation of perversion and the appearance of this word in, for instance, Saint Augustine's moral theology. Thus one will fail to see, as Mino Bergamo has put it, that discontinuity can be "dissimulated under the veil of a lexical permanence."[28] Bergamo is one of a small number of historians of thought who have clearly understood (in his case, using Foucault's methodological suggestions to study the history of French mysticism) the way in which the field of stabilization of a statement both assures it a repeatability that distinguishes it from the "pure event, singular and unrepeatable," of enunciation, while at the same time imposing on this very repeatability "particularly burdensome restrictions," thus distinguishing the statement from the infinitely repeatable phrase.[29] Some of the most remarkable moments in the history of thought are precisely those in which an old phrase or word is stabilized in a new way, resulting in the production of a new set of concepts and a new realm of statements. This is, I would claim, exactly what happened when nineteenth-century psychiatric reasoning invented a new field of stabilization, a new scheme of utilization, for the moral-theological-juridical ideas of perversion and the unnatural. And analytic philosophers have failed to recognize the transformation of thought that took place because they treated these concepts as if they were both self-stabilizing and permanently stabilized.

It is important to insist that new statements and new concepts do not appear at will. An individual does not just decide to create a new statement.

The field of utilization or field of stabilization that creates the *conditions of possibility* for a new statement is typically very elaborate, and, under these circumstances, we should expect to find not just a single new statement or a single new individual concept, but a whole new field of possibilities. As Foucault realized, this kind of transformation often seems to be exhibited simultaneously in the writings of a number of different individuals, making a new field of stabilization appear as a collective, even anonymous, structure. It is only within this new field of stabilization that a statement or concept will obey new conditions of inscription, thus modifying its identity. As Bergamo has remarked,

> in order for a new statement to appear it will be necessary that a new field of stabilization is organized, that new schemes of utilization and new series of relations are given, and that, in short, the conditions of inscription of the sentence are transformed.[30]

A change in enunciative value is produced as a result of the new system of inscription, which because it is organized, systematic, has wide-ranging, yet regulated, effects. The concept of perversion is inscribed differently in nineteenth-century psychiatry than in medieval moral theology. Reconstructing the field of stabilization that accounts for the new kind of inscription allows us to understand why a nineteenth-century psychiatrist could not have used the concept of perversion to make new statements about diseases without also employing the related concepts of the natural, the deviant, function, and so on, concepts that are related to one another by a network of uses that are neither arbitrary nor eternal. Concepts and statements are indeed stable, but this stability is created by an interdependent set of practices, a field, or style of reasoning, whose existence confers a specific role or function on our words, allows them to exhibit certain "strategic potentialities."

Many analytic philosophers have recognized that a bad picture of concepts can have profoundly obfuscating consequences in the philosophy of mind and the philosophy of language. But many fewer have seen that a fixated picture of concepts, as free-standing, self-identifying entities, can have, and does have, deep consequences on how one writes the history of systems of thought. The idealization and decontextualization of concepts strips the history of thought of its different possibilities, draws one to a historiography of the everlasting, as if to write the history of thought is to write a history of successive instantiations of the same, as though a clearly circumscribed number of thoughts, our thoughts now, must eternally recur. Jacques Bouveresse has described Wittgenstein as belonging to Robert Musil's category of "men of the possible" rather than "men of the actual";

> he belongs, that is, to those who are particularly sensitive to the contingency and precariousness of what exists and particularly disposed to discern everything that could perfectly well exist in its place.[31]

What Bouveresse has called Wittgenstein's anthropological method consists in bringing to light, in *describing*, other possibilities than those to which we are attached; thus the fundamental work of philosophy consists in part in "the capacity to perceive reality on a ground of possibilities much broader than that of the usual conception."[32] In *Remarques mêlées (Culture and Value)*, Wittgenstein writes,

> ⌐ If we employ an ethnological point of view, does that mean we are making philosophy an ethnology? No, it only means that we are taking up a position far outside so as to be able to see things *more objectively* . . . One of the most important methods I use is to imagine a historical development of our ideas different from what really occurred. If we do this, we see the problem from an entirely new view.[33]

Wittgenstein was a genius at being able to imagine concretely, to describe in detail, other possibilities, to think through what might have been and what might be, and so to allow us to see our own actualities from an entirely new point of view. Foucault, in my view, made use of *history* in such a way as to let us glimpse other possibilities, wrote history so as to free us from the habit of identifying what happens, intellectually and socially, with what must have happened and what must continue to happen. His histories were intended to play a strategic role, both epistemologically and politically; they were meant to disclose epistemological and political possibilities the existence of which we might not even have imagined. In an interview from 1983, Foucault weaves together the historical, epistemological, and political dimensions of his work in a series of remarkable responses. Following the Kantian question "Was ist Aufklärung?" and declaring that "the task of philosophy is to say what 'today' is and to say what 'we are today,'" he says "with respect to this function of diagnosis concerning the present,"

. . . it does not consist in simply characterizing what we are, but in following the lines of fragility of the present, in coming to grasp in what way that which is and how that which is could no longer be that which is. And it is in this sense that the description should always be made according to that kind of virtual rupture that opens a space of freedom, understood as a space of concrete freedom, that is to say, of possible transformation . . .

And I would say that the work of the intellectual is indeed in a sense to speak about that which is while making it appear as capable of not existing or capable of not being as it is. And that is why this designation and this description of reality never has the value of a prescription under the form "since this is, that will be"; that is also why it seems to me that the recourse to history—one of the great facts of philosophical thought in France for at least about twenty years—takes on its import to the extent that history has for its function to show that that which exists didn't always exist, that is to say, that it is always at the confluence of encounters, of accidents, through the course of a fragile, precarious history that things are formed that give us the impression of being the most obvious. What reason experiences as its necessity or rather what different forms of rationality present as their necessary condition one can perfectly well do the history of, and recover the networks of contingencies from which it has emerged; which does not mean however that these forms of rationality were irrational; it means that they rest on a base of human practice and of human history and since these things have been made, they can, provided that one knows how they were made, be unmade.[34]

Without pausing to comment in detail on this text, I simply want to emphasize that Foucault did not claim that writing the history of forms of rationality had the effect of turning the rational into the irrational, as if his goal was to put reason on trial.[35] Rather, his recourse to history was meant to show how our forms of rationality depended on human practices, to indicate that these practices were neither necessary nor self-evident, and thus to provide a space to help to free us from a sense of fatalism. The analysis of concepts, I have been arguing, need not be fatal, if we learn to return our concepts to our human practices, the practices from which they emerged and which sustain them. Notwithstanding the enormous differences in political attitude and sensibility between Foucault and Wittgenstein, it remains the case that, as Bouveresse has pointed out, Wittgenstein too was struck by "the sense of the historical and cultural relativity of concepts which obliges us to abandon entirely the search for eternal essences for the technique of comparison."[36] Thus Wittgenstein's work never stops reminding us that "concepts like those of science, philosophy, religion, art, thought, rationality and many others of the same type do not possess the kind of constancy and universality that our philosophy is inclined to attribute to them."[37] One goal of Wittgenstein's method is to get us to turn toward ourselves, to see ourselves in the uses we make of our concepts, as if our typical philosophical posture is to deny the humanity of our practices. He writes, for instance:

> The only way for us to avoid having our assertions be distorted or vacuous consists in taking the ideal in our reflections for what it *is,* namely an object of comparison—a yardstick [*Maßstad*], as it were—instead of making of it a prejudice to which everything *must* conform. It is in this that lies the dogmatism into which philosophy so easily falls.[38]

Even the ideals of our theoretical activity are to be treated as objects of comparison, and so much of Wittgenstein's work consists in getting us to see that not everything *must* conform to these ideals, attempting, in example after example, to get us to divorce ourselves from the impulse to end our remarks with a philosophical *must.* Hence Wittgenstein's writing so often takes the form of a *comparative description* of language games.[39] These descriptions are meant as a kind of defense against dogmatism, and what unites both Wittgenstein and Foucault to the Kantian tradition in philosophy is precisely their recurrent warnings about, and searching out of, the various guises that this dogmatism takes.

In the "Introduction" to *L'Usage des plaisirs* Foucault describes his motivation as deriving from that kind of curiosity that "allows one to detach oneself from oneself" and he explains the profound change in his project for *Histoire de la sexualité* as resulting from one of those "moments in life in which the question of knowing if one can think otherwise then one thinks and perceive otherwise then one sees is indispensable in order to continue to look or to reflect."[40] This *otherwise* is, I have tried to show, a constant theme of Foucault's writing; it confronts us, in different forms, from *Histoire de la folie* until his final works. Foucault's history of the present was always also a history of other possibilities. No one can read the amazing opening section of *Surveiller et punir* without experiencing that anthropological estrangement that allows us to view our own history more objectively while showing us that "everything that is possible in this ambit could be real, but also that everything that is real is possible and conceivable."[41] What Bouveresse has labeled Wittgenstein's "speculative anthropology" and what Foucault has described as his analysis of "'games of truth,' of games of truth and falsity through which being constitutes itself historically as experience, that is, as able to be and having to be thought," both function as methods of making us see and feel the entanglement of the possible and the actual, of bringing to light the status of the actual by situating it against the background of other possibilities.[42]

Foucault claimed that it was the right of the philosopher "to explore that which, in his own thought, can be changed by the exercise that he makes of a knowledge which is foreign to him."[43] This is a right whose genuine exercise is as difficult to realize as is the ability to gain a satisfying perspective on ourselves. I have tried to show how a history of concepts that profits from Foucault's work can offer us opportunities for such explorations that would otherwise be blocked. And so I think that the two metaphilosophical questions that Foucault poses to himself at the beginning of *L'Usage des plaisirs* can serve as a kind of emblem for what we, as philosophers, can continue to learn from him:

> But what therefore is philosophy today—I mean philosophical activity— if it is not the critical work of thought on itself. And if it does not consist, instead of legitimating what one already knows, *in undertaking to know how and how far it would be possible to think otherwise.*[44]

No doubt this is why I have long believed that a powerful summary of the "Foucaultian moment" in philosophy can be found in the remark of René Char that appears on the back cover of Foucault's last books: "The history of humanity is the long succession of synonyms for the same word. To contradict it is a duty."

8

On Epistemology and Archeology: From Canguilhem to Foucault

ONE OF THE GREATEST difficulties in trying to situate Michel Foucault's work is that he was one of his own best interpreters. At each stage of his career he gave retrospective reinterpretations of the entire corpus of his work, redescribing the projects he had undertaken from the perspective of his current concerns, and so shifting his focus, highlighting different aspects of his previous work, and employing a terminology that overlapped with but was distinct from that which he had used in earlier periods. Thus in giving an account of Foucault's position one must be acutely aware from which point in Foucault's own career one is drawing one's characterization. Since my main concern is to try to understand Foucault's relation to and significance for the history and philosophy of science, and, more specifically, to clarify his place in the French tradition of historical epistemology that includes Gaston Bachelard, Georges Canguilhem, and, to a lesser extent, certain strata of the work of Louis Althusser, I will focus on Foucault's writings that most directly articulate his so-called archeological project. There is a widespread misinterpretation that Foucault eventually came to reject his archeological investigations, that he came to believe that archeology suffered from some intrinsic methodological failure. It will become clear as I proceed why I think that this is a profound misdescription of Foucault's progression from archeology to genealogy.

Moreover, Foucault always considered his own work in the history and philosophy of science as owing a significant debt to the orientation of Georges Canguilhem, one of the small number of people, alongside Georges Dumézil and Jean Hyppolite, to whom he pays explicit homage in his inaugural lecture to the Collège de France. Thus the need to examine the connections and differences between Foucault's archeology and Canguilhem's epistemology is especially evident if one wants to understand the import of Foucault's archeological enterprise. Furthermore, the growth of the practice of historical epistemology in the English-speaking world and its continued practice in France makes it all the more interesting to try to determine Foucault's role in this methodologically distinctive strain of the history and philosophy of science. I will therefore group my remarks here around the theme of the relation between epistemology and archeology, and I will conclude by taking up the question of the relation between archeology and genealogy.

Let me begin by stating, simply and straightforwardly, that for Foucault I believe that *science* stands to *epistemology* as *knowledge* (savoir), which I think Foucault often uses interchangeably with *discursive formations,* stands to *archeology.* (In Foucault's last writings, which I shall not discuss here, the relevantly marked pair is *thought* and *problematization*.)[1] That is to say, the object of epistemology is science as the object of archeology is discursive formations or knowledge (savoir). And between the two methods and their corresponding objects there are both analogies and displacements. This is how François Delaporte, one of the most accomplished inheritors of the French tradition of historical epistemology, describes the relation between Canguilhem and Foucault:

> Canguilhem indeed does the history of "veridical discourses," of discourses that effect upon themselves an entire work of elaboration oriented by the task of stating the truth. Foucault does instead the history of a discipline, showing how medicine effects upon itself an entire work oriented by the task of constituting a space in which one must situate one-

self in order to be "in the truth." In short, Foucault displaces the preponderance of scientific discourse toward the discipline, the history of the formation of scientific discourse toward the history of the formation of the discipline, and the "stating the truth" of the norm-governed discourse toward the being "in the truth" of the discipline [et du "dire vrai" du discours normé vers le "dans le vrai" de la discipline].[2]

With the exception of wanting to substitute the concept of *knowledge* (savoir) for that of *discipline* (the latter is perhaps more consonant with *Naissance de la clinique,* but is clearly set aside by the use of *savoir* in *Les Mots et les choses* and *L'Archéologie du savoir*), I am in deep agreement with this description of Delaporte.

Notice that in this description the emphasis is placed not on differences in methodological procedure, but on the differences in object, such that we have a contrast between scientific discourse and discipline, between the "'stating the truth' of the norm-governed discourse" and the "'being in the truth' of the discipline." Moreover, following Delaporte's description, Foucault is concerned with the constitution of "a space in which one must situate oneself in order to be 'in the truth'" and this space must certainly be related to the "'stating the truth'" of Canguilhem's "norm-governed [scientific] discourse." But precisely how should we understand this relation?

I want to turn, first, to a little-known text of Foucault, a text that is explicitly engaged with the history and philosophy of science, a text written in 1969 and published in 1970. In this brief, but dense discussion, Foucault distinguishes between different levels of analysis, which he calls *épistémonomique, épistémocritique, épistémologique,* and a fourth level that he identifies as his own without naming it, and that we can call *archéologie.* Here is Foucault's characterization of the epistemological level of analysis: "the analysis of the theoretical structures of a scientific discourse, the analysis of the conceptual material, the analysis of the fields of application of these concepts and the rules of usage of these concepts."[3] Foucault goes on to remark, "it seems to me that the studies that have been done, for example, on the history of the reflex answer to this epistemological level," obviously referring to Canguilhem's *La Formation du concept de réflexe aux xviie et xviiie siècles,* and thus giving us his understanding of Canguilhem's procedures. The level at which Foucault places himself, "the analysis of transformations of fields of knowledge," allows him forcefully to disassociate two levels of analysis. The first level concerns the "system of truths and errors," that by which the assertions in a given scientific text can be distinguished from what today we can affirm as true and false; the second level, that of epistemological modifications, concerns the set of modifications that one can grasp at work in scientific texts, "modifications that are not so much modifications of objects, of concepts, and of theories, but modifications of the rules according to which [biological] discourses formed their objects, defined their concepts, constituted their theories. It is this modification of rules that I am trying to isolate."[4] Foucault goes on to say that such an epistemological transformation would be distinct from the truth of scientific affirmations. An epistemological transformation passes through, takes hold in, a system of scientific affirmation. But such a transformation can take place even through a system of affirmations that turn out to be scientifically false.

> One must distinguish, in the density of a scientific discourse, that which belongs to the order of the true or false scientific assertion and that which would belong to the order of the epistemological transformation. That certain epistemological transformations pass through, take shape, in a set of scientifically false propositions seems to me a historical claim that is perfectly possible and necessary.[5]

An epistemological transformation is the condition of possibility for the existence of a (new) system of scientific affirmations, affirmations that may turn out to be either true or false. One might say that an epistemological transformation is the condition of possibility for the emergence of a domain of scientific discourse, with its theoretical structures, conceptual material, fields of application for its concepts and rules for the usage of these concepts. The problem, to which I shall return at length, is how to characterize more fully these conditions of possibility, but as an initial approximation it will suffice to say that an epistemological transformation, as understood by Foucault, is the condition of possibility for the truth-or-falsity of a domain of scientific discourse.[6]

Foucault's placement of his own analysis at the level of epistemological transformations should nevertheless not lead one to lose sight of the fact that he and Canguilhem share the view that a domain of scientific discourse is, in its internal economy, norm-governed (normé), that it does possess "a well-defined regularity."[7] In his inaugural lecture to the Collège de France, Foucault said that he owed to Canguilhem the idea "that one can, one must do the history of science as that of a set, at the same time coherent and transformable, of theoretical models and conceptual instruments."[8] I want to emphasize the phrase "coherent and transformable" since it marks out the level of rules or norms, rules that both give a well-defined regularity to a scientific discourse and allow for a wide, if limited, range of transformations within the discourse. A central task of epistemology à la Canguilhem is to find the set of rule-governed regularities that provide coherence, that set forth the underlying structure and limits, for a specifiable scientific discursive domain, and that can be found within the science itself, that, as it were, internally regulate what can be produced as a scientific statement within the science. This system of rules, which provides for the coherence and transformability of a domain of scientific discourse, is what I shall henceforth call the *internal* condition of possibility for the production of scientific statements. Without the articulation of some such system, from an epistemological point of view one will not understand why certain statements, both true and false, are produced within a scientific discourse at a given time, while others are not.

To Canguilhem's question, repeated to Foucault by the "Cercle d'épistémologie" in 1968, "Concerning theoretical knowledge, is it possible to consider [penser] it in the specificity of its concept without reference to some norm?" both Canguilhem and Foucault responded with a clear *no,* a "no" that was one basis of their methodological innovations.[9] If Canguilhem looked for the internal norms that governed the specificity of concepts and theories of science, while Foucault looked at other levels for other kinds of norms, from the perspective of the historiography of the history and philosophy of science, their common orientation was more decisive than their divergences. This is one fundamental reason why their work was the site of such fruitful exchange.

Foucault, as I have said, placed his work at a different level of analysis, at a level, as he described it in his "Titres et travaux" prepared for his candidacy at the Collège de France,

of domains of knowledge that could not be identified exactly with sciences, without however being simple mental habits . . . between opinion and scientific knowledge [connaissance], one can recognize the existence of a specific level that I propose to call that of knowledge [savoir] . . . it includes in fact rules that belong to it in its own right, thus characterizing its existence, its functioning, and its history; certain of these rules are specific to a single domain, others are common to several; it may happen that others are general for an epoch.[10]

Thus what is methodologically central is that "a system of knowledge . . . has its own equilibrium and coherence."[11] What distinguishes Foucault's work from Canguilhem's is the "specific level" at which he conducted his analyses; what links his work to Canguilhem's is the articulation of rules and norms that provide for characteristic types of "equilibrium and coherence."

Here is what I think of as perhaps Foucault's best brief description of the method of archeological analysis, which I quote at length since it condenses so much of his thought. It appears in his "summary" for his first course at the Collège de France, 1970–71.

Previous investigations have allowed us to recognize a singular level among all of those that enable us to analyze systems of thought: the level of discursive practices. One finds there a systematicity that is neither of the logical nor of the linguistic type. Discursive practices are characterized by the carving out of a field of objects, by the definition of a legitimate perspective for the subject of knowledge, by the fixing of norms for the elaboration of concepts and theories. Each discursive practice thus implies a play of prescriptions that governs the exclusions and choices.

Now these sets of regularities do not coincide with individual works; even if they are manifested through them, even if it happens that they stand out, for the first time, in one of them, these regularities go largely beyond them, while often regrouping a considerable number of them. But neither do they necessarily coincide with what we usually call sciences or disciplines, although their boundaries may be sometimes provisionally the same; it happens more frequently that a discursive practice brings together diverse disciplines or sciences, or, again, that it traverses a certain number of them and regroups into a sometimes unapparent unity several of their regions.[12]

In the terms I was just using, Foucault's first paragraph describes his methodological or analytical commitments—the search for a specific kind of "systematicity" and for "a play of prescriptions that governs the exclusions and choices," commitments he shares with Canguilhem. Foucault's second paragraph describes the level at which he employs his analytical tools—neither individual works, nor sciences or disciplines, but "discursive practices" that constitute knowledge (savoir), a level that separates his work from that of epistemological historians of science, such as Canguilhem.

I have characterized the task of epistemology as that of finding the internal conditions of possibility for the production of a given domain of scientific statements. But if archeology bears to epistemology the relation I have been suggesting, then there must be some role for the notion of conditions of possibility in archeological analysis as well, although these conditions of possibility will have to be differently located than those of epistemology. Indeed, in "Sur l'archéologie des sciences," in a significant passage, Foucault does in fact distinguish two orders of conditions of possibility, "two heteromorphous systems" of conditions of possibility. The first system "defines the conditions of the science as science." These conditions of possibility are relative to a given science with its objects, theories, and concepts; they define "the rules . . . that are required in order for a statement to belong to this science." Since these conditions of possibility and the rules they define are internal to the domain of science, I have dubbed them internal conditions of possibility. As Foucault says, "the conditions of possibility are internal to the scientific discourse in general, and can only be defined by it."[13] The second system of conditions of possibility I shall call the external conditions of possibility, since they are external with respect to the given scientific domain. Foucault writes, "The other system concerns the possibility of a science in its historical existence. It is external to it and not superimposable. It is characterized by a field of discursive ensembles that have neither the same status, nor the same delimitation, nor the same organization, nor the same functioning as the sciences to which they give rise."[14] These discursive ensembles neither consist of false knowledge that science has relegated to its dark prehistory, nor outline some future science that is only able to express itself in this not yet fully articulated form until it sprouts forth as scientific knowledge. That is to say, these discursive ensembles are neither pseudo-sciences nor quasi-sciences, since they do not get their coherence by reference to the internal norms of scientificity. Rather, as Foucault says,

> it is a matter of figures that have their own consistency, their laws of formation and their internal arrangement. To analyze discursive formations,

the positivities and the knowledge that corresponds to them, is not to assign forms of scientificity; it is to traverse a field of historical determination that must give an account of discourses in their appearance, their persistence, their transformation, and, if need be, their effacement, some of which are still recognized today as scientific, others of which have lost this status, certain of which have never acquired it, others of which, finally, have never claimed to acquire it. In short, knowledge is not science in the successive displacement of its internal structures; it is the field of its actual history.[15]

Thus *knowledge* stands to *science* as *field* stands to *internal structure,* which is another way of saying that these discursive ensembles are the external conditions of possibility for the structures of scientificity. The actual production of scientific statements takes place within a rule-governed structure that provides the conditions of possibility for these statements; the entire domain of these statements takes place within a field of knowledge that provides the conditions of possibility for the existence of this domain. In both cases we have conditions of possibility, but each is located at a different discursive level.

Another way of trying to characterize the relations between archeology and epistemology is to make a distinction between the "will to know" (volonté de savoir) and the "will to truth" (volonté de vérité), a distinction that Foucault sometimes (although not always) at least implicitly observed.[16] Within a given scientific domain, there is always a particular division (partage) of truth and falsity, a set of rules or norms that determines which statements count as candidates of either truth or falsehood. Within this division some statements will be true, others false, but a false statement will be what Foucault once called a "disciplined error," since it will be part of the rule-governed domain of this scientific discourse; it will lie within the limits of the particular "will to truth."[17] A statement that violates these rules or norms will not, strictly speaking, be false, but incoherent; it will fall into "pure and simple linguistic monstrosity."[18] These monstrous statements do not meet the internal conditions of possibility of the scientific discourse, and so from within the structure of this discourse they are repelled and must inhabit what Foucault once called "an entire teratology of knowledge."[19] Since epistemology is concerned with these very conditions of possibility, its task is, among other things, to describe the underlying division—truth and falsity, on the one side, and monstrosity, on the other.

This epistemological task will be historical, since not all sciences share the same division of truth and falsity, nor does the history of a single science necessarily exhibit an identical division of truth and falsity. These divisions may be more or less extensive and stable, but they are neither universal nor permanent. That is why the shape that these monsters take will change when a different form of the will to truth emerges; a new form will bring with it a new division of truth and falsity and thus will reshape the boundaries of the teratology of truth. One form of scientific revolution takes place precisely when a new form of the will to truth is established.

That a given scientific domain has one division of truth and falsity rather than another, and that these divisions are subject to transformations, cannot be accounted for within the scientific discourse itself. In trying to give an account of the existence of a specific division or of a transformation which brings about a new division, a central position that needs to be circumscribed rests at the level of knowledge (savoir); we need to look for conditions of possibility that lie at the stratum of knowledge (savoir). That is, we should start to look for a description of the history, of the changing forms, of the will to truth (volonté de vérité) by repositioning ourselves within the space of the history of the will to know (volonté de savoir). Foucault insisted, first of all, that in our history the *volonté de savoir* has predominantly taken the form of a *volonté de vérité*, so that knowledge has decisively appeared to us in the form of scientific truth, and he emphasized that this very fact itself needed to be the object of historical investigation.[20] Moreover, Foucault claimed that an established division of truth and falsity and the transformations of such divisions depend on the existence and transformation of discursive ensembles of knowledge (savoir). A reorganization of *savoir* brings about the possibility of a new form of the will to truth. Here is an example of this phenomenon as described by Foucault:

> At the turn of the sixteenth and seventeenth century (and above all in England) a will to know appeared that, anticipating its actual contents, delineated schemes of possible, observable, measurable, classifiable objects; a will to know that imposed on the knowing subject (and in a certain way before all experience) a certain position, a certain gaze and a certain function (to see rather than to read, to verify rather than to comment on); a will to know that prescribed (and in a mode more general than any determinate instrument) the technical level where knowledge would have to invest itself in order to be verifiable and useful.[21]

It is clear that Foucault is here describing not changes within a science, but rather changes of *savoir* that are preconditions for the emergence of new divisions of truth and falsity, divisions that exhibit new norms and rules, new internal structures of a science. I have myself argued that in the nineteenth century a new division of truth and falsity, what I have sometimes called a new style of reasoning, made possible psychiatric statements about sexual perversion that had no scientificity at all before this time. An internal condition of possibility for these statements was a transformation in the will to truth (volonté de vérité) that brought about new rules for the production of true discourses, new categories of true-and-false statements. If one were to ask what were the conditions of existence for this markedly new form of the *volonté de vérité,* one would want to look at the transformations of *savoir* that provided external conditions of possibility for this new distribution of truth-and-falsity. For example, one would look for "the carving out of a field of objects" (such as the individual, personality), "the definition of a legitimate perspective for the subject of knowledge" (in this instance, the psychiatrist), "the fixing of norms for the elaboration of concepts and theories" (norms for the elaboration of the concepts of the natural and unnatural, for the theory of degeneration).[22] This level of discursive formation has a different status, organization, functioning, and historicity than the discursive practices of the science itself. And yet it is related to these practices exactly as Foucault indicates—as "the field of its actual history."[23]

As should be evident, this level of knowledge (savoir) is broader or more extensive than that of any given science, and transformations in the discursive ensembles of *savoir* can make possible changes, even if the effects are realized in different ways, in the discursive practices of more than one science. If there is a knowledge (savoir) common to more than one science, if there is an order of knowledge uniting different sciences, then this system of knowledge constitutes what Foucault called an *épistémè.* Isolating the discursive regularities of given sciences may allow one to discover that there is a set of relations that unites these discursive practices; this set of relations provides the "epistemological space" for these sciences, their *épistémè.*[24] Thus an *épistémè* is "a global configuration" that organizes "in a coherent way an entire region of empirical knowledge."[25] The *épistémè* marks out the relations and communication between the different sciences; it is located neither at the level of accumulated empirical knowledge (connaissance) nor at that of the internal norms of a science that provide the framework for this *connaissance,* but is rather to be found precisely at the level of the discursive formations of *savoir*. As Foucault remarks, "It is all these phenomena of relations between the sciences or between the different discourses in the diverse scientific sectors that constitute what I call the episteme of an epoch."[26] *Les Mots et les choses* is the study of the classical *épistémè*, what natural history, economics, and grammar shared in common in the classical age:

> Without their having been conscious of it, the naturalists, the economists, and the grammarians used the same rules to define the objects proper to their field of study, to form their concepts, construct their theories. These are rules of formation that never had a distinct formulation and are only perceived through extremely different theories, concepts, and objects of study, rules that I have tried to bring to light, while isolating, as their specific locus, a level that I have called, perhaps in a manner a bit arbitrary, archeological.[27]

Thus the archeological system common to these scientific discourses, their shared rules of formation, is the *épistémè* of the classical age.

If we correctly situate the level at which the *épistémè* of a particular age is to be found, then Canguilhem's apparently paradoxical remark "the episteme is not an object for the epistemologist" becomes fully intelligible.[28] The epistemologist, concerned with the internal norms and rules of a science, cannot, qua epistemologist, have the *épistémè* of a particular epoch as an object of his conceptualization, since it is located below or behind the objects, concepts, and theories of a given scientific discourse. It is a condition of possibility for an entire set of diverse scientific objects, concepts, and theories, and can never be excavated while maintaining oneself at their level. The epistemologist cannot see such conditions of possibility without modifying his own position with respect to his domain of investigation, and such modification is what transforms him from epistemologist to archeologist, takes him from *science* to *savoir*, to the level at which the very constitution of an *épistémè* can first be articulated. The *épistémè* does not lie on the epistemologist's geometric plane; it is not so much unseen as unseeable from his point of view. Thus the *épistémè* can no more be superposed on the dimension of epistemological analysis than the external conditions of possibility can be collapsed into the internal conditions.

In claiming that the discursive formations of knowledge (savoir) provide the (external) conditions of possibility for the (internal) structures of scientificity, one must be careful not to misinterpret the notion of conditions of possibility. *Savoir* is a condition of *possibility,* not of actuality, for the existence of a scientific discourse. As Foucault notes, a field of *savoir* can characterize discourses some of which are still considered scientific today, others of which have either lost this status, or have failed to acquire it, or have never even aspired to scientificity.[29] Within the space of *savoir* certain additional modifications need to take place in order for a scientific discourse to emerge. Without this epistemological space our scientific discourse would not exist as such, but this space does not provide sufficient conditions for the appearance of any actual scientific discursive practice. Moreover, different scientific discourses, even though they may share an *épistémè,* will emerge as scientific discourses by instantiating this *épistémè* in distinct ways. Scientific discourses are modified instantiations of *savoir,* never unmediated expressions of it. In order for it to cross the threshold of scientificity, numerous constraints must be imposed on a discursive formation, constraints additional to the conditions of possibility defined at the level of *savoir.* These constraints, with all of their detail, will have to be described separately for each scientific discipline and for each relevant stage of historical development. Thus, between archeology and epistemology, there is the historical problem, indicated by Foucault in his "Titres et travaux," of how *savoir* is elaborated as scientific discourse, of how a dimension of *savoir* can come to assume the status and function of "scientific knowledge" (connaissance scientifique).[30] To go from *savoir* to *science* requires modifications the extent and nature of which can only be determined historically. Specific such modifications are part of the history of the relationship between the will to know (volonté de savoir) and the will to truth (volonté de vérité). That Foucault could pose this problem so lucidly was due in part to his methodological innovations, to his delimitation and description of an archeological territory, a territory that made it possible to formulate the question of the relation between *savoir* and *science,* to isolate discursive formations that make scientific discourses possible without determining their actual shapes.

In speaking of archeology and epistemology, I have spoken in both cases of discursive practices, since, strictly speaking, archeology and epistemology take as their only objects of analysis differently located discursive practices. To approach Foucault's quite fundamental concern with the relations between discursive and nondiscursive practices, we would have to turn to the question of the relationship between archeology and genealogy, since the latter focuses on the formation of discursive practices on the basis of "incitations, centers, techniques and procedures" of power, on the relation, that is to say, between knowledge (savoir) and power (pouvoir).[31] Both *Histoire de la folie* and *Naissance de la clinique* were not only archeological, but genealogical *avant la lettre*, since these two books dealt with "invested knowledges" (savoirs investis), knowledge as it entered into complex relations with nondiscursive practices that were productive and sustaining of this knowledge, and that, in turn, were affected by it.[32] *Les Mots et les choses* was the purest archeological investigation pursued by Foucault, since in that book he undertook to neutralize the nondiscursive aspect in order to isolate the discursive domains of *savoir*.[33] The relationship of these three books to Foucault's developing methodological positions has often been the source of misunderstandings. But Foucault himself was quite clear about what he had been doing. In 1972 he said,

> I repeat to you . . . *Les Mots et les choses* is situated at a purely descriptive level that leaves entirely aside all analysis of the relations of power that underlie and make possible the appearance of a type of discourse. If I wrote this book, I wrote it after two others, one concerning the history of madness, the other the history of medicine . . . precisely because in these first two books, in a manner a little confused and anarchical, I had tried to treat all the problems together.[34]

Les Mots et les choses was the clearest realization of Foucault's archeological project, and as he developed in a less confused and more systematic form his genealogical aspirations, he could return more articulately to the "analysis of the relations of power that underlie and make possible the appearance of a type of discourse" in *Surveiller et punir* and the first volume of *Histoire de la sexualité*. As Foucault came to see that "if one wants to do the history of certain types of discourse, bearers of knowledge, one cannot not take into account the relations of power that exist in the society in which this discourse functions," he had to develop an analysis of power to go along with his analysis of discursive practices so that ultimately he would have the conceptual resources to pose the question of the kinds of relations that exist between systems of knowledge and networks of power.[35]

Even before Foucault definitively settled on the Nietzschean notion of genealogy to describe the work he began after *L'Archéologie du savoir*, he was fully aware of the differences between his earlier work and what he was undertaking at the beginning of the 1970s. He described the contrast as that between the archeology and the dynastics of knowledge:

> What I call the "archeology of knowledge" is precisely the marking out and the description of types of discourse, and what I call the "dynastics of knowledge" is the relationship that exists between these main types of discourse that one can observe in a culture and the historical conditions, the economic conditions, the political conditions of their appearance and their formation.[36]

Foucault was certainly not a linguistic idealist; he did not believe that everything was discourse and that all that one could do was to analyze the relations between discursive practices. But he did believe that discursive practices had their own specificity, that one could isolate "normative and rule-governed forms of discourse" even if ultimately one was interested in analyzing the relations between these forms and nondiscursive social practices.[37] And he identified with Dumézil's type of analysis rather than with Claude Lévi-Strauss's structuralism exactly because for Dumézil "there is . . . not an absolute privilege accorded to the verbal myth, to the myth as a verbal production, but he acknowledges that the same relations can occur in a discourse as well as in a religious ritual or a social practice."[38] Dumézil's method allowed "a comparison between theoretical discourses and practices," the kind of comparative perspective that Foucault would employ when he analyzed the relations between systems of knowledge and networks of power.[39]

Foucault distinguished among three kinds of dependencies or relations—intradiscursive, interdiscursive, and extradiscursive.[40] If, roughly speaking, epistemology deals with the intradiscursive relations within a scientific discourse, and archeology with the interdiscursive relations of knowledge (savoir), then genealogy marks out the extradiscursive dependencies between knowledge and power. Indeed, Foucault developed the notion of a *dispositif*, an apparatus, a theoretically central notion in the first volume of *Histoire de la sexualité*, in order to be able to study the linkages or network that exists among elements within "a resolutely heterogeneous ensemble," an ensemble consisting of both discursive and nondiscursive elements.[41] The *dispositif* of sexuality, for example, is a strategically connected heterogeneous ensemble of "relations of force supporting types of knowledge and supported by them."[42] Thus Foucault says that "the apparatus is . . . always inscribed in a game of power, but also always linked to one or several boundaries of knowledge that are born from it but, just as much, condition it."[43] So when Foucault remarks that a *dispositif* is "a much more general case of the episteme," what he means is that while an *épistémè* is a network of relations among specifically discursive elements, a *dispositif* exhibits such linkages among elements both "discursive and nondiscursive, its elements being much more heterogeneous."[44] These considerations, however, already take us beyond Foucault the archeologist, which is the focus of this essay. My purpose has been to emphasize that archeology, like epistemology, deals with discursive practices, and that in this respect they are both distinct from genealogy. At the same time, while granting archeology its theoretical autonomy, as Foucault did, I have wanted to point to some of the ways in which genealogy affected the significance and lessons to be drawn from Foucault's earlier analyses.

I began by acknowledging how difficult it is to provide an adequate characterization of Foucault's thought, given his own constant movement and the elaborations and reinterpretations he gave of his own work. But I realize now that these intellectual difficulties are compounded for me by a somewhat guilty conscience. For my interpretations of Foucault most often conclude with my hearing his voice, accompanied by his unmistakable laugh. And he is uttering those stinging words that end his introduction to *L'Archéologie du savoir*:

> Don't ask me who I am and don't tell me to remain the same: it's for the morality of the civil state to administer our papers. Would that it leave us alone when it's a matter of writing.[45]

APPENDIX:
FOUCAULT, PSYCHOANALYSIS, AND PLEASURE

Despite the genuine complexities and real ambiguities that characterize Michel Foucault's attitude toward psychoanalysis, one can at least say with confidence that the Freudian discovery of the unconscious represented for him a decisive epistemological achievement with respect to the philosophy with which he was surrounded, that is to say, with respect to phenomenology and existentialism. It was the psychoanalytic discovery of the unconscious that, as Foucault emphasizes in "The Death of Lacan," allowed one to question the old theory of the subject; whether described in Cartesian or phenomenological terms this theory of the subject was incompatible with the concept of the unconscious, an incompatibility that Jean-Paul Sartre embraced and carried to its ultimate conclusion in *Being and Nothingness*. Thus, for Foucault, in spite of their overlapping philosophical formation, Lacan and Sartre appeared as "alternate contemporaries," unable to inhabit the same epistemological space.[1] Foucault would therefore see as one of the defining features of existentialism the attempt "to show how human consciousness or the subject or human freedom came to penetrate everything that Freudianism had described or designated as unconscious mechanisms."[2] Since Foucault, in consonance with Lacan, understood the unconscious as a system of logico-linguistic structures, he could oppose the primacy of the subject, of psychological forms, to the search for logical structures, structures that could not be understood or explained in psychological terms and whose existence could not be reconciled with the Sartrean sovereignty of the subject. Structuralism could be understood as "the search for logical structures everywhere that they could occur," and if they could be located within the subject, then the epistemological primacy of consciousness would be overthrown.[3] Such were the fundamental stakes in the philosophical debate between existentialism and structuralism, as Foucault conceived it. However odd it may sound, the existence of the unconscious was a decisive component in Foucault's *antipsychologism.* Moreover, Foucault's interest in linguistics and in the search for linguistic structures played the same kind of epistemological role in his thought, since the existence of these structures would show that language could not be understood by reference to the intentionality of consciousness, thus further limiting the powers of the subject. The space of the psyche was threatened by this alternative space—the space of logic, of logical and linguistic structures, rules, operations—and this threat was one that Foucault was committed to pursuing. He took Jacques Lacan to be committed to a similar pursuit. So that in another brief interview about Lacan, Foucault says that reading Lacan's first texts in the fifties helped him to discover that one "had to try to free everything that hides itself behind the apparently simple use of the pronoun 'I.'"[4] If the structures of the unconscious helped one to realize this aim, so too did Foucault's archeological histories. And thus Foucault could only have been grateful for Lacan's intervention at the very end of the discussion period following his presentation of "What Is an Author?" to the Société française de philosophie. Lacan remarked:

> . . . structuralism or not, it seems to me that, in the field vaguely determined by this label, it is nowhere a question of the negation of the subject. It is a matter of the subordination (dépendance) of the subject, which is extremely different; and quite particularly, at the level of the return to Freud, of the subordination of the subject with respect to something truly elementary, and which we have attempted to isolate under the term "signifier."[5]

The same general kind of subordination is a theme that pervades Foucault's *The Archaeology of Knowledge,* and, in both Lacan's case and Foucault's, a certain form of humanism, exemplified but hardly limited to Sartre, is a constant target of attack.

It should come as no surprise then that even after the publication of the first volume of *The History of Sexuality*, often misinterpreted as a full-scale rejection of psychoanalysis, Foucault always insisted on the significance of the psychoanalytic theory of the unconscious and wanted, in effect, to detach its significance from the much more suspect psychoanalytic theory of sexuality. As he said,

> What is important is not the *Three Essays on the Theory of Sexuality*, but the *Traumdeutung* . . . It is not the theory of development, it is not the sexual secret behind the neuroses and psychoses, it is a *logic of the unconscious*.[6]

This brings me to "The West and the Truth of Sex," Foucault's brief sketch of some of the main themes of the first volume of *The History of Sexuality*.[7] We know that Foucault had originally intended to entitle this volume *Sex and Truth*, and that he thought of its central problems as revolving around the question of how the domain of sex came to be placed within the field of true discourse, that is to say, how in the West sexual behaviors became the objects of a science of sexuality, and of how these true discourses were linked to different mechanisms of power.[8] Without trying to take up these general questions, I want to underline the distinction, highlighted by Foucault in this brief essay, between an erotic art and a science of sexuality, a distinction that raises a series of issues that most commentators on *The Will to Know* have failed to develop. One underlying, fundamental motivation for this distinction is precisely to undermine, from a new angle, the old theory of the subject as it had come to be incorporated into psychoanalytic and other related types of psychological theory. Although Foucault is not everywhere consistent in his terminology, I would claim that we should draw the conclusion from his discussions, here and elsewhere, that while *ars erotica* is organized around the framework of body-pleasure-intensification, *scientia sexualis* is organized around the axis of subject-desire-truth. It is as if one could say that the imposition of true discourses on the subject of sexuality leads to the centrality of a theory of sexual desire, while the discourse of pleasure and the search for its intensification are exterior to a science of sexual desire. Just as Foucault wanted to divorce the psychoanalytic theory of the unconscious from the theory of sexuality, so he wants to detach the experience of pleasure from a psychological theory of sexual desire, of sexual subjectivity.[9] The modification of the subject aimed at by the true discourse of the science of sexuality uses the conceptual structure of *desire* to excavate the real identity of the subject, and so to delimit the domain of psychological intervention. Desire has psychological *depth;* desire can be latent or manifest, apparent or hidden; desire can be repressed or sublimated; it calls for decipherment, for interpretation; true desire expresses what one really wants, who one really is, while false desire hides or masks identity, one's true subjectivity. No doubt this is a main part of the reason why Foucault could not bear the word *desire.*[10] Although we have no difficulty talking about and understanding the distinction between true and false desires, the idea of true and false pleasures (and Foucault understood this point even if he never put it in exactly this way) is conceptually misplaced. Pleasure is, as it were, exhausted by its surface; it can be intensified, increased, its qualities modified, but it does not have the psychological depth of desire. It is, so to speak, related to itself and not to something else that it expresses, either truly or falsely. There is no coherent conceptual space for the science of sexuality to attach itself to pleasure, and no primacy of the psychological subject in the experience of pleasure. Structures of desire lead to forms of sexual orientation, kinds of subjectivity; different pleasures do not imply orientation at all, require no theory of subjectivity or identity formation. The circumscription of true desire is a procedure of individualization; the production of pleasure is not. In a famously enigmatic passage of *The Will to Know* Foucault identifies bodies and pleasure, in contrast to sex-desire, as the point of support for the counterattack against the apparatus of sexuality.[11] Whereas desire and the science of sexuality are internal to this apparatus, pleasure can function as a point or line of resistance to the structures and mechanisms of that very apparatus. Foucault is less enigmatic about this contrast in his interview "Le Gai savoir," originally conducted in 1978:

> I advance this term [pleasure] because it appears to me to escape those medical and naturalistic connotations that this notion of desire bears within itself. That notion was used as a tool, a setting of intelligibility, a calibration in terms of normality: "Tell me what your desire is and I will tell you who you are, if you are normal or not; I will therefore be able to admit or disqualify your desire." One certainly finds this "hold" ["prise"] which goes from the notion of Christian concupiscence to the Freudian notion of desire, while passing through the notion of the sexual instinct

in the 1840s. Desire is not an event, but a permanence of the subject, on which all this psychologico-medical armature is grafted. The term "pleasure," on the other hand, is free of use, almost devoid of meaning. There is no "pathology" of pleasure, no "abnormal" pleasure. It is an event "outside the subject," or at the limit of the subject, in that something which is neither of the body nor of the soul, which is neither inside nor outside, in short, a notion not assigned and not assignable.[12]

Desire allows a hold or grip on the subject which is central to the constitution of a science of sexuality, while pleasure escapes the discourse of pathology and abnormality, the discourse of *scientia sexualis;* its "location" at the limit of the self in fact disturbs, disrupts, the primacy of the subject. This is one philosophical context in which we should place Foucault's extraordinary remarks delivered in 1979 at the meeting of Arcadie:

> Pleasure is something that passes from one individual to another; it is not a secretion of identity. Pleasure has no passport, no identity card.[13]

We can easily invert Foucault's remarks and say that desire is a secretion of identity; it does possess an identity card. And as with other kinds of passports, it can be authentic or counterfeit, representing more or less faithfully who one is. Pleasure does not represent anything; there are no counterfeit pleasures.

Although other texts of Foucault could be cited to support this interpretation, these claims do directly raise the question of how one is to understand Foucault's remarks, both in "The West and the Truth of Sex" and in *The Will to Know,* about that other pleasure, the "pleasure of analysis."[14] For this specific pleasure seems to belie the conceptual division between desire and pleasure on which I have insisted. Indeed, Foucault's invocation of the pleasure of analysis is intended to complicate the strict distinction between *ars erotica* and *scientia sexualis,* leading us to ask whether, "at least in certain of its dimensions," *scientia sexualis* may not function as an *ars erotica.*[15] Without denying the numerous relations between this art and this science, I want to note that Foucault's own remarks question the status of this "pleasure of analysis" in ways that mark it out as not being homogeneous with the pleasures that can function as points of resistance to the apparatus of sexuality. In addition to placing this pleasure within question marks, Foucault explicitly refers to this category as containing "ambiguous pleasures," a characterization used nowhere else.[16] But even more important, his characterization of this pleasure employs verbs all of which partake of the grammar of desire—in "The West and the Truth of Sex," "fouiller," "traquer," "interpréter"; in *The Will to Know,* verbs such as "exposer," "découvrir," "débusquer." These are all activities whose object is typically *desire* and not pleasure, and this is the only instance in which Foucault attaches them to "pleasure," evidence enough of the ambiguous status of this pleasure. Moreover, in "The West and the Truth of Sex," speaking of the way in which the science of sex still belongs to the erotic art, Foucault himself refers not to the pleasure of analysis but to people who "spend so much money to buy the biweekly right to laboriously formulate *the truth of their desire,* and to patiently await the *benefit of interpretation*" (my emphasis), as if to say that the formulation of true desire and the benefit of interpretation fill in the content of the pleasure of analysis.[17] At the end of his discussion in *The Will to Know* Foucault raises a set of questions that already indicate the gap between this pleasure and the body-pleasure-intensification axis that I have previously discussed. After identifying the pleasure of analysis, he asks:

> Should one believe that our *scientia sexualis* is but a singularly subtle form of *ars erotica* and that, of this apparently lost tradition, it is the Western and quintessential version? Or should one suppose that all these pleasures are but the by-products of a sexual science, a benefit that supports its innumerable efforts?[18]

This latter question can only be coherently asked of the pleasures of analysis, and that fact alone shows the distinctiveness, the peculiarity, of this kind of pleasure. It is a pleasure that has neither the epistemological nor the political force of those other pleasures advanced by Foucault; in a word, it does not disrupt the sovereignty of the subject.

Foucault's interest in the dissolution of the psychological subject of *scientia sexualis* is not only compatible with but, in my view, required by his final concern with ethical subjectivation. But rather than pursuing these latter concerns, I want to give a final example of the stakes involved in the dissolution of the psychological subject. Perhaps the clearest exemplification of this dissolution remains Pierre Guyotat's *Eden, Eden, Eden,* to which Foucault devoted a very brief but brilliant and theoretically powerful text. Guyotat's book, without saving "the subject, the self, the soul," without protecting the "primacy of the subject, the unity of the individual," without representing sexuality as the "fundamental or primitive desire of the individual," is able to enact a rupture.[19] In this book the individual

> is but the precarious extension of sexuality, provisional, quickly effaced; the individual, in the end, is but a pallid form that arises for a few moments from a great repetitive, persistent source. Individuals, the quickly retracted pseudopods of sexuality. If we want to know what we know, we must give up what we suppose about our individuality, our self, our subject position. In your text, it is perhaps the first time that the relations of the individual and of sexuality are plainly and decidedly reversed . . . : sexuality passes to the other side of the individual and ceases to be "subjected" ["assujettie"].[20]

The inaccessibility of *Eden, Eden, Eden*, its unreadability, its new form of extremeness, are marks of its conceptual exteriority, and of its resistance to the apparatus of sexuality. Our inability to imagine what this text sounds like attests to the hold of that "anthropological slumber" that Foucault was ceaselessly combating.[21] We should not underestimate, as we so often do, the severe difficulty of dissolving the subject. If psychology, in all of its forms, has been an "absolutely inevitable and absolutely fatal impasse" of our thought since the nineteenth century, then its rupture will be experienced as a kind of death.[22] So let us not forget, in this context, these shocking remarks of Foucault:

> I think that pleasure is a very difficult behavior . . . I would like and I hope I'll die of an overdose of pleasure of any kind. Because I think it's really difficult, and I always have the feeling that I do not feel *the* pleasure, the complete total pleasure, and, for me, it's related to death . . .
>
> Because I think the kind of pleasure I would consider as *the* real pleasure would be so deep, so intense, so overwhelming that I couldn't survive it. I would die.[23]

I hope we are in a position to take Foucault's remarks conceptually, and not psychologically, and use them to ask ourselves a question he often asked himself, a question to which we still do not have a satisfactory answer: What is the pleasure of sex, what does it do to us?

NOTES

Preface

1. Georges Canguilhem, "Introduction to *Penser la Folie: Essais sur Michel Foucault*" in *Foucault and His Interlocutors,* ed. and introduced by Arnold I. Davidson (Chicago: University of Chicago Press, 1997). A helpful discussion of Foucault's relation to psychoanalysis in *Histoire de la folie* and *La Volonté de savoir* can be found in Ernani Chaves, *Foucault e a psicanálise* (Rio de Janeiro: Forense-Universitéria, 1988). However, in discussing the passages from *La Volonté de savoir* that I go on to cite, Chaves' interpretation blurs the differences between Foucault's archeological and genealogical projects and leads him to mischaracterize the significance of Foucault's remarks on psychoanalysis.

2. Michel Foucault, *Histoire de la sexualité,* vol. 1: *La Volonté de savoir* (Paris: Gallimard, 1976), p. 157.

3. Michel Foucault, *The History of Sexuality,* vol. 1: *An Introduction* (New York: Pantheon Books, 1978), p. 119.

4. Foucault, *La Volonté de savoir,* p. 157.

5. Ibid., p. 158.

6. On this topic, see Ian Hacking, "Language, Truth, and Reason" in *Rationality and Relativism,* ed. Martin Hollis and Steven Lukes (Cambridge: MIT Press, 1982).

1. Closing Up the Corpses

This essay was first published in a festschrift for Hilary Putnam and takes up issues that go back to Putnam's famous 1962 discussion of analytic and a priori truths in "It Ain't Necessarily So." In a series of papers published in the 1970s, Putnam extends and develops this discussion, and his arguments are directly relevant to my own philosophical motivations in writing a history of the concepts and theories of psychiatry. I offer here an extended case study of the way in which the status of statements is relative to a body of knowledge, what I call a "style of reasoning." More specifically, I want to show that some claims cannot even be conceived without the development of a new style of reasoning. Thus the very possibility of conceiving of certain statements as part of the domain of scientific knowledge depends upon the historically specific formation of new concepts, and new forms of reasoning and argumentation. So I hope to begin to demonstrate how the history of concepts is relevant to problems about the epistemological status of scientific statements.

Among Putnam's papers most central to my motivations, see especially, "It Ain't Necessarily So," in *Mathematics, Matter, and Method, Philosophical Papers,* vol. 1 (Cambridge: Cambridge University Press, 1975); "'Two Dogmas' Revisited," "There Is at Least One *A Priori* Truth," and "Analyticity and Apriority: Beyond Wittgenstein and Quine," in *Realism and Reason, Philosophical Papers,* vol. 3 (Cambridge: Cambridge University Press, 1983).

I am grateful to Michael Lavin, John McNees, and Alan Stone for comments on an earlier version of this essay. I owe two special debts of gratitude. Conversations with Michel Foucault in 1976 were crucial in helping me to conceptualize these issues. And discussions with Ian Hacking contributed to this essay in a multitude of different ways.

1. Michel Foucault, *The Birth of the Clinic* (New York: Vintage Books, 1973).
2. Quoted in ibid., p. 140.
3. Quoted in ibid., p. 146, from Bichat's *Anatomie générale.*
4. Ibid.
5. See, for example, the brief remarks of Michel Foucault, "The Confession of the Flesh," in *Power/Knowledge* (New York: Pantheon Books, 1980), pp. 221–222.
6. Dr. Michea, "Des déviations maladives de l'appétit vénérien," *Union Médicale,* 17 (July 1849). The case of Sergeant Bertrand provoked a number of discussions, of which Michea's is the most instructive.
7. Ibid., p. 339.
8. Ibid.
9. Ibid.
10. J. G. Kiernan, "Sexual Perversion and the Whitechapel Murders," *The Medical Standard,* 4, no. 5 (November 1888), 129–130, and 4, no. 6 (December 1888), 170–172.
11. The phrase "principle of atavism" is used by Morton Prince in his discussion

and critique of Kiernan and related views in "Sexual Perversion or Vice? A Pathological and Therapeutic Inquiry," *Journal of Nervous and Mental Diseases,* April 1898. Reprinted in *Psychotherapy and Multiple Personality: Selected Essays* (Cambridge: Harvard University Press, 1975), pp. 89–90.

12. Kiernan, "Sexual Perversion," p. 129.

13. Ibid., p. 130.

14. G. Frank Lydston, "Sexual Perversion, Satyriasis, and Nymphomania," *Medical and Surgical Reporter,* 61, no. 10 (September 7, 1889), 253–258, and 61, no. 11 (September 14, 1889), 281–285. The quotation is from p. 255.

15. Ibid., p. 253; my emphasis. See also E. Gley, "Les Aberrations de l'instinct sexuel," *Revue Philosophique,* January 1884, pp. 88–89.

16. Julien Chevalier, *De l'inversion de l'instinct sexuel au point de vue médico-légal* (Paris: O. Doin, 1885). Chevalier summarizes his conclusions at the end of chap. 6.

17. Wilhelm Griesinger, *Mental Pathology and Therapeutics* (London: The New Sydenham Society, 1867), p. 1. The first edition was published in German in 1845, the second enlarged edition in 1861.

18. Ibid., p. 8.

19. Ibid., p. 4.

20. Ibid., p. 206; my emphasis.

21. Paul Moreau (de Tours), *Des aberrations du sens génésique* (Paris: Asselin, 1880), p. 146.

22. Eugene Kraepelin, *Clinical Psychiatry: A Textbook for Students and Physicians* (London: Macmillan, 1907), pp. 115–116.

23. Another discussion of cerebral pathology that bears attention is Richard von Krafft-Ebing, *Textbook of Insanity* (Philadelphia: G. A. Davis, 1904). See especially pp. 20–24.

24. See Ian Hacking, "Language, Truth, and Reason," in *Rationality and Relativism,* ed. S. Lukes and M. Hollis (Oxford: Blackwell Books, 1982), and Michel Foucault, "Truth and Power," in *Power/Knowledge.*

25. See Kiernan, "Sexual Perversion," p. 130, and Griesinger, *Mental Pathology,* pp. 5–7.

26. Krafft-Ebing, *Textbook of Insanity,* p. 21.

27. The same set of problems surrounds J. M. Charcot's introduction of the ambiguous notion of "dynamic lesion" in reference to hysteria. See *Diseases of the Nervous System,* vol. 3 (London: The New Sydenham Society, 1889), pp. 12–14. I briefly discuss this notion in "Assault on Freud," *London Review of Books,* 6, no. 12 (1984).

28. Moriz Benedikt, *Anatomical Studies upon Brains of Criminals* (New York: Wm. Wood, 1881). Published in German in 1878.

29. Ibid., pp. v and vii.

30. Ibid., p. 157; emphasis in the original.

31. Ibid., p. 158.

32. Paul Magnan, "Des anomalies, des aberrations et des perversions sexuelles," *Annales Médico-Psychologiques,* 7th ser., 1 (1885), 447–474.

33. J. M. Charcot and P. Magnan, "Inversion du sens génital," *Archives de Neurologie,* 3, no. 7 (January 1882), 53–60, and 4, no. 12 (November 1882), 296–322.

34. See, for example, Paul Sérieux, *Recherches cliniques sur les anomalies de l'instinct sexuel* (Paris: Lecrosnier et Babé, 1888).

35. Griesinger, *Mental Pathology,* p. 41.

36. Richard von Krafft-Ebing, *Psychopathia Sexualis* (New York: Stein & Day, 1965; translation of the twelfth German edition), p. 17. There are significant differences between the first edition of *Psychopathia Sexualis* (1886) and later editions; when referring to the first edition, I shall so indicate.

37. Ibid., pp. 17–21. The quotation is from p. 21. Mackenzie's paper appears in the *Journal of Medical Science,* April 1884.

38. M. P. Legrain, *Des anomalies de l'instinct sexuel et en particulier des inversions du sens génital* (Paris: Carré, 1896), p. 36.

39. Moreau (de Tours), *Des aberrations du sens génésique,* p. 2.

40. Ibid., p. 3. Moreau classifies as "perversion génitale absolue" bestiality, the profanation of corpses, and rape. He also discusses erotomania, satyriasis, and nymphomania. Remarkably, he has no discussion of contrary sexual instinct.

41. *Oxford English Dictionary* (Oxford: Clarendon Press, 1933), vol. 7, p. 739.

42. Krafft-Ebing, *Textbook on Insanity,* p. 79. Krafft-Ebing considers abolition to be the extreme case of diminution.

43. Ibid., pp. 77–81.

44. Ibid., p. 81. This same classification is given in *Psychopathia Sexualis,* p. 34.

45. Krafft-Ebing, *Textbook on Insanity,* pp. 83–86, and *Psychopathia Sexualis,* pp. 34–36. I discuss masochism in Essay 2 in the present volume.

46. Krafft-Ebing, *Psychopathia Sexualis,* pp. 16, 52–53. See also *Textbook on Insanity,* p. 81. For other representative statements see Albert Moll, *Perversions of the Sex Instinct* (Newark: Julian Press, 1931), pp. 172 and 182 (originally published in German in 1891); and Dr. Laupts (pseudonym of G. Saint-Paul), *L'homosexualité et les types homosexuels: Nouvelle édition de Perversion et perversités sexuelles* (Paris: Vigot, 1910).

47. In eighteenth-century medicine, masturbation was considered exclusively as a causal factor, omnipresent of course, in the genesis of disease processes. It was not considered a distinct and autonomous disease. See S. A. Tissot, *L'Onanisme, dissertation sur les maladies produites par la masturbation* (Paris: Bechet, 1823); originally published in Latin in 1758. In the nineteenth cen-

tury, masturbation came to be thought of as both a distinct morbid entity and a significant causal factor in the genesis of other diseases. For the later understanding, see Moreau (de Tours), *Des aberrations du sens génésique,* p. 168.

48. It is instructive to compare this conception of perversion with Aquinas' treatment of unnatural vice. Saint Thomas believed that there was a distinct kind of lustful vice, "contrary to the natural order of the venereal act as becoming to the human race: and this is called the unnatural vice." He considered onanism, bestiality, sodomy, and the sin of not observing the right manner of copulation all to be unnatural vices. He thought them to be not only distinct from but also worse than incest, adultery, rape, and seduction. See *Summa Theologica,* II-II, question 154, articles 11 and 12. One must be careful, however, not to assimilate this moral conception of perversion to the nineteenth-century medical conception. For discussion see Essay 2 in the present volume. I am indebted to John McNees for discussion on this point.

49. Carl Westphal, "Die conträre Sexualempfindung," *Archiv für Psychiatrie und Nervenkrankheiten,* 2 (1870), 73–108.

50. See note 33. A case reported by Legrand du Saulle appears in *Annales médico-psychologiques* in 1876, vol. 4. But this case is not nearly as well documented as those of Charcot and Magnan.

51. Arrigo Tamassia, "Sull'inversione dell'istinto sessuale," *Revista sperimentale di freniatria,* 1878, pp. 87–117.

52. Julius Krueg, "Perverted Sexual Instincts," *Brain,* 4 (October 1881), 368–376.

53. J. C. Shaw and G. N. Ferris, "Perverted Sexual Instinct," *Journal of Nervous and Mental Diseases,* 10, no. 2 (April 1883), 198. A useful discussion of the nineteenth-century medical literature can be found in Chevalier, *De l'inversion de l'instinct sexuel,* chap. 2.

54. Shaw and Ferris, "Perverted Sexual Instinct." This article is the most comprehensive early article to appear in English.

55. Ibid., p. 100.

56. See Sérieux, *Recherches cliniques,* p. 37 (quoting Magnan), and Kiernan, "Sexual Perversion," p. 130.

57. Krafft-Ebing, *Psychopathia Sexualis,* p. 186.

58. Ibid., pp. 35–36.

59. Moll, *Perversions of the Sex Instinct,* p. 171.

60. Michel Foucault, *The History of Sexuality,* vol. 1: *An Introduction* (New York: Pantheon Books, 1978), chap. 2.

61. Krafft-Ebing, *Textbook on Insanity,* p. 85. By the fourth category Krafft-Ebing seems to have in mind those cases where "the secondary physical sexual characteristics approach that sex to which the individual, according to his instinct,

belongs." He refers to these cases as pseudohermaphroditism. See *Psychopathia Sexualis*, p. 36.

62. Legrain, *Des anomalies de l'instinct sexuel*, p. 51.

63. Ibid., pp. 37–38.

64. Kraepelin, *Clinical Psychiatry*, p. 510.

65. Ibid., pp. 510–514.

66. American Psychiatric Association, *Diagnostic and Statistical Manual of Mental Disorders*, 3rd ed. (Washington, D.C.: APA, 1980), pp. 6–8.

67. Morton Prince, "Habit Neuroses as True Functional Diseases," *Boston Medical and Surgical Journal*, 139, no. 24 (1898), 589–592. Alfred Binet's "Le Fetichisme dans l'amour," *Revue Philosophique*, 24 (1887), must be mentioned as one of the earliest articulations of the associationist point of view. However, his associationism still left room for the notion of congenital morbid states, which he also invoked as part of his explanation of fetishism.

68. Prince, "Habit Neuroses," p. 589.

69. Ibid., p. 590.

70. Sigmund Freud, "Some Points in a Comparative Study of Organic Hysterical Paralyses," *Early Psychoanalytic Writings*, ed. Philip Rieff (New York: Collier Books, 1963).

71. I have deliberately left aside Freud's views on the perversions. The best brief discussion of this topic is the entry on perversion in J. Laplanche and J. B. Pontalis, *The Language of Psychoanalysis* (New York: Norton, 1973), pp. 306–309. Also see Essay 3 in the present volume.

72. Stanley Cavell, "Knowing and Acknowledging," in *Must We Mean What We Say?* (New York: Charles Scribner's Sons, 1969), p. 265.

73. Krafft-Ebing, *Textbook on Insanity*, p. 81; my emphasis. This is one theme of Foucault's writings on the history of sexuality.

74. Laupts, *L'homosexualité et les types homosexuels*.

75. Ibid., pp. 200–201.

76. Krafft-Ebing, *Psychopathia Sexualis*, p. 53.

77. Immanuel Kant, *Anthropology from a Pragmatic Point of View* (The Hague: Martinus Nijhoff, 1974), pp. 82–89.

78. Immanuel Kant, *The Doctrine of Virtue* (Philadelphia: University of Pennsylvania Press, 1964), pp. 87–89.

79. Ibid., p. 89.

80. Charcot was greatly disturbed by critics who claimed that hysteria was an artificial creation, not to be found in nature, but rather learned through imitation by "patients" who visited the Salpètrière. He vigorously affirmed that the truth is "que la grande attaque dont j'ai formulé les caractères, est bel et bien un type morbide naturel; ce n'est pas un création artificielle; elle

appartiennent à tous les ages, à tous les pays." J. M. Charcot, *Leçons du Mardi à la Salpêtrière. Policlinique 1887–1888,* vol. 1 (Paris: Aux Bureaux du Progrès Médical, 1892), p. 105.

81. Of course, the general doctrine of scientific realism has come under increasingly detailed attack. For some of the most important recent critiques, see Hilary Putnam, *Meaning and the Moral Sciences* (London: Routledge & Kegan Paul, 1978), *Reason, Truth and History* (Cambridge: Cambridge University Press, 1981), and *Realism and Reason* (Cambridge: Cambridge University Press, 1983); Nancy Cartwright, *How the Laws of Physics Lie* (New York: Oxford University Press, 1983); and Ian Hacking, *Representing and Intervening* (Cambridge: Cambridge University Press, 1983).

82. Moreau, *Des aberrations du sens génésique,* pp. 67–68.

83. E. Littré, "Un fragment de médicine rétrospective," *Philosophie Positive,* 5 (1869), 103–120.

84. J. M. Charcot and Paul Richer, *Les Démoniaques dans l'art* (Paris: Delahaye et Lecrosnier, 1887). See especially "Preface," p. vi. Charcot's retrospective medicine is discussed in Jan Goldstein, "The Hysteria Diagnosis and the Politics of Anticlericalism in Late Nineteenth Century France," *Journal of Modern History,* 54, no. 2 (June 1982).

85. B. A. Morel, *Traité des dégénérescences physiques, intellectuelles et morales de l'espèce humaine* (Paris: J. B. Ballière, 1857), pp. 4–5. Morel also uses the notion of a functional lesion *(lésion functionnelle),* p. 53. For some examples of the use of the theory of degeneracy, see Jacques Borel, *Du concept de dégénérescence à la notion d'alcoolisme dans la médicine contemporaine* (Montpellier: Caues et cie, 1968), and Alan Corbin, *Les Filles de noce: Misère sexuelle et prostitution (19ᵉ et 20ᵉ siècles)* (Paris: Aubier Montaigne, 1978).

86. Foucault, *The History of Sexuality,* p. 139.

87. Krafft-Ebing, *Psychopathia Sexualis,* p. 32.

88. Kraepelin, *Clinical Psychiatry.*

89. Morton Prince, "Sexual Perversion or Vice?" p. 85.

90. Ibid. One of the first persons to recognize this consequence of the degeneracy theory of perversion was A. von Schrenck-Notzing, *Therapeutic Suggestion in Psychopathia Sexualis* (Philadelphia: F. A. Davis, 1895) (published in German in 1894). See, for example, p. 145.

91. Quoted by von Schrenck-Notzing, *Therapeutic Suggestion,* p. 145.

92. Ibid.

93. Ibid., p. 304.

94. Ibid., p. v.

95. Ibid., p. 146.

96. Ibid., p. 305.

97. Prince, "Sexual Perversion or Vice?" p. 85.
98. Ibid., p. 95.
99. See Krafft-Ebing's preface to the first edition of *Psychopathia Sexualis,* p. xiv.
100. Prince, "Sexual Perversion or Vice?" p. 95.
101. Ibid.
102. Ibid., p. 96.
103. Immanuel Kant, *Critique of Pure Reason* (New York: St. Martin's Press, 1929), B68-B69.
104. Michel Foucault, "Sexuality and Solitude," *London Review of Books,* 3, no. 9 (1981), 5.
105. Ian Hacking, "Biopower and the Avalanche of Numbers," *Humanities in Society,* 5, nos. 3/4 (1982). See also Hacking's "The Invention of Split Personalities," *I & C,* nos. 10/11 (1988).
106. Westphal, "Die conträre Sexualempfindung." See also Gley, "Les Aberrations de l'instinct sexuel," pp. 83–84, footnote.
107. Ian Hacking, "How Should We Do the History of Statistics?" *I & C,* no. 8 (Spring 1981), 17. See also Hacking's *The Emergence of Probability* (Cambridge: Cambridge University Press, 1975), and his Dawes Hicks Lecture on Philosophy, "Leibniz and Descartes: Proof and Eternal Truths," *Proceedings of the British Academy* (London: Oxford University Press, 1974).
108. Hacking, "Leibniz and Descartes: Proof and Eternal Truths," p. 188.

2. Sex and the Emergence of Sexuality

I am indebted to Stanley Cavell, Lorraine Daston, Peter Galison, Ian Hacking, Erin Kelly, John McNees, and Joel Snyder for conversations on the topics of this essay.

1. Philippe Ariès and André Béjin, eds., *Western Sexuality: Practice and Precept in Past and Present Times* (Oxford, 1985).
2. Michel Foucault, "Omnes et Singulatum: Towards a Criticism of 'Political Reason,'" in *The Tanner Lectures on Human Values,* ed. Sterling M. McMurrin (Salt Lake City, 1981), p. 239.
3. Ibid., p. 240.
4. Foucault wrote several different prefaces or introductions to the second volume of *The History of Sexuality.* This one appears in *The Foucault Reader,* ed. Paul Rabinow (New York, 1984), p. 338.
5. Ibid., p. 339; my emphasis.
6. Paul Veyne, "Homosexuality in Ancient Rome," in *Western Sexuality,* p. 29.
7. See Foucault, introduction to *Herculine Barbin, Being the Recently Discovered Memoirs of a Nineteenth-Century French Hermaphrodite,* trans. Richard

McDougal (New York, 1980), pp. vii-viii; all further references to this work, abbreviated *HB,* will be included in the text.

8. For a critique of some of Foucault's claims, see Lorraine Daston and Katharine Park, "Hermaphrodites in Renaissance France," *Critical Matrix: Princeton Working Papers in Women's Studies,* 1, no. 5 (1985).

9. See Ambroise Paré, *Des monstres et prodiges,* ed. Jean Céard (Geneva, 1971), pp. 24–27.

10. Tardieu's book was published in 1874. Parts of it had previously appeared in the *Annales d'hygiène publique* in 1872.

Controversies concerning the identity of an individual's sex often revolved around questions of the person's reproductive capabilities and ultimate suitability for marriage. By the nineteenth century, these determinations subordinated physiological considerations to anatomical ones. To base classifications of hermaphroditism on physiological rather than anatomical facts was thought to be "completely inadmissable in the present state of science." See Isidore Geoffroy Saint-Hilaire, *Histoire générale et particulière des anomalies de l'organisation chez l'homme et les animaux,* 3 vols. (Paris, 1832–37), vol. 3, p. 34n. For a more general discussion of some of these issues, see Pierre Darmon, *Le Tribunal de l'impuissance: Virilité et défaillances conjugales dans l'ancienne France* (Paris, 1979). I am indebted to Joel Snyder for clarifications on this point.

11. Havelock Ellis, "Sexo-Aesthetic Inversion," *Alienist and Neurologist,* 34 (1913), 156.

12. Ibid., p. 159.

13. For an explanation of this terminology, see Ian Hacking, "Language, Truth, and Reason," in *Rationality and Relativism,* ed. Martin Hollis and Steven Lukes (Oxford, 1982), pp. 48–66.

14. American Psychiatric Association, Task Force on Nomenclature and Statistics, *Diagnostic and Statistical Manual of Mental Disorders,* 3rd ed. (Washington, D.C., 1980), p. 261.

15. Ariès, "Thoughts on the History of Homosexuality," in *Western Sexuality,* p. 66.

16. Stanley Cavell, *The Claim of Reason: Wittgenstein, Skepticism, Morality, and Tragedy* (New York, 1979), p. 78.

17. Ibid., p. 77.

18. Leo Steinberg, *The Sexuality of Christ in Renaissance Art and in Modern Oblivion* (New York, 1983); all further references to this work, abbreviated *SC,* will be included in the text.

19. André Chastel, "A Long-Suppressed Episode," review of *The Sexuality of Christ in Renaissance Art and in Modern Oblivion* by Leo Steinberg, trans. Da-

vid Bellos and Christopher Benfry, *New York Review of Books,* Nov. 22, 1984,
p. 35n2.

20. Charles Hope, "Ostentatio Genitalium," *London Review of Books,* Nov. 15–
Dec. 5, 1984, p. 20.

21. Steinberg's entire excursis 18 is relevant here.

22. A useful discussion of the iconography of madness can be found in Sander L.
Gilman, *Seeing the Insane* (New York, 1982).

23. S. Lindner, "Das Saugen an den Fingern, Lippen etc. bei den Kindern
(Ludeln). Eine Studie," *Jahrbuch für Kinderheilkunde und physische Erziehung,*
14 (1879), 68; see Sigmund Freud, *Three Essays on the Theory of Sexuality, The
Standard Edition of the Complete Psychological Works of Sigmund Freud,* ed. and
trans. James Strachey, 24 vols. (London, 1953–1974), vol. 7, pp. 179–181.

24. These articles originally appeared in *The Medical Annual,* vol. 12 (1894), vol.
15 (1897), and vol. 21 (1903). They were republished as *The Physiognomy of
Mental Disease and Degeneracy* (Bristol, 1903). The quotation is from the
latter.

25. Ibid.

26. Georges Canguilhem, "Introduction: L'Objet de l'histoire des sciences,"
Etudes d'histoire et de philosophie des sciences (Paris, 1983), pp. 9–23.

27. Richard von Krafft-Ebing, *Psychopathia Sexualis, with Especial Reference to the
Antipathic Sexual Instinct: A Medico-Forensic Study,* trans. Franklin S. Klaf
(New York, 1965), p. 34; all further references to this work, abbreviated *PS,*
will be included in the text.

28. D. M. Rozier, *Des habitudes secrètes ou des maladies produites par l'onanisme
chez les femmes* (Paris, 1825). This frontispiece first appears by the time of the
third edition in 1830.

In reading through this essay, while preparing it for publication in this
book, it now seems to me that the remarks in this paragraph concerning the
drawing that appears in Rozier's book contain a significant, and instructive,
misinterpretation. The drawing of the habitual female masturbator, at least as
understood by Rozier, does not participate in the conceptual space of the psychiatric style of reasoning. Rozier's work belongs rather to the eighteenth-
century regime of discourse about masturbation, the most influential exemplification of which was Tissot's *L'Onanisme,* which I discuss in Essay 4.
Rozier's masturbators practice the solitary vice, engage in secret habits that are
the concern of morality and theology, even though this practice does also produce pathophysiological and anatomical effects. The habitual masturbator is
taken to be not a psychopathological personality type, but a vicious person
whose solitary habit had to be combated. The drawing does not show "her
psyche, her personality, disintegrating before our eyes," but rather a disorder

of the soul, depicted in her eyes and on her face. Between this defectively ordered soul and the disintegration of the personality, between 1825 and 1870, there is all of the distance of a conceptual break, the distance marked by the emergence of the subject of sexuality. Although later treatises could appropriate the Rozier drawing, redescribing it, misdescribing it, unhinged from its original conceptual context, so as to make it fit into the psychiatric style of reasoning, it is crucial to recognize that this redescription is as epistemologically distorting as is Charcot's redescription of demonic possession as instances of convulsive hysteria.

I have marked this misinterpretation at length because it also recapitulates, from a different angle, some of the issues that appear in my critique of Steinberg. And it reemphasizes the difficulties that surround the use of visual evidence, and underlines the problem of the relationship between visual depiction and conceptual representation.

29. Michel Foucault, "The Confession of the Flesh," *Power/Knowledge: Selected Interviews and Other Writings, 1972–1977,* ed. Colin Gordon, trans. Gordon et al. (New York, 1980), p. 221.

30. Essay 1 in the present volume.

31. Ian Hacking, "Five Parables," in *Philosophy in History: Essays on the Historiography of Philosophy,* ed. R. Rorty, J. B. Schneewind, and Q. Skinner (Cambridge, 1984), pp. 122 and 124.

32. See Ian Hacking, "The Invention of Split Personalities," *Human Nature and Natural Knowledge,* ed. Alan Donagan, Anthony N. Perovich, Jr., and Michael V. Wedin (Dordrecht, 1986), pp. 63–85, and "Making Up People," in *Reconstructing Individualism: Autonomy, Individuality, and the Self in Western Thought,* ed. Thomas C. Heller, Morton Sosna, and David E. Wellbery (Stanford, Calif., 1986), pp. 222–236. Hacking attributes the doctrine of dynamic nominalism to me in this latter paper on the basis of my "Closing Up the Corpses" (Essay 1 in the present volume).

33. Johann Heinrich Meibom, *On the Use of Flogging in Venereal Affairs* (Chester, Pa., 1961), p. 19; all further references to this work, abbreviated *FVA,* will be included in the text. The English translation of this Latin treatise first appeared in 1801.

34. The copy of the text I have cited is mispaginated; p. 23 is followed by p. 30.

35. For further discussion of this terminology, see Hacking's essays cited in note 32.

36. Augustine, *Concerning the City of God against the Pagans* (New York, 1972), bk. 12.

37. Thomas Aquinas, *Summa Theologica,* trans. Fathers of the English Dominican Province (Westminster, Md., 1911), vol. 4, p. 1819.

38. Richard von Krafft-Ebing, *Text-book of Insanity Based on Clinical Observations,* trans. Charles Gilbert Chaddock (Philadelphia, 1904), p. 81.

39. Foucault, "The Confession of the Flesh," p. 221. Foucault uses this expression in a different context than mine, though a related one.

40. Michel Foucault, *The Archaeology of Knowledge and the Discourse on Language,* trans. A. M. Sheridan Smith (New York, 1972), p. 190.

41. Ibid.

3. How to Do the History of Psychoanalysis

Discussions, both recent and ancient, with Dan Brudney, Nancy Cartwright, Peter Galison, Erin Kelly, and David Wellbery have greatly benefited this essay. Conversations with Stanley Cavell about how to approach the texts of Freud were enormously helpful. A version of this essay was given as a talk to the Institute for Psychoanalytic Training and Research in New York, and I am grateful for the discussion that followed my presentation.

1. The sketch that follows reproduces, with some omissions and additions, the beginning of my "Archaeology, Genealogy, Ethics," in *Michel Foucault: A Critical Reader,* ed. David Hoy (London, 1986), pp. 221–234.

2. Michel Foucault, "Truth and Power," *Power/Knowledge: Selected Interviews and Other Writings, 1972–1977,* ed. Colin Gordon, trans. Gordon, Leo Marshall, John Mepham, and Kate Soper (New York, 1980), p. 133.

3. Michel Foucault, "History of Systems of Thought," *Language, Counter-Memory, Practice: Selected Essays and Interviews,* ed. Donald F. Bouchard, trans. Bouchard and Sherry Simon (Ithaca, New York, 1970), p. 199.

4. Michel Foucault, *The Order of Things: An Archaeology of the Human Sciences* (New York, 1970), p. ix.

5. See Ian Hacking, "Michel Foucault's Immature Science," *Noûs,* 13 (March 1979), 39–51.

6. Foucault, *The Order of Things,* p. xi.

7. Foucault, "History of Systems of Thought," p. 200.

8. See Essays 1 and 2 in the present volume.

9. I discuss this notion at length in my paper "Styles of Reasoning, Conceptual History, and the Emergence of Psychiatry," in *The Disunity of Science,* ed. Peter Galison and David Stump (Palo Alto, 1995), as well as in Essay 5 in the present volume.

10. See Heinrich Wölfflin, *Principles of Art History: The Problem of the Development of Style in Later Art,* trans. M. D. Hottinger (New York, 1950).

11. See Paul Veyne, *L'Inventaire des différences: Leçon inaugurale au Collège de France* (Paris, 1976); and Arnold Hauser, *The Philosophy of Art History*

(Evanston, Ill., 1985). Hauser is referring to Wölfflin's own phrase, "Kuntsgeschichte ohne Namen," which appears in the foreword to the first edition of *Principles of Art History.* This foreword was omitted from later editions, and from the English translation of Wölfflin's book.

12. Wölfflin, *Principles,* p. ix.

13. I have discussed some of these issues in relation to hysteria in my "Assault on Freud," *London Review of Books,* July 5–19, 1984, pp. 9–11.

14. In what follows, I recount, with some additional quotations, parts of Essay 1 in the present volume. More detailed historical documentation for my claims can be found in that essay.

15. See Michel Foucault, *The History of Sexuality,* vol. 1: *An Introduction,* trans. Robert Hurley (New York, 1978).

16. See Paul Moreau (de Tours), *Des aberrations du sens génésique,* 2nd ed. (Paris, 1880), p. 2.

17. See ibid., p. 3.

18. *Oxford English Dictionary,* s.v. "perversion."

19. Richard von Krafft-Ebing, *Text-book of Insanity Based on Clinical Observations,* trans. Charles Gilbert Chaddock (Philadelphia, 1904), p. 79; further references to this work, abbreviated *TI,* will be included in the text. Krafft-Ebing considers abolition to be the extreme case of diminution.

20. This same classification is given in Richard von Krafft-Ebing, *Psychopathia Sexualis, with Especial Reference to the Antipathic Sexual Instinct: A Medico-Forensic Study,* trans. Franklin S. Klaf (New York, 1965), p. 34; all further references to this work, abbreviated *PS,* will be included in the text.

21. See also *TI,* p. 81.

22. See Frank J. Sulloway, *Freud, Biologist of the Mind* (New York, 1979), esp. chap. 8.

23. Albert Moll, *Perversions of the Sex Instinct: A Study of Sexual Inversion,* trans. Maurice Popkin (Newark, N.J., 1931), pp. 171–172; my emphasis.

24. For some French examples of this understanding, see Maurice Paul Legrain, *Des anomalies de l'instinct sexuel et en particulier des inversions du sens génital* (Paris, 1896), and Dr. Laupts (pseudonym of Georges Saint-Paul), *L'Homosexualité et les types homosexuels: Nouvelle édition de Perversion et perversité sexuelles* (Paris, 1910).

25. Moll, *Perversions of the Sex Instinct,* p. 180.

26. Sigmund Freud, *Three Essays on the Theory of Sexuality, The Standard Edition of the Complete Psychological Works of Sigmund Freud,* ed. and trans. James Strachey, 24 vols. (London, 1953–1974), vol. 7, p. 135; further references to this work, abbreviated *T,* will be included in the text.

27. In my discussion, I shall leave aside Freud's comments about popular opinion

concerning the absence of infantile sexuality. The question of the relationship between popular and learned opinion on this issue is too complex to take up here.

28. For a useful overview, see Sulloway, *Freud, Biologist of the Mind.*

29. The German is "Die Erfahrung an den für abnorm gehaltenen Fällen lehrt uns . . ." (Freud, *Gesammelte Schriften* [Vienna, 1924], vol. 5, p. 20).

30. For one recent example, see Bruno Bettelheim, *Freud and Man's Soul* (New York, 1982). I have criticized Bettelheim's claims in "On the Englishing of Freud," *London Review of Books,* Nov. 3–16, 1983.

31. Iwan Bloch, *Anthropological Studies on the Strange Sexual Practises of All Races and All Ages* (New York, 1933), pp. 5 and 6; all further references to this work, abbreviated *AS,* will be included in the text. This is a translation of vol. 1 of Bloch's *Beiträge zur Aetiologie der Psychopathia Sexualis* (Dresden, 1902–3). I believe that Sulloway does not adequately see the role of Bloch's work in Freud's *Three Essays.*

32. Iwan Bloch, *Anthropological and Ethnological Studies in the Strangest Sex Acts in Modes of Love of All Races Illustrated* (New York, 1935), pt. 2, p. 4. This is a translation of vol. 2 of Bloch's *Beiträge zur Aetiologie der Psychopathia Sexualis.*

33. The German is "Die Grenze dieses Ekels ist aber häufig rein konventionell" (*Gesammelte Schriften,* vol. 5, p. 25).

34. Pain and horror are mentioned, respectively, on pp. 159 and 161; aesthetic and moral ideals are listed on p. 177.

35. Freud uses the term "erotogenic instincts" once on p. 193. The German is "erogenen Trieben" (*Gesammelte Schriften,* vol. 5, p. 68).

36. Freud uses this notion of uniformity in two crucial passages. See *T,* pp. 148 and 162. For the German uses of "gleichförmig," see *Gesammelte Schriften,* vol. 5, pp. 21 and 36.

37. Freud uses the word pathogenic *(pathogene)* in this context.

38. The German passage appears in *Gesammelte Schriften,* vol. 5, pp. 34–35.

39. The corresponding German passage appears in *Gesammelte Schriften,* vol. 5, p. 113.

40. Useful introductions to the history of mentalities can be found in Jacques LeGoff, "Les Mentalités: Une histoire ambigue," in *Faire de l'histoire: Nouveaux objets,* ed. LeGoff and Pierre Nora (Paris, 1974), and Roger Chartier, "Intellectual History or Sociocultural History? The French Trajectories," in *Modern European Intellectual History: Reappraisals and New Perspectives,* ed. Dominick LaCapra and Steven L. Kaplan (Ithaca, New York, 1982), pp. 13–46. The notion of mentality is invoked for the history of science in some of the essays in *Occult and Scientific Mentalities in the Renaissance,* ed. Brian Vickers (London, 1984).

4. The Horror of Monsters

Among the many people who have offered comments and suggestions on earlier versions of this chapter, I am especially grateful to Daniel Brudney, Nancy Cartwright, Justine Cassell, Stanley Cavell, Lorraine Daston, Peter Galison, Jan Goldstein, Joel Snyder, and David Wellbery.

1. Lucien Febvre, "Sensibility and History: How to Reconstitute the Emotional Life of the Past," *A New Kind of History* (London: Routledge and Kegan Paul, 1973), p. 24.

2. This essay is a fragment of a much longer manuscript entitled "The History of Horror: Abominations, Monsters, and the Unnatural." That manuscript is a comparative historical analysis of the three concepts mentioned in the title, linking each of them to the reaction of horror and thus taking a first step toward writing a history of horror. I then use this comparative history to consider both the phenomenology of horror and its moral analysis, interlacing historical and philosophical concerns throughout.

3. Jean Delumeau, *La Peur en Occident: Une cité assiégée* (Paris: Fayard, 1978), and *Le Péché et la peur: La culpabilisation en Occident* (Paris: Fayard, 1983).

4. For useful discussion, see, among many others, Jacques Le Goff, "Mentalities: A History of Ambiguities," in Jacques Le Goff and Pierre Nora, eds., *Constructing the Past* (Cambridge: Cambridge University Press, 1985); Robert Mandrou, "L'histoire des mentalités," in the article "Histoire," *Encyclopedia Universalis* (Paris: Encyclopedia Universalis France, 1968); Jean Delumeau, "Déchristianisation ou nouveau modèle de christianisme," *Archives de Science Sociales des Religion,* 40 (July–December 1975); and Carlo Ginzburg, *The Cheese and the Worms* (New York: Penguin Books, 1980), "Preface to the Italian Edition."

5. This is emphasized by Alphonse Dupront in his seminal essay, "Problèmes et méthodes d'une histoire de la psychologie collective," *Annales* (January–February 1961).

6. I have tried to do this for the history of sexuality in Essays 1–3 in the present volume.

7. See Dupront, "Problèmes et méthodes," p. 9.

8. Martin Luther, *Werke* (Weimar: H. Böhlau, 1930–1985), vol. 11, pp. 370–385.

9. In my interpretation of this pamphlet, I follow Jean Céard, *La Nature et les prodiges* (Geneva: Librarie Droz, 1977), pp. 79–84.

10. Martin Luther and Phillip Melancthon, *Of Two Wonderful Popish Monsters,* trans. John Brooke (Imprinted at London: Colophon, 1579). I have modernized spelling and punctuation. The quotation comes from the first page of Brooke's preface, which is unpaginated in the 1579 edition of the pamphlet.

11. Ibid.

12. Ibid. The quotation comes from the second page of Brooke's preface.

13. Delumeau, *Le Péché et la peur*, p. 153.

14. I am following Delumeau's account here. Ibid., pp. 152–158. But Delumeau's chap. 4 as a whole should be read in this context.

15. Quoted in Delumeau, *Le Péché et la peur*, p. 155.

16. Ambroise Paré, *Des monstres et prodiges*, annotated critical edition by Jean Céard (Geneva: Librarie Droz, 1971). There is an English translation under the title *On Monsters and Marvels* (Chicago: University of Chicago Press, 1982). I have tried to follow the English translation in my quotations, but I have altered it whenever I felt it was necessary to preserve Paré's meaning. For some inexplicable reason, the English renders *prodiges* as "marvels" rather than "prodigies," a translation that cannot help but result in obfuscation.

17. Céard, *La Nature et les prodiges*.

18. Katharine Park and Lorraine J. Daston, "Unnatural Conceptions: The Study of Monsters in Sixteenth- and Seventeenth-Century France and England," *Past and Present*, 92 (August 1981). For some premedieval treatments of monsters, see Bruce MacBain, *Prodigy and Expiation: A Study in Religion and Politics in Republican Rome* (Brussels: Collection Latomus, 1982); Raymond Bloch, *Les Prodiges dans l'antiquité classique* (Paris: Presses Universitaire de France, 1963); and E. Leichty, "Teratological Omens," in *La Divination en Mésopotamie ancienne et dans les régions voisines* (Paris: Presses Universitaire de France, 1966).

19. Thomas Aquinas, *The Summa Theologica*, trans. the Fathers of the English Dominican Province (New York: Benziger Brothers, 1981), Part II-II, question 153, article 2. I have generally followed this translation, although in paraphrasing Aquinas, I have also consulted the Latin and facing-page English translation of the *Summa* by the Blackfriars (New York: McGraw-Hill, 1964–1980). I have appropriated terminology from each of the translations when I thought it appropriate.

20. Ibid., pp. 157–158.

21. Ibid., II-II, q. 154, art. 12, reply.

22. Ibid., p. 161.

23. Ibid., II-II, q. 154, art. 12, rep. obj. 4.

24. Ibid., p. 160. A useful discussion of this part of Aquinas can be found in John Boswell, *Christianity, Social Tolerance, and Homosexuality* (Chicago: University of Chicago Press, 1980). See esp. chap. 11.

25. Paré, *On Monsters and Marvels*, p. 3. In 1579, Paré added a third category to that of monsters and marvels, namely, the maimed *(les mutilez)*. I shall not discuss this category, since, as Céard notes, after the preface, Paré no longer uses the concept of the maimed. See Paré, *Des monstres et prodiges*, p. 151.

26. Céard, *La Nature et les prodiges,* pp. 304–305.
27. On this topic, see Stuart Clark, "The Scientific Status of Demonology," in Brian Vickers, ed., *Occult and Scientific Mentalities in the Renaissance* (Cambridge: Cambridge University Press, 1984).
28. Paré, *On Monsters,* p. 152.
29. Céard, *La Nature et les prodiges,* pp. 293–295.
30. Paré, *On Monsters,* p. 5. In this chapter, Paré also considers the monsters that are produced when a man copulates with a woman during her period; he analogizes such activity to bestiality, since "it is a filthy and brutish thing to have dealings with a woman while she is purging herself." Without discussing this important topic here, I simply note that the same chapter of Leviticus which prohibits bestiality also prohibits intercourse with a woman during her period (the relevant chapter is Leviticus 18, not 16 as Paré states).
31. Paré, *Des monstres,* chap. 9. This chapter appears as chap. 20 in the English translation.
32. Paré, *On Monsters,* p. 67.
33. Ibid., p. 73.
34. See Delumeau, *Le Péché et la peur,* p. 156.
35. Quoted in John Block Friedman, *The Monstrous Races in Medieval Art and Thought* (Cambridge: Harvard University Press, 1981), p. 182. Friedman's book is a useful introduction to the topic of monstrous races, a topic I shall not discuss here.
36. Paré, *On Monsters,* p. 8.
37. For an English example, see John Sadler's *The Sicke Woman's Private Looking-Glasse,* relevant portions of which are excerpted in Paré, *On Monsters,* pp. 174–176.
38. Lorraine Daston, "The Decline of Miracles," unpub. ms., p. 12.
39. Paré, *On Monsters,* p. 69. The practice of killing both the human being and the beast involved in bestial copulation has a long history that goes back to the law of Leviticus 20:15–16. I have been able to find a few exceptions where the beast was spared. The most interesting of these exceptions is reported as follows: "E. P. Evans states that at Vanvres in 1570 one Jacques Verrons was hung for copulation with a she-ass. The animal was acquitted on the grounds that she was a victim of violence and had not participated of her own free will. The prior of the local convent and several citizens of the town signed a certificate saying that they had known said she-ass for four years, and that she had always shown herself to be virtuous both at home and abroad and had never given occasion of scandal to anyone. This document was produced at the trial and is said to have exerted a decisive influence upon the judgment of the court." Quoted in Harry Hoffner, "Incest, Sodomy, and Bestiality in the Ancient Near East," ed. Harry Hoffner, *Orient and Occident,* vol. 22 of *Alter*

Orient und Altes Testament (Germany: Verlag Butzon & Bercker Kevelaer, 1973), p. 83, note 13. This exceptional case should not misdirect one to think that trials for bestiality required the ascription of moral responsibility to animals. For discussion, see J. J. Finkelstein, *The Ox That Gored* (Philadelphia: The American Philosophical Society, 1981) esp. pp. 69–72.

40. Edward Tyson, "A Relation of two Monstrous Pigs, with the Resemblance of Human Faces, and two young Turkeys joined by the Breast," *Philosophical Transactions of the Royal Society,* 21 (1669), 431. I have modernized spelling and punctuation.

41. Ibid., p. 434.

42. Both Treves's memoir and the relevant medical reports are reprinted in Ashley Montagu, *The Elephant Man* (New York: E. P. Dutton, 1979).

43. See Aquinas' discussion in *Summa Theologica,* pt. I-II, q. 91, art. 2, and q. 94.

44. I have taken my list from art. I, sec. 4, of S. Tissot, *L'Onanisme: Dissertation sur les maladies produites par la masturbation,* 5th ed. (Lausanne: Marc Chapuis, 1780). Tissot's list is entirely representative of other eighteenth-century discussions. An English translation of Tissot's book appeared in 1832: *Treatise on the Diseases Produced by Onanism* (New York: Collins and Hennay, 1832). I have often found it necessary to modify the English translation. For discussions of the masturbation literature, see T. Tarczylo, "*L'Onanisme* de Tissot," *Dix-huitième Siècle,* 12 (1980), and *Sexe et liberté au siècle des Lumières* (Paris: Presses de la Renaissance, 1983); J. Stengers and A. Van Neck, *Histoire d'une grande peur: La masturbation* (Brussels: Editions de l'Université de Bruxelles, 1984).

45. A representative example is Alfred Hitchcock, "Insanity and Death from Masturbation," *Boston Medical and Surgical Journal,* 26 (1842).

46. Tissot, *L'Onanisme,* p. 33.

47. See, e.g., the last paragraph of the introduction to *L'Onanisme.*

48. Ibid., p. 3.

49. Ibid., p. 121.

50. Pierre Guiraud, *Dictionnaire historique, stylistique, rhétorique, étymologique, de la littérature érotique* (Paris: Payot, 1978), p. 76.

51. Ibid., p. 215.

52. Ambroise Tardieu, *Etude médico-légale sur les attentats aux moeurs,* 7th ed. (Paris: J. B. Ballière, 1878), p. 198. The category of sodomy has proven notoriously flexible and has been used to encompass a variety of activities. However, despite the flexibility, I believe that this category has more conceptual unity than has sometimes been attributed to it. I discuss this issue in the manuscript of which this essay is an excerpt.

53. Ibid., p. 255.

54. Ibid., p. 195.
55. Ibid., p. 237.
56. Ibid., p. 236.
57. Ibid., p. 258.
58. Ibid., p. 260.
59. Michael Mitchell, *Monsters of the Guilded Age: The Photographs of Charles Eisenmann* (Toronto: Gauge Publishing, 1979), pp. 28 and 30. I am indebted to Ian Hacking for providing me with this book.

5. Styles of Reasoning

1. See Essays 1–3 in the present volume.
2. J. L. Austin, "Intelligent Behaviour: A Critical Review of *The Concept of Mind*," in *Ryle: A Collection of Critical Essays,* ed. Oscar P. Wood and George Pitcher. (New York: Anchor Books, 1970), p. 51.
3. I should mention that an analysis of fashion which is methodologically closer to what I am attempting here can be found in Roland Barthes, *Système de la mode* (Paris: Editions du Seuil, 1967).
4. Michel Foucault, "Truth and Power," *Power/Knowledge.* (New York: Pantheon Books, 1980), p. 133.
5. Veyne's remark occurs in a discussion of Foucault by some of France's leading historians, *Magazine littéraire,* April 1977, p. 21.
6. Ian Hacking, "Language, Truth, and Reason," *Rationality and Relativism,* ed. Martin Hollis and Steven Lukes (Cambridge: MIT Press, 1982), pp. 64–65.
7. Ibid., p. 60.
8. Meyer Schapiro, "Style," in *Aesthetics Today,* ed. Morris Philipson and Paul J. Gudel (New York: New American Library, 1980).
9. For some general remarks, see sec. 2 of Schapiro's "Style."
10. Meyer Schapiro, *Words and Pictures: On the Literal and the Symbolic in the Illustration of a Text* (The Hague: Mouton, 1973), p. 41.
11. Ibid., pp. 42–43.
12. Ibid., p. 43.
13. Ibid., p. 44.
14. Heinrich Wölfflin, *Principles of Art History: The Problem of the Development of Style in Later Art* (New York: Dover Publications, 1950), "Preface to the Sixth Edition," p. vii.
15. Some of the problems with Wölfflin's account are discussed in sec. 5 of Schapiro's "Style."
16. Wölfflin, *Principles of Art History,* p. 12.
17. Ibid.

18. Ibid., p. 227.

19. Paul Frankl, *Principles of Architectural History: The Four Phases of Architectural Style, 1420–1900* (Cambridge: MIT Press, 1968).

20. Wölfflin, *Principles of Art History,* p. ix. The thesis is repeated on p. 11.

21. Ibid., p. 228. My emphasis.

22. See Essays 1–3 in the present volume.

23. Michael Baxandall, *Painting and Experience in Fifteenth Century Italy* (Oxford: Oxford University Press, 1972). See also Michael Baxandall, *The Limewood Sculptures of Renaissance Germany* (New Haven: Yale University Press, 1981). Especially relevant is chap. 6.

24. Baxandall, *Painting and Experience in Fifteenth Century Italy,* p. 152.

25. Ibid., pp. 29–30.

26. Paul Veyne. *L'Inventaire des différences* (Paris: Editions du Seuil, 1976), p. 31.

27. Ibid., p. 32.

28. Ibid., p. 33.

29. Ibid.

30. Ibid.

31. Ibid., p. 34.

32. Ibid.

33. Ibid., p. 49.

34. See especially Essay 1 in the present volume.

35. Ibid.

36. Pierre Hadot, *Porphyre et Victorinus* (Paris: Etudes Augustiniennes, 1968), vol. 1, p. 38.

37. Ibid., p. 39.

38. Mino Bergamo, "Il problema del discorso mistico. Due sondaggi," *Asmodee Asmodeo,* vol. 1 (Florence: Il Ponte alle Grazie, 1989), p. 13.

39. Ibid., p. 10.

40. Ibid., p. 19.

41. Augustine, *Confessions* (Oxford: Oxford University Press, 1991), II, VI (14), p. 32.

42. Augustine, *The City of God Against the Pagans* (Cambridge: Harvard University Press, 1966), bk. XII, VIII, p. 36.

43. Ibid., bk. XIV, XII, pp. 335–337. The internal quotation is from *Ecclesiastes* 10:13.

44. Ibid., bk. XII, IX, p. 41.

45. See, for example, the classic discussion of Richard von Krafft-Ebing, *Psychopathia Sexualis* (New York: Stein and Day, 1965). For additional treatment, see Essay 1 in the present volume.

46. Mino Bergamo, *La Scienza dei santi* (Florence: Sansoni, 1983), p. 51. Bergamo's remarks take as their point of departure a discussion of Michel

Foucault, *L'Archéologie du savoir* (Paris: Gallimard, 1969), p. 136. For more extensive treatment, see Essay 7 in the present volume.

47. Bergamo, *La scienza dei santi,* pp. 51–52.

48. Ibid., p. 52.

6. The Epistemology of Distorted Evidence

All translations, except where otherwise indicated, are my own.

1. Carlo Ginzburg, *Il giudice e lo storico: Considerazioni in margine al processo Sofri* (Turin, 1991), pp. 109–110.

2. Ginzburg's historiographical writings are cited in the first footnote of "Checking the Evidence: The Judge and the Historian," in *Questions of Evidence,* ed. J. Chandler, A. I. Davidson, and H. Harootunian (Chicago: University of Chicago Press, 1994), p. 290; hereafter abbreviated "CE." I have used all of these sources, as well as others I shall mention shortly, in writing this essay.

3. Carlo Ginzburg, "Montrer et citer: La Vérité de l'histoire," *Le Débat,* 56 (September– October 1989), 43–54; hereafter abbreviated "MC." See especially secs. 4–7.

4. On Griffet, see also Carlo Ginzburg, "Just One Witness," in *Probing the Limits of Representation: Nazism and the Final Solution,* ed. Saul Friedlander (Cambridge, 1992), p. 85.

5. Ginzburg, *Il giudice e lo storico,* p. 110.

6. Carlo Ginzburg, "Proofs and Possibilities: In the Margins of Natalie Zemon Davis' *The Return of Martin Guerre,*" trans. Anthony Guneratne, *Yearbook of Comparative and General Literature,* 37 (1988), 115.

7. For what follows, see "Just One Witness," pp. 85–86.

8. John Rawls, *A Theory of Justice* (Cambridge, 1971), p. 3.

9. On the distinction between concepts and conceptions, see ibid., pp. 5–6. See also Ginzburg, "Checking the Evidence," p. 302.

10. For a discussion of some recent philosophical attempts to debunk truth and on the problems with these attempts, see Cora Diamond, "Truth: Defenders, Debunkers, Despisers," in *Commitment in Reflection: Essays in Literature and Moral Philosophy,* ed. Leona Toker (New York, 1994), pp. 195–221.

11. Quoted in Natalia Ginzburg, *Serena Cruz o la vera giustizia* (Turin, 1990), p. 95; hereafter abbreviated *SC.*

12. See Ginzburg, *Il giudice e lo storico,* pp. 110–111.

13. Ginzburg, "Just One Witness," p. 93.

14. On these issues, see many of the essays in Hilary Putnam, *Realism with a Human Face,* ed. James Conant (Cambridge, 1990). I note especially the last paragraph of the essay "William James's Ideas."

15. The best discussion of this topic is Stanley Cavell, *The Claim of Reason: Wittgenstein, Skepticism, Morality, and Tragedy* (New York, 1979), pt. 1.

16. Pierre Vidal-Naquet, *Assassins of Memory: Essays on the Denial of the Holocaust,* trans. Jeffrey Mehlman (New York, 1992), p. xxiv.

17. Peter Galison, "History, Philosophy, and the Central Metaphor," *Science in Context* 2 (Spring 1988), 207.

18. Ibid., secs. 2–3.

19. See Ginzburg, "Just One Witness," p. 89.

20. See Galison, "History, Philosophy, and the Central Metaphor," sec. 4. See also Galison, *How Experiments End* (Chicago, 1987).

21. Carlo Ginzburg, "The Inquisitor as Anthropologist," *Clues, Myths, and the Historical Method,* trans. John and Anne C. Tedeschi (Baltimore, 1989), pp. 158–159; hereafter abbreviated "IA."

22. Carlo Ginzburg, *The Night Battles: Witchcraft and Agrarian Cults in the Sixteenth and Seventeenth Centuries,* trans. John and Anne Tedeschi (New York, 1985), p. xiv; hereafter abbreviated *NB.*

23. See also, more generally, Carlo Ginzburg, *Ecstasies: Deciphering the Witches' Sabbath,* trans. Raymond Rosenthal (New York, 1991).

24. For some of Ginzburg's later doubts about the notion of mentality, see *The Cheese and the Worms: The Cosmos of a Sixteenth-Century Miller,* trans. John and Anne Tedeschi (New York, 1982), pp. xxiii-xxiv; hereafter abbreviated *CW.*

25. Paola Zambelli's interpretation can be found in her "Uno, due, tre, mille Menocchio?" *Archivio storico italiano,* 137, no. 499 (1979), 51–90.

26. Ian Hacking, "Making Up People," in *Reconstructing Individualism: Autonomy, Individuality, and the Self in Western Thought,* ed. Thomas C. Heller et al. (Stanford, Calif., 1986), pp. 228 and 236; hereafter abbreviated "MP."

27. See Essays 1 and 2 in the present volume.

28. For his earliest work on multiple personality, see Ian Hacking, "The Invention of Split Personalities," in *Human Nature and Natural Knowledge: Essays Presented to Marjorie Grene on the Occasion of Her Seventy-Fifth Birthday,* ed. Alan Donagan, Anthony N. Perovich, Jr., and Michael V. Wedin (Dordrecht, 1986), pp. 63–86. For his most recent contribution to this subject, see "Two Souls in One Body," in *Questions of Evidence,* pp. 433–462.

29. See Pierre Janet, "Les Actes inconscients et le dédoublement de la personnalité pendant le somnambulisme provoqué," *Revue Philosophique,* 22 (December 1886), 577–592.

30. Cited by Ginzburg in "Checking the Evidence," pp. 300–301. See also "Proofs and Possibilities," p. 116.

31. I have reversed the order of Ginzburg's two sentences in my quotation of them.

32. Ginzburg, "Proofs and Possibilities," p. 117.

33. Giovanni Levi, "Les Usages de la biographie," *Annales,* no. 6 (November–December 1989).

34. Ibid., sec. 9.

35. Ibid., p. 1334.

36. Ibid., pp. 1333–1334. For a discussion of some of these problems from a different perspective, see Michel Foucault, "The Subject and Power," Afterword to Hubert Dreyfus and Paul Rabinow, *Michel Foucault: Beyond Structuralism and Hermeneutics* (Chicago, 1982), and Michel Foucault, *Histoire de la sexualité,* vol. 1: *La Volonté de savoir* (Paris: Editions Gallimard, 1976), pt. 4.

37. Levi, "Les Usages de la biographie," pp. 1329–1330.

38. Ibid., pp. 1331–1332.

39. Ginzburg's specific target is Michel Foucault's treatment of the case of Pierre Rivière. See *The Cheese and the Worms,* sec. 5. Levi seems to share Ginzburg's judgment about Foucault. See "Les Usages de la biographie," p. 1332.

40. Levi, "Les Usages de la biographie," p. 1333.

41. Ibid., secs. 8 and 10.

42. Arsenio Frugoni, *Arnaldo da Brescia nelle fonti del secolo XII* (Turin, 1989), p. xxi. Ginzburg discusses Frugoni in "Checking the Evidence," pp. 83–84, and "Proofs and Possibilities," pp. 123–124.

43. In approaching Frugoni's historiography, I have been greatly helped by Giuseppe Sergi's introduction to the 1989 edition of Frugoni's book.

44. Frugoni, *Arnaldo da Brescia,* p. xxiii.

45. Cited by Giuseppe Sergi in his introduction to Frugoni's *Arnaldo da Brescia* (from Frugoni's 1940 work *Papato impero e regni occidentali* [*dal periodo carolingio a Innocenzo III*]), p. xiii.

46. Ginzburg, "Proofs and Possibilities," p. 123.

47. The concepts of "anomalies" and "cracks" appear in Ginzburg, *Ecstasies,* p. 10.

48. In my account of Marcus Aurelius' *Meditations,* I closely follow Pierre Hadot's chapter on Marcus in his *Philosophy as a Way of Life: Spiritual Exercises from Socrates to Foucault,* ed. Arnold I. Davidson (Oxford, 1993). The quotation is from p. 186. See also Pierre Hadot, "Marc Aurèle était-il opiomane?" in *Mémorial André-Jean Festugiere,* ed. E. Lucchesi and H. D. Saffrey (Geneva: Patrick Cramer, 1984).

49. Hadot, *Philosophy as a Way of Life,* p. 186.

50. Ibid., p. 187. My emphasis.

51. Pierre Hadot, "Forms of Life and Forms of Discourse in Ancient Philosophy," *Critical Inquiry,* 16 (Spring 1990), 500.

52. Ibid., p. 502.

53. Philippe Lejeune, *On Autobiography* (Minneapolis, 1989). See especially chaps.

7, 8, and 10. Lejeune uses the notion of "implicit code" on, for example, p. 141.

54. Arnaldo Fortini, *Francis of Assisi* (New York: Crossroad, 1992), p. 558. This is an abridged translation of *Nova vita di San Francesco* (Assisi, 1959).

55. *The Little Flowers of St. Francis* (New York, 1958), pp. 191–192.

56. Thomas of Celano, *Saint Francis of Assisi* (Chicago, 1988), *The First Life of St. Francis*, bk. 2, chap. 3, secs. 94–96, pp. 84–87.

57. Ibid., Prologue, sec. 1, p. 2.

58. Fortini, *Nova vita di San Francesco,* vol. 2, p. 446.

59. See Fortini's endorsement of Renan's remarks in ibid., p. 447.

60. André Vauchez, "Les Stigmates de Saint François et leurs detracteurs dans les derniers siècles du moyen âge," *Mélanges d'Archéologie et d'Histoire, Ecole Française de Rome,* 80 (1968), 599–600.

61. Ibid., pp. 612–618.

62. Ibid.

63. Carlo Ginzburg, *The Enigma of Piero* (London, 1985).

64. Ibid., p. 11.

65. Ibid., pp. 11–12.

66. Ibid., p. 12; my emphasis.

67. Cited by Ginzburg in "Checking the Evidence," p. 299.

68. Ginzburg, *Il giudice e lo storico,* p. 106.

69. See also *Il giudice e lo storico,* p. 106.

70. Ginzburg, *Il giudice e lo storico,* p. 106, and "Checking the Evidence," p. 299.

71. Ginzburg, *Il giudice e lo storico,* p. 106.

72. Ibid.

73. Ginzburg, *Il giudice e lo storico,* p. 106.

74. See Ginzburg's discussion in "Just One Witness," especially his remarks on Vidal-Naquet and de Certeau, pp. 86 and 94.

75. Ginzburg, "Proofs and Possibilities," p. 121.

76. Ibid., p. 122.

77. The relevant Italian footnote reads, "Si noti che nella frasa precedente 'certamente' significa 'molto probabilmente' (è un vizio diffuso tra gli storici; non so se lo sia anche tra i giudici)," *Il giudice e lo storico,* p. 117, note 72.

78. Cited in Ginzburg, "Proofs and Possibilities," p. 123.

79. Ginzburg, "Proofs and Possibilities," pp. 116–117.

80. See also "Proofs and Possibilities," p. 123.

81. Ginzburg, "Proofs and Possibilities," p. 117.

82. Ibid., p. 119.

83. Ibid., p. 120.

84. Ibid., p. 121.

85. Cited in ibid., p. 123.

86. Ibid., p. 124.
87. Ibid., p. 119.
88. Ibid., p. 124.

7. Foucault and the Analysis of Concepts

This essay was written for the conference "Ecrire, Diffuser, Traduire: Foucault Dix Ans Après," organized by the Centre Michel Foucault in 1994. I would like to thank Yves Duroux and Daniel Defert for our conversations about Foucault and analytic philosophy. All translations, except where otherwise indicated, are my own.

1. Michel Foucault, *Dits et écrits, 1954–1988* (Paris: Editions Gallimard, 1994), vol. 4, p. 170.
2. Hilary Putnam, "Philosophie analytique et philosophie continentale: Entretien avec Joëlle Proust," *Philosophie*, 35 (Summer 1992), 49.
3. Michel Foucault, *L'Ordre du discours* (Paris: Editions Gallimard, 1971), p. 16.
4. Ibid., p. 18.
5. See Essays 1–3 in this volume.
6. Foucault, *Dits et écrits*, vol. 3, p. 160.
7. Ibid., vol. 4, p. 286.
8. See my "Styles of Reasoning, Conceptual History, and the Emergence of Psychiatry," *The Disunity of Science*, ed. Peter Galison and David Stump (Palo Alto: Stanford University Press, 1995).
9. Ian Hacking, "How Should We Do the History of Statistics?" *I & C*, 8 (Spring, 1981), 17.
10. Jacques Bouveresse, "L'animal cérémoniel: Wittgenstein et l'anthropologie," in Ludwig Wittgenstein, *Remarques sur "Le Rameau d'Or" de Frazer* (Montreux: Editions l'Age d'Homme, 1982), p. 103. A fuller consideration of Wittgenstein's perspective should also take into account the uses made of it by Carlo Ginzburg in *Storia notturna* (Turin: Einaudi, 1989). See especially pp. xxviii–xxx.
11. My understanding, in what follows, of conceptual connections that are revisable is indebted to Hilary Putnam, "Pragmatism," in *Proceedings of the Aristotelian Society*, 95, pt. 3 (1995), and "Rethinking Mathematical Necessity" in *Words and Life* (Cambridge: Harvard University Press, 1994).
12. Foucault, *Dits et écrits*, vol. 4, p. 633.
13. See my discussion in "Styles of Reasoning, Conceptual History, and the Emergence of Psychiatry."
14. Jacques Bouveresse, "Wittgenstein antropologo," in Ludwig Wittgenstein, *Note sul "Ramo d'oro" di Frazer* (Milan: Adelphi, 1975), pp. 80–81. The internal quotations come from Wittgenstein, *Philosophical Investigations* (Oxford:

Basil Blackwell, 1958), sec. 316, and *The Blue and Brown Books* (Oxford: Basil Blackwell, 1958), p. 5.

15. Pierre Hadot, "Jeux de langage et philosophie," *Revue de Métaphysique et de Morale,* 64 (1960), 331.

16. Ibid., p. 340.

17. Ibid., pp. 342–343.

18. Ibid., pp. 339–340. The internal quotations come, first, from Nietzsche, and then from A. de Waelhens. See the notes to p. 340 for further specification.

19. Ibid., p. 342.

20. For the contrast between a "determinate discourse" and an "ideal and absolute discourse," see ibid., p. 342.

21. Ibid., p. 342. On ancient philosophy, see pp. 340–342.

22. Michel Foucault, *L'Archéologie du savoir* (Paris: Editions Gallimard, 1969), p. 136.

23. Ibid.

24. Ibid.

25. Ibid., pp. 136–137.

26. Ibid., p. 137. The contrast with an "ideal form" can be found on p. 138.

27. Pierre Hadot, *Porphyre et Victorinus* (Paris: Etudes Augustiniennes, 1968), vol. 1, p. 30.

28. Mino Bergamo, "Il problema del discorso mistico. Due sondaggi," in *Asmodee Asmodeo,* vol. 1 (Florence: Il Ponte Alle Grazie, 1989), p. 13.

29. Mino Bergamo, *La Scienza dei santi* (Florence: Sansoni, 1983), pp. 51–52. Bergamo cites the same passages from *L'Archéologie du savoir* that I have cited.

30. Bergamo, *La Scienza dei santi,* p. 52.

31. Bouveresse, "Wittgenstein antropologo," p. 63. Of course, Bouveresse also recognizes that this did not imply for Wittgenstein that we can change these things as we please. For Wittgenstein's views on the natural and the conventional, the best discussion remains Stanley Cavell, *The Claim of Reason* (Oxford: Oxford University Press, 1979), chap. 5.

32. Jacques Bouveresse, "L'Animal cérémonial: Wittgenstein et l'anthropologie," p. 51. For another use of Wittgenstein's anthropological method, see Sandra Laugier-Rabaté, *L'Anthopologie logique de Quine* (Paris: Vrin, 1992), as well as her "Bouveresse anthropologue," *Critique,* 567–568 (August–September, 1994).

33. Ludwig Wittgenstein, *Remarques mêlées* (Mauvezin: Editions T.E.R., 1990), p. 53. The first remark is cited by Bouveresse, "L'Animal cérémoniel: Wittgenstein et l'anthropologie," p. 53.

34. Foucault, *Dits et écrits,* vol. 4, pp. 448–449.

35. Ibid., vol. 4, p. 135.
36. Bouveresse, "L'Animal cérémoniel: Wittgenstein et l'anthropologie," p. 102.
On Wittgenstein's political sensibility, see especially secs. 2 and 3 of
Bouveresse's essay.
37. Ibid., p. 85.
38. Wittgenstein, *Remarques mêlées,* p. 41.
39. On the role of comparative description in Wittgenstein, see Bouveresse,
"L'Animal cérémoniel: Wittgenstein et l'anthropologie," p. 102.
40. Michel Foucault, *L'Usage des plaisirs* (Paris: Editions Gallimard, 1984), p. 14.
41. Bouveresse, "Wittgenstein antropologo," p. 64, describing Wittgenstein's
philosophical work.
42. For the notion of "speculative anthropology" with respect to Wittgenstein,
see ibid., p. 63. For the quotation from Foucault, see *L'Usage des plaisirs,*
pp. 12–13.
43. Foucault, *L'Usage des plaisirs,* p. 15.
44. Ibid., pp. 14–15, my emphasis.

8. On Epistemology and Archeology

This essay was first presented at the Boston Colloquium for the Philosophy
of Science conference "French History and Philosophy of Science," 1996. It
was prompted, in part, by François Delaporte's paper "Foucault,
l'épistémologie, et l'histoire," also presented at that conference. All translations, except where otherwise indicated, are my own.

1. See, for example, Michel Foucault, "Introduction" to *L'Usage des plaisirs*
(Paris: Gallimard, 1984); "Polémique, politique et problématisations" in *Dits
et écrits, 1954–1988,* vol. 4 (Paris: Gallimard, 1994); "Osservazioni conclusive"
in *Discorso e verità nella Grecia antica* (Rome: Donzelli, 1996).
2. François Delaporte, "Foucault, l'épistémologie et l'histoire," unpublished
manuscript, p. 5. Delaporte draws his description largely, although not exclusively, from the terrain of Foucault's *Naissance de la clinique.* Since his own
work primarily concerns the life sciences, we can read his discussion of
Foucault and Canguilhem as shedding light on the kind of methodological
choices he has had to make, choices that have been crucial in producing his
own distinctive and important works.
3. Michel Foucault, "Discussion" in *Dits et écrits,* vol. 2, p. 28. In what follows
throughout this essay, my remarks about the epistemology of science are determined by Foucault's understanding of Canguilhem's work. For my purposes here, I need not consider all of the complications and subtleties of
Canguilhem's own views.

4. Ibid., pp. 28–29.

5. Ibid., p. 29.

6. For further discussion of some of this terminology, see Ian Hacking, "Language, Truth, and Reason" in *Rationality and Relativism,* ed. Martin Hollis and Steven Lukes (Oxford: Blackwell Books, 1982); and Essay 5 in the present volume.

7. Michel Foucault, "Préface à l'édition anglaise [of *Les Mots et les choses*]" in *Dits et écrits,* vol. 2, p. 7.

8. Michel Foucault, *L'Ordre du discours* (Paris: Gallimard, 1971), p. 74.

9. Michel Foucault, "Sur l'archéologie des sciences: Réponse au Cercle d'épistémologie" in *Dits et écrits,* vol. 1, p. 696, note 1.

10. Michel Foucault, "Titres et travaux" in *Dits et écrits,* vol. 1, pp. 843–844.

11. Ibid., p. 843.

12. Michel Foucault, "La Volonté de savoir" in *Dits et écrits,* vol. 2, pp. 240–241.

13. Foucault, "Sur l'archéologie des sciences: Réponse au Cercle d'épistémologie," p. 724.

14. Ibid., pp. 724–725.

15. Ibid., p. 725.

16. Foucault, "La Volonté de savoir," and *L'Ordre du discours,* pp. 15–19.

17. Foucault, *L'Ordre du discours,* pp. 36–37.

18. Ibid., p. 35.

19. Ibid.

20. Ibid., pp. 16–18, and "La Volonté de savoir," p. 244.

21. Foucault, *L'Ordre du discours,* pp. 18–19.

22. The quoted words come from Foucault, "La Volonté de savoir," p. 240.

23. Foucault, "Sur l'archéologie des sciences: Réponse au Cercle d'épistémologie," p. 725.

24. For the quoted phrase, see Foucault, "Préface à l'édition anglaise [of *Les Mots et les choses*]," p. 9.

25. Foucault, "Titres et travaux," p. 843.

26. Michel Foucault, "Les problèmes de la culture. Un débat Foucault—Preti" in *Dits et écrits,* vol. 2, p. 371.

27. Foucault, "Préface à l'édition anglaise [of *Les Mots et les choses*]," p. 10.

28. Quoted by Delaporte in "Foucault, l'épistémologie et l'histoire," p. 12.

29. Foucault, "Sur l'archéologie des sciences: Réponse au Circle d'épistémologie," p. 725.

30. Foucault, "Titres et travaux," p. 845.

31. The quoted words are from Michel Foucault, "L'Occident et la vérité du sexe" in *Dits et écrits,* vol. 3, p. 105.

32. For the notion of "savoirs investis" see Foucault, "Titres et travaux," pp. 842–843.

33. Ibid., p. 843.
34. Michel Foucault, "De l'archéologie à la dynastique" in *Dits et écrits*, vol. 2, p. 409.
35. Ibid. To take up adequately the question of the relationship between archeology and genealogy, I would have to make a further distinction, namely a distinction between discursive conditions of possibility and nondiscursive conditions of possibility. One distinctive dimension of genealogical analysis concerns the role of nondiscursive conditions of possibility.
36. Ibid., p. 406.
37. Ibid., p. 405.
38. Michel Foucault, "La vérité et les formes juridiques" in *Dits et écrits*, vol. 2, pp. 635–636.
39. Ibid., p. 637. See also Foucault, *L'Ordre du discours*, p. 73.
40. Michel Foucault, "Réponse à une question" in *Dits et écrits*, vol. 1, p. 680. See also Foucault, "La Volonté de savoir," p. 241.
41. Michel Foucault, "Le Jeu de Michel Foucault" in *Dits et écrits*, vol. 3, p. 299.
42. Ibid., p. 300.
43. Ibid.
44. Ibid., pp. 300–301.
45. Michel Foucault, *L'Archéologie du savoir* (Paris: Gallimard, 1969), p. 28.

Appendix

This essay was originally written as an introduction to the translation of two brief texts by Michel Foucault, "The Death of Lacan" and "The West and the Truth of Sex." All translations, except where otherwise indicated, are my own.

1. Michel Foucault, "The Death of Lacan," in *Homosexuality and Psychoanalysis*, ed. Tim Dean and Christopher Lane (Chicago: University of Chicago Press, 2001), p. 57.
2. Michel Foucault, "Interview avec Michel Foucault" in *Dits et écrits*, ed. Daniel Defert and François Ewald with the collaboration of Jacques Lagrange (Paris: Editions Gallimard, 1994), vol. 1, p. 654. Hereafter abbreviated as *DE*, followed by volume and page number.
3. Ibid., p. 653. I discuss this topic at greater length in "Structures and Strategies of Discourse: Remarks Towards a History of Foucault's Philosophy of Language" in *Foucault and His Interlocutors*, ed. Arnold I. Davidson (Chicago: University of Chicago Press, 1997).
4. Michel Foucault, "Lacan, le 'liberateur' de la psychanalyse" in *DE*, vol. 4, p. 205.
5. Michel Foucault, "Qu'est-ce qu'un auteur?" in *DE*, vol. 1, p. 820.

6. Michel Foucault, "Le Jeu de Michel Foucault" in *DE,* vol. 3, p. 315; my emphasis.

7. Michel Foucault, "The West and the Truth of Sex," in *Homosexuality and Psychoanalysis,* ed. Dean and Lane, pp. 51–56.

8. Foucault, "Le Jeu de Michel Foucault," vol. 3, p. 312, in conjunction with Michel Foucault, "Sexualité et vérité" in *DE,* vol. 3, p. 137.

9. In what follows, I restrict my discussion to the desire and pleasure of sexual experience.

10. Gilles Deleuze, "Desire and Pleasure" in *Foucault and His Interlocutors,* p. 189.

11. Michel Foucault, *Histoire de la sexualité,* vol. 1: *La Volonté de savoir,* p. 208. (Paris: Editions Gallimard, 1976). Hereafter abbreviated as *VS.*

12. The French text is quoted in David M. Halperin, *Saint Foucault: Towards a Gay Hagiography* (New York: Oxford University Press, 1995), p. 217, note 181. Halperin's book remains the indispensable discussion of Foucault on desire and pleasure.

13. The French text is cited in Didier Eribon, *Michel Foucault et ses contemporains* (Paris: Fayard, 1994), p. 271.

14. Foucault, *VS,* p. 94–96.

15. Ibid., p. 95.

16. Foucault, "The West and the Truth of Sex," p. 53.

17. The corresponding sentence in *VS* does refer instead to the "pleasure of analysis." See pp. 95–96.

18. Foucault, *VS,* p. 96.

19. Michel Foucault, "Il y aura scandale, mais . . ." in *DE,* vol. 2, p. 75. I am indebted to Daniel Defert for having first made me aware of this text.

20. Ibid. The fact that Foucault here singles out a literary text merits further discussion.

21. Michel Foucault, "Philosophie et psychologie" in *DE,* vol. 1, p. 448.

22. Ibid.

23. Michel Foucault, "Michel Foucault: An Interview by Stephen Riggins" in *Ethics, Subjectivity and Truth,* ed. Paul Rabinow (New York: The New Press, 1997), p. 129. This interview was conducted in English.

CREDITS

INDEX